EMPLOYMENT DISCRIMINATION LAW

VISIONS OF EQUALITY IN THEORY AND DOCTRINE

SECOND EDITION

By

GEORGE RUTHERGLEN

John Barbee Minor Distinguished Professor of Law
Edward F. Howrey Research Professor
University of Virginia

CONCEPTS AND INSIGHTS SERIES

FOUNDATION PRESS
2007

© 2001 FOUNDATION PRESS
© 2007 By FOUNDATION PRESS
       395 Hudson Street
       New York, NY 10014
       Phone Toll Free 1–877–888–1330
       Fax (212) 367–6799
       foundation–press.com
Printed in the United States of America
ISBN 978–1–59941–239–9

TEXT IS PRINTED ON 10% POST CONSUMER RECYCLED PAPER

For Jessica

*

PREFACE

This book is intended as an introduction to the field of employment discrimination law, both at the abstract level of theory and at the concrete of level of doctrine. It is an introduction as much for experienced lawyers and scholars who come to this field with a thorough knowledge of other aspects of the law as for law students who have just begun on their careers. My hope is that it will convey to everyone within this broad audience the basic structure of this field, and more importantly, the fundamental questions that animate it. These are questions, I believe, that go to the heart of our nation's commitment to civil rights and of the struggle among competing visions of equality in American life. This introductory text cannot attempt to answer these questions. Its aim, instead, is to reveal the influence that they have exercised over both the form and content of employment discrimination law. Technical legal rules, as much as grand statements of principle, have been shaped by the different perspectives that can be taken on the fundamental questions in this field.

In attempting to demonstrate the influence of abstract propositions over concrete cases and doctrines, I have drawn on assistance from many sources. All of these are connected in one way or another to my colleagues and students at the University of Virginia School of Law. For their continuing challenges, criticisms, and inspiration, I am very grateful. The Federal Judicial Center first gave me the opportunity to try to develop a comprehensive introduction to employment discrimination law, and more immediately, several research assistants have been indispensable to the task of composing this book. Jennifer Swize suggested innumerable stylistic improvements; and Ross Goldman, Molly Mitchell, Terrica Redfield, and Deborah Prisinzano assisted in the crucial final stages of preparing the manuscript. My principal debt, however, remains to my colleagues on the faculty who, in a multitude of workshops, individual conversations, and comments on previous drafts have assisted me in developing the views put forward in this manuscript. Ken Abraham, Barry Cushman, Earl Dudley, John Jeffries, Pam Karlan, Mike Klarman, Daryl Levinson, Liz Magill, Chuck McCurdy, Greg Mitchell, Dan Ortiz, and Rip Verkerke are only some of the individuals who have assisted with different parts of this book. I am grateful to all of them.

GEORGE RUTHERGLEN

Charlottesville, Virginia
January 2007

*

TABLE OF CONTENTS

TABLE OF CONTENTS

*

EMPLOYMENT DISCRIMINATION LAW

VISIONS OF EQUALITY IN THEORY AND DOCTRINE

*

INTRODUCTION

Over the latter half of the twentieth century, the field of employment discrimination law grew from a minor specialty into a flourishing branch of legal practice. It began, modestly enough, with the passage of fair employment practice statutes in several states before the decision in *Brown v. Board of Education.* That decision, in 1954, changed the landscape of civil rights law, and much else besides. By the end of the decade that followed, nearly half the states had passed fair employment practice laws and Congress had passed the most important civil rights legislation in American history, the Civil Rights Act of 1964. Title VII of this act contained the first general prohibition against employment discrimination in federal law, and from this point forward, Title VII, together with the constitutional decision in *Brown,* provided the framework for the subsequent development of employment discrimination law. This body of law is almost wholly statutory, but it is deeply influenced by the active role taken by the judiciary in enforcing the constitutional principle against discrimination derived from *Brown.* The Civil Rights Act of 1964 extended this principle in a variety of different directions: to public accommodations, to recipients of federal funds, and in Title VII, to private employment. Subsequent legislation has extended it still further, to grounds of discrimination not recognized in constitutional law, such as age and disability, and through a combination of judicial interpretation and statutory amendment, to obligations not imposed by constitutional law, such as to avoid employment practices with disparate impact upon particular groups. All of these innovations, however, bear the marks of their origins in constitutional law and some directly raise constitutional questions, such as the permissibility of certain forms of affirmative action. All of these innovations also harken back to the original provisions of Title VII of the Civil Rights Act of 1964, which themselves have been amended by subsequent legislation, the most important of which is the Civil Rights Act of 1991.

Decisions interpreting the laws against employment discrimination have multiplied, as have the books and articles commenting on these developments. As the law in this field has become more complex and technical, it also has become less accessible. In such a large and growing field, any attempt at detailed analysis across the full range of significant issues would require a lengthy treatise or casebook, and several have been published. This book has a differ-

1

ent aim: to provide a critical introduction to the field. Just as this book must be selective in its coverage, it must also be critical in its analysis of arguments and positions. Criticism must inevitably be offered from one perspective rather than another. I have tried to identify and analyze the unifying principles in this body of law and to provide a framework for understanding the most important issues that they raise. Advocates from different points of view often take controversial positions on these issues, and while it is impossible to remain wholly neutral, I have tried to present each point of view fairly in its own terms.

My own perspective emerges clearly enough in what follows. Within the limits of a realistic appraisal of what the law can accomplish in changing social practices, I believe that the laws against employment discrimination play a useful role in remedying some of the persistent inequalities of American life. To say this is not to say very much. It is necessary also to identify the specific forms of equality that are worth pursuing and the means that the law might provide for doing so. It is at this point where the most fundamental disputes break out over the aims and methods of employment discrimination law. Disputes over the kind of equality to be achieved are the flip side of disputes over the kinds of discrimination to be prohibited: equality is the end and prohibitions against discrimination are the means. My purpose in this book is not to offer an extended argument for my own beliefs on these questions, but to describe the law as it is and as it is likely to develop: to provide an introduction to the statutes and decisions, and the animating principles and arguments, so that the reader can make sense of the law of employment discrimination to his or her own satisfaction. If the reader emerges with a better appreciation of the controversial questions in this field, and with better means of answering them (even with answers different from mine), this book will have accomplished its purpose.

Accordingly, this book begins with a brief historical survey of the development of the law in this field. It is immediately followed by an exposition and analysis of the major theoretical approaches to the law as it has developed. From these abstract considerations of history and theory, the next chapters move to concrete questions of interpretation and enforcement of the major statute in this field, Title VII of the Civil Rights Act of 1964. The substantive provisions of Title VII are examined initially with an emphasis on their application to discrimination on the basis of race, with other grounds of discrimination considered as they introduce exceptions and qualifications to these basic prohibitions. Separate chapters examine procedures and remedies under Title VII, topics of some complexity but also of great practical significance. The following chapters examine statutes enacted entirely separately from Title VII. Some of these statutes, such as the various Reconstruction civil rights acts, are closely modeled on the constitutional prohibitions against racial discrimination. Others are only distantly related to prohibitions against discrimination on the basis of race, such as the Age Discrimination in Employment Act and the Americans with Disabilities Act. The chapter on each of these statutes also contains a discussion of the procedures for enforcement and the remedies available under each act. This book then ends where it began, with the state fair employment practice laws that once provided the model for Title VII and may now provide the model for future developments.

Chapter I

DEVELOPMENT OF THE LAW

A. Constitutional Law

The single most important fact about the laws against employment discrimination is so obvious that it has often been minimized or overlooked entirely. It is that these laws derive from the principle against discrimination recognized in *Brown v. Board of Education*.[1] This principle seeks to establish racial equality, mainly for the benefit of racial and ethnic minorities and mainly by prohibiting race as a basis for decisions by government officials. This principle did not spring into existence full-blown in *Brown*, which was itself the culmination of a series of decisions eroding the doctrine of "separate but equal" established over half a century earlier in *Plessy v. Ferguson*.[2] This series of decisions had ramifications outside of constitutional law as well, and most directly for employment discrimination law, in the enactment of "fair employment practice" laws in several states after World War II. These laws provided the model for numerous bills introduced in successive sessions of Congress, one of which eventually became Title VII of the Civil Rights Act of 1964. Nevertheless, these state laws were not effectively enforced, or even widely adopted, until after the decision in *Brown*. That decision is rightly regarded as the foundation of modern civil rights law, including employment discrimination law.

The decision in *Brown*, of course, was controversial at the time and its implications remain controversial even today, another half century later. It is, for instance, still an open question whether the principle against discrimination allows any form of affirmative action, or, even more fundamentally, what constitutes "intentional discrimination" prohibited by the Constitution. These disputes in constitutional law have spread throughout civil rights law, even to areas dominated by statutes such as Title VII. Under this statute, just as under the Constitution, the permissibility of affirmative action and the meaning of "intentional discrimination" have been matters of intense debate. Yet these controversies could not have arisen if the constitutional principle had not been accepted as the foundation for modern civil rights law. It is a foundation whose content remains inherently contested, but for that very reason, one

1. 347 U.S. 483 (1954). **2.** 163 U.S. 537 (1896).

whose support and influence extend far beyond the proper boundaries of constitutional law itself.

If the influence of the constitutional principle against discrimination cannot be doubted, neither can the limitations on its immediate operation as a doctrine of constitutional law. These limitations derive from the principle's source in the Fifth and Fourteenth Amendments, which apply only to discrimination by government and do not reach discrimination by private individuals and organizations. Moreover, these amendments cover only grounds of discrimination prohibited by the Constitution, such as race or religion, and not other grounds, such as age or disability, which are left almost entirely free of judicial review under the Constitution. Of still greater significance, these amendments have been interpreted to prohibit only "intentional discrimination," which explicitly takes account of race, and not discrimination in the form of neutral practices with discriminatory effects.

The statutes prohibiting employment discrimination go beyond all of these doctrinal limitations on constitutional law, while retaining the same fundamental purpose and many of the same qualities as the constitutional principle against discrimination. The common fundamental purpose of both sources of law is to promote equality: to provide equal opportunity in public life without regard to characteristics such as race or sex. In the statutes prohibiting employment discrimination, this purpose is carried beyond government action to private employment; beyond race and sex to other grounds of discrimination, such as age, and disability; and beyond intentional discrimination to neutral practices with discriminatory effects. The shared qualities of both statutory and constitutional law are the abstract and open-ended nature of the prohibitions. The Constitution simply requires "due process" and "equal protection of the laws," while the statutory prohibitions simply prohibit discrimination, although in a variety of different verbal formulations. Judges accordingly have been given a prominent role in interpreting and enforcing the law, for instance, in defining such crucial concepts as discrimination itself, in allocating the burden of proof to establish a violation of the law, and in devising the appropriate remedies once a violation is established. After enacting the federal statutes prohibiting employment discrimination, Congress has returned only occasionally to revise judicial interpretations of its work, and even then, it has confined itself usually to choosing among alternatives already considered by the courts.

B.   The Civil Rights Act of 1964

If the modern civil rights era began with *Brown*, the passage of the Civil Rights Act of 1964 marked the highest point of civil rights activism. In its provisions in Title VII,[3] the act created the most important of the statutory prohibitions against employment discrimination and the one that most clearly expanded upon the protection offered by the Constitution. The act as a whole prohibited discrimination by a wide range of private entities beyond the reach of the Fifth and Fourteenth Amendments. In addition to Title VII, Title II of the act prohibited racial discrimination in public accommodations, whether these were operated by private entities or by the government,[4] and Title VI prohibited racial discrimination by recipients of federal funds, again regardless of who received these funds.[5] Against the background of these other titles, Title VII simply extended the constitutional principle to discrimination by private employers.[6] In doing so, Title VII enacted into federal law the prohibitions—and indeed, much of the exact language—found in state fair employment practice laws.[7] These prohibitions were exceedingly broad, covering all aspects of employment: hiring, discharge, compensation, fringe benefits, conditions of work, and anything else connected with employment.

Title VII also extended the prohibition against discrimination in another direction: to additional grounds of discrimination. In addition to race, Title VII prohibits discrimination on the basis of national origin, religion, and sex. The first two of these additional grounds have a solid foundation in the Constitution: national origin because it is treated the same as race in constitutional decisions under the Fifth and Fourteenth Amendments[8] and religion because

---

3. Civil Rights Act of 1964, codified as §§ 701–718, 42 U.S.C. §§ 2000e to–17 (2000).

4. § 201, codified as 42 U.S.C. § 2000a (2000).

5. § 601, codified as 42 U.S.C. § 2000d (2000).

6. § 703(a), codified as 42 U.S.C. § 2000e–3(a) (2000). Title VII also covers unions, employment agencies, and joint labor-management committees. § 703(b)–(d), codified as 42 U.S.C. §§ 2000–e(b)–(d) (2000). These terms are technically defined in the statute, imposing further limits on coverage. For instance, only employers with 15 or more employees fall within the scope of

the statute. § 701, codified as 42 U.S.C. § 2000e (2000).

7. Michael Evan Gold, *Griggs'* Folly: An Essay on the Theory, Problems, and Origin of the Adverse Impact Definition of Employment Discrimination and a Recommendation for Reform, 7 Indus. Rel. L.J. 429, 568–72 (1985).

8. Korematsu v. United States, 323 U.S. 214, 217 (1944) (exclusion of Japanese treated as racial exclusion); Adarand Constructors, Inc. v. Pena, 515 U.S. 200, 223 (1995) (treating affirmative action on the basis of race and national origin the same).

it is protected by the religion clauses of the First Amendment. When Title VII was enacted, however, sex was not recognized as a constitutionally prohibited basis of discrimination in areas outside of voting.[9] It was only later that the Supreme Court generally prohibited sex discrimination,[10] and even then, under narrower circumstances than racial discrimination.[11] The addition of sex to Title VII resulted from a legislative maneuver that was designed to defeat the bill by adding what opponents of Title VII thought to be a ridiculous provision protecting women to the same extent as racial minorities. This maneuver backfired in one of the great ironies of American civil rights law, as supporters of women's rights saw an opportunity to enact the first general prohibition against sex discrimination in employment. The addition of this prohibition raised the question whether prohibitions against racial discrimination should furnish the model for prohibitions against other forms of discrimination.

This question first arose with respect to the "BFOQ" exception in Title VII, so called because it allows "bona fide occupational qualifications" on the basis of national origin, religion, and sex. Despite its application to these three grounds of discrimination, this exception does not allow discrimination on the basis of race, suggesting that different grounds for discrimination require different forms of regulation. As applied to sex, the BFOQ exception eventually received a narrow interpretation,[12] applying only to such positions that involve concerns about physical privacy, such as a locker room attendant or nurse. Other differences between race and sex also generated controversy over the scope of the prohibition against sex discrimination. The most salient of these is pregnancy, which involves the most obvious biological difference between women and men. The Supreme Court initially put pregnancy entirely outside the scope of Title VII by holding that discrimination on this basis was different from discrimination on the basis of sex.[13] These decisions led Congress to amend Title VII to provide explicitly that these two grounds of discrimination were the same.[14]

9. *E.g.*, Hoyt v. Florida, 368 U.S. 57, 61 (1961) (women could rationally be excluded from juries in criminal cases).

10. Reed v. Reed, 404 U.S. 71 (1971) (preference for men in administering estates held unconstitutional).

11. United States v. Virginia, 518 U.S. 515, 531 (1996) (sex discrimination permitted only if based on an "exceedingly persuasive" justification).

12. United Auto. Workers v. Johnson Controls, Inc., 499 U.S. 187, 201 (1991); Dothard v. Rawlinson, 433 U.S. 321, 333–34 (1977).

13. General Electric Co. v. Gilbert, 429 U.S. 125 (1976).

14. The amending statute was the Pregnancy Discrimination Act, which added § 706(k), codified as 42 U.S.C. § 2000e(k) (2000).

Similar problems arose in interpreting special provisions concerned with religion, and in particular, the provision imposing a duty on employers to reasonably accommodate the religious practices of their employees.[15] The latter provision was shaped by developments that were, in many ways, the opposite of those concerned with pregnancy. The administrative agency charged with enforcing Title VII, the Equal Employment Opportunity Commission (EEOC), first proposed the duty of reasonable accommodation in a regulation including religious practices in the definition of "religion," which was then adopted by Congress in an amendment to Title VII. The Supreme Court, however, narrowly interpreted this duty to impose only minimal burdens upon employers, apparently to avoid favoring one religion over another.[16] That concern has its basis in the distinctive treatment of religion in the Constitution, which requires government both to protect the free exercise of religion and to avoid the establishment of any one religion over another.

C. Age and Disability

As the example of religion illustrates, the question whether to follow the model of racial discrimination has been raised anew with each new statutory prohibition against discrimination on a different ground. After Title VII, this question came up again with the Age Discrimination in Employment Act (ADEA),[17] later with the Rehabilitation Act,[18] and most recently with the Americans with Disabilities Act (ADA).[19] These acts expanded on the constitutional principle to reach grounds of discrimination that receive no special treatment at all under the Constitution. Classifications based on either age or disability receive only the most lenient form of judicial review under the Fourteenth Amendment, requiring only a rational basis in some legitimate government purpose.[20] The main prohibitions in these statutes were taken, almost verbatim, from Title VII, leaving the difference between race and other grounds for discrimination to be recognized in the form of exceptions and other special provisions. These departures from the general prohibitions in Title

15. § 701(j), codified as 42 U.S.C. § 2000e(j) (2000).

16. Trans World Airlines v. Hardison, 432 U.S. 63, 84 (1977).

17. Codified as 29 U.S.C. §§ 621–634 (2000).

18. Codified as 29 U.S.C. §§ 701–796i (2000).

19. Codified as 42 U.S.C. §§ 12101–12213 (2000).

20. Massachusetts Bd. of Retirement v. Murgia, 427 U.S. 307, 313–14 (1976) (per curiam) (age); City of Cleburne v. Cleburne Living Center, 473 U.S. 432, 442–47 (1985) (disability); New York City Transit Auth. v. Beazer, 440 U.S. 568, 587–94 (1979).

VII become more complex and elaborate as the resemblance to race grows more and more attenuated.

In the ADEA, the exceptions take on a life of their own in detailed statutory provisions, as well as in accompanying regulations and interpretations, all of which are far removed from issues of racial discrimination. The ADEA begins by adopting the BFOQ defense in terms that have led the Supreme Court to emphasize the similarity between permissible classifications on the basis of age and those on the basis of sex.[21] Other provisions in the ADEA, however, go beyond the analogy between age and sex as grounds of discrimination and allow age to be taken into account in retirement and pension plans,[22] areas of employment in which Title VII does not allow sex to be considered at all.[23]

Beneath all of these technicalities lies a fundamental question of policy: To what extent can a changing characteristic, such as age, be treated like an unchanging characteristic, such as race or sex? As the coverage of individuals protected by the ADEA has expanded, initially from those between ages 40 and 65 to all those now 40 and over,[24] the unique characteristics of age discrimination have become more apparent. In particular, the ADEA does not protect a group whose members have suffered systematic disadvantages in the past, such as racial minorities, certain ethnic minorities, and women. The ADEA instead protects everyone who is fortunate enough to live into middle age. With this change in scope comes the need for a change in justification.

The same basic question arises under the statutes that protect individuals with disabilities, the Rehabilitation Act and the ADA. These acts also recognize special exceptions that allow discrimination on the basis of disability, in the ADA in explicit provisions like that excluding individuals with disabilities based on risks to the health or safety of other workers.[25] Of greater significance, both practical and theoretical, is the duty imposed upon employers to reasonably accommodate disabled individuals, a duty adopted from the definition of "religion" in Title VII.[26] As applied to disabilities, the duty of reasonable accommodation can be broadly formulated and broadly interpreted, without any constitutional constraints like

---

21. § 4(f)(1), codified as 29 U.S.C. § 623(f)(1) (2000); Western Air Lines v. Criswell, 472 U.S. 400, 412 (1985).

22. § 4(f)(2)(B), (j)–(*l*), codified as 29 U.S.C. § 623(f)(2)(B), (j)–(*l*) (2000).

23. City of Los Angeles, Dep't of Water & Power v. Manhart, 435 U.S. 702, 712–13 (1978).

24. § 12(a), codified as 29 U.S.C. § 631(a) (2000).

25. § 103(b), codified as 42 U.S.C. § 12113(b) (2000).

26. §§ 101(9), (10), 102(b)(5), codified as 42 U.S.C. §§ 12111(9), (10), 12112(b)(5) (2000).

those imposed by the religion clauses on accommodation of religious practices. Yet it has also become a major source of litigation because it is codified in only the most open-ended terms. The statutory language itself creates a fundamental ambiguity about the nature of the duty of reasonable accommodation: whether it constitutes a duty not to discriminate, as it has usually been understood, or a duty to engage in affirmative action on behalf of the disabled.

D. Judicial Interpretation and Legislative Amendment

In fact, all of the provisions concerned with particular forms of discrimination raise a question, addressed neither in the text of the Constitution nor, until recently, in legislation: Just what constitutes prohibited discrimination? It is on this question that courts have taken the largest role in interpreting the statutory prohibitions against employment discrimination. Characteristically, this role emerged most clearly on a question of extending the constitutional principle in yet another direction: from intentional discrimination to neutral practices with discriminatory effects. In the landmark case of *Griggs v. Duke Power Co.*,[27] the Supreme Court recognized the theory of disparate impact, which imposes liability upon employers for neutral practices, such as general ability tests, that have a disproportionate adverse effect on minority groups or women. Employers can retain such practices only if they are "job related for the position in question and consistent with business necessity."[28] The details of this theory and the defenses available to employers were worked out in a series of cases and eventually codified, with important modifications, by the Civil Rights Act of 1991. Less dramatically, the Supreme Court has also developed different standards for proving intentional discrimination, both on claims by individual plaintiffs and on claims on behalf of entire classes.[29] Here, too, a series of judicial decisions were eventually codified, again with modifications in the Civil Rights Act of 1991.[30]

These developments illustrate how employment discrimination law is based on, but different from, constitutional law as it has evolved from *Brown v. Board of Education*. Because employment discrimination law is primarily statutory, Congress always has the

---

27. 401 U.S. 424 (1971).

28. § 703(k), codified as 42 U.S.C. § 2000e–2(k) (2000).

29. McDonnell Douglas Corp. v. Green, 411 U.S. 792, 802–04 (1973); Ha-

zelwood School Dist. v. United States, 433 U.S. 299, 307–09 (1977).

30. §§ 701(m), 706(g), codified as 42 U.S.C. §§ 2000e(m),–5(g) (2000).

final say over how far the principle against discrimination should be extended in the workplace. Unlike constitutional decisions, judicial decisions interpreting the laws against employment discrimination can be overridden by Congress, as they have been on several occasions. But if Congress has the final say, the courts often have the initial say, most prominently on the issue of what constitutes prohibited discrimination. In giving the concept of discrimination a central role in employment discrimination law, Congress also gave the courts a leading role in defining what that concept means. By invoking the concept of discrimination, Congress also invoked the tradition of judicial activism associated with civil rights law. Activist decisions have not always reached conventionally liberal results, although many did in the first decade or so after passage of Title VII. What they have achieved is an initial—and often decisive—influence on what the law is and how it is to be applied.

As originally enacted, Title VII contained no general definition of prohibited discrimination. Subsequently enacted statutes followed the same pattern: they contained broadly worded prohibitions against discrimination without any attempt to define what that term means. Only recently has this gap in the statutes been filled, mainly by the Civil Rights Act of 1991, but only in response to judicial decisions attempting to define what constitutes prohibited discrimination.[31] Congress may have been reluctant to do so because of the difficulty of codifying the meaning of so controversial a term. Certainly Congress was aware of the controversy over *Brown v. Board of Education* when it enacted the Civil Rights Act of 1964, not to mention the controversy over that legislation itself. The broadly worded prohibitions in Title VII reflect a concern with evasion and pretexts that might have resulted from any narrower versions of the statute, including any provision that attempted to give an exhaustive definition of prohibited discrimination. At this point, the broad purpose of extending the constitutional principle against discrimination merged with the need to rely upon the judiciary to prevent evasion of any newly enacted prohibition. The result was to give the courts an active role in interpreting and enforcing the statute analogous to the role that they played in constitutional litigation over school desegregation.

Almost every leading decision in employment discrimination law returns to the question of what constitutes prohibited discrimination and how it is to be proved. This tendency is apparent in cases concerned with such diverse issues as affirmative action, seniority, the treatment of pregnant workers, replacement of older

---

31. § 703(k)–(m), codified as 42
U.S.C. § 2000e–2(k)–(m) (2000).

workers, and the qualifications of disabled individuals. Its influence is more subtle, but no less influential, in the pervasive concern with allocating the burden of proof in employment discrimination cases. Early on in interpreting Title VII, the Supreme Court turned to the burden of proof to define what constitutes a violation of the statute: what facts the plaintiff must establish in order to recover and what facts the defendant might use to make out a defense. These decisions are extraordinarily intricate, as Chapters III and IV discuss in more detail. What they accomplished is a judicial definition of the concept of discrimination as it is actually applied in almost every litigated case.

A more dramatic, and no less significant, form of judicial activism appears in the curious history of the Civil Rights Act of 1866, better known in its codified form as section 1981.[32] As its name indicates, this statute was first enacted immediately after the Civil War. It was then reenacted and codified in the nineteenth century, and late in the twentieth century, it was significantly amended by the Civil Rights Act of 1991. Section 1981 prohibits employment discrimination as part of a more general prohibition against discrimination in any form of contracting. It provides that "[a]ll persons within the jurisdiction of the United States shall have the same right in every State and Territory to make and enforce contracts ... as is enjoyed by white citizens...." Because of its origin in debates over the Fourteenth Amendment, section 1981 was thought for over a century to apply, just like that amendment, only to discrimination by the states. In 1968, the Warren Court radically revised this understanding of the statute to extend its scope far beyond state action to all forms of private discrimination in contracting.[33] The revival of this statute, after a century in which it was treated as little more than a statutory predecessor to the Fourteenth Amendment, testifies eloquently to the judicial activism inspired by *Brown v. Board of Education*.

The judicial extension and revival of section 1981 has been sharply criticized.[34] Yet it has supported a developing body of judicial decisions which were modified by Congress only when the

32. 42 U.S.C. § 1981 (2000).

33. Jones v. Alfred H. Mayer Co., 392 U.S. 409, 412 (1968). This case concerned a provision in the original act that prohibits discrimination with respect to real estate transactions, which is now codified in 42 U.S.C. § 1982 (2000). Nevertheless, the reasoning in this case applies equally to discrimination in contracting and was soon extended to claims of employment discrimination. *See* Johnson v. Railway Express Agency, 421 U.S. 454, 460 (1975).

34. Charles Fairman, VI History of the Supreme Court of the United States: Reconstruction and Reunion: Part One 1207 (1971); Gerhard Casper, *Jones v. Mayer*: Clio, Bemused and Confused Muse, 1968 Sup. Ct. Rev. 89.

Supreme Court tried to narrow the broad interpretation of the statute first offered by the Warren Court. As with proof of discrimination, these decisions are analyzed in detail in Chapter X. Even a cursory description of these decisions reveals how large a role judicial interpretation has played in the development of the law under section 1981, placing Congress in the position mainly of reacting to what the courts have done. Judicial activism on this scale can only be explained by the comparable activism found in interpreting the constitutional principle against discrimination. It is worth emphasizing again that such activism need not result in conventionally liberal decisions. In recent years, the more activist decisions, on issues such as affirmative action, have been obviously conservative. Judicial decisions and judicial reasoning, whether liberal or conservative, have set the agenda and course of employment discrimination law far more frequently than has Congress in the details of statutory language.

Like all trends, this one might have run its course. The most recent major statute, the Civil Rights Act of 1991, displays a new level of congressional concern with the interpretation and enforcement of the laws against employment discrimination. This most recent statute did not add any new grounds of discrimination to those previously prohibited, but it elaborated on issues of greater significance and in greater detail than any previous amending legislation. Although enacted primarily in response to judicial decisions, the Civil Rights Act of 1991 succeeded in removing many issues from reconsideration by the judiciary. This process of gradual codification could continue, and conceivably accelerate, with Congress assuming a greater role in the elaboration and implementation of employment discrimination law. Nevertheless, as decisions under the Civil Rights Act of 1991 have revealed, even the most technical and detailed amendments have required further judicial interpretation. Congress is not likely—and perhaps is not able, as a practical matter—to greatly restrict the role of the courts in deciding what constitutes prohibited discrimination.

For this reason, the influence and content of the constitutional principle against discrimination has to be more precisely defined. The next chapter takes up this topic at the abstract level of defining the overall goal of the laws against employment discrimination, followed by two chapters that examine how this goal is implemented at the concrete level of defining prohibited discrimination. At both levels of analysis, the similarities between constitutional law and the interpretation of statutory law are striking and important.

Chapter II

DISCRIMINATION AND EQUALITY

Disputes over discrimination are the flip side of disputes over equality: discrimination identifies what is prohibited; equality is what should be achieved. The laws against employment discrimination were passed in order to promote equality, first for racial and ethnic groups and then for other disfavored groups. Just as the nature of prohibited discrimination is contested, so is the kind of equality to be achieved. Many different versions of equality have been proposed and defended, but they can be organized around the emphasis that they give to three different perspectives: historical, economic, and remedial. Speaking very broadly, each of these perspectives is associated with a moderate, conservative, or liberal position on employment discrimination law, but varying political positions can be taken within each perspective and the perspectives themselves overlap to some degree.

The main difference among the perspectives lies in the factors they deem to be relevant and the questions they consider to be crucial. The historical perspective focuses on the events surrounding the enactment of the various civil rights laws and, in particular, the precise form of the prohibitions against employment discrimination that have been enacted and the evils to which these prohibitions were addressed. It invites a comparison between the issues that arise today and the issues that confronted the legislatures that enacted the civil rights laws. The crucial question from this perspective is how a claim of discrimination asserted today resembles the kind of discrimination that the legislature meant to eliminate. In this respect, the historical perspective confines itself to a narrow version of political history, emphasizing the official legislative record, made up of the statutory text and its legislative history, rather than the social movements, political coalitions, and intellectual trends that generate profound changes in society, such as that achieved by the civil rights laws.

If the historical perspective focuses on the immediate past, the economic perspective focuses on the near future, examining the consequences of enforcing legal prohibitions against employment discrimination. The crucial question from this perspective is whether the gains from eliminating discrimination outweigh the costs of legal enforcement, and in particular, whether a legal prohibition is superior to deterring discrimination through the competitive pressure of the market. This question can receive different answers depending upon the kind of discrimination prohibited, the remedies available for enforcement, the likely reaction of employers, and a multitude of other factors. From the economic perspective, everything depends upon an assessment of the consequences. Nothing depends upon any presumption that discrimination is a particularly serious evil that must be eliminated.

The remedial perspective, however, does take a position on this question and emphasizes the degree to which the consequences of past discrimination are likely to persist in the absence of broad and vigorous enforcement of the civil rights laws. The remedial perspective adds to the historical perspective a deeper inquiry into the social consequences of past discrimination and to the economic perspective a greater weight attached to the cost of discrimination in any form. Its focus is upon the question whether any vestige of past subordination of disfavored groups continues to persist, and if so, how the law can be interpreted and enforced to provide a remedy for it. To paraphrase a famous school desegregation decision, past discrimination and its effects must be "eliminated root and branch."[1]

Each of these perspectives provides a separate means of analyzing the laws against employment discrimination, but not one that is complete in itself. In any fully developed theory of employment discrimination law, components from each perspective are necessary, with the differences mainly a matter of emphasis from one theory to another. Thus, a typical moderate view does not rely solely on the history of the civil rights laws and the types of discrimination that were common immediately before their enactment. It also must be pluralistic, at least to the extent of offering an account of the economic costs and benefits of preventing future discrimination, as well as a position on the adequacy of existing remedies for the continuing effects of past discrimination. And conversely, any fully developed theory based on the economic or remedial perspective must also offer an account of how the laws against employment discrimination came to be enacted and the evils to which they were addressed. Only the emphasis differs from a theory based on one perspective to a theory based on another, although such differences in emphasis invariably are significant and often are crucial.

A. The Historical Perspective: Equality as Colorblindness

What is distinctive about the historical view, and the moderate political position associated with it, is the decisive weight that it

1. Green v. County School Bd., 391 U.S. 430, 438 (1968).

attaches to the enactment of the laws against employment discrimination. The passage of these laws, and particularly Title VII of the Civil Rights Act of 1964, brought to a close the era in American history in which discrimination could be openly practiced and widely condoned and transformed discrimination into a phenomenon that is now receding into the past. This optimistic conclusion arises naturally from any account of the development of the law, like that set forth in the preceding chapter, in which progressively broader grounds of discrimination have been identified and prohibited. The enactment and expansion of laws like Title VII demonstrate a national commitment to leave the era of customary discrimination behind, supporting an historical perspective that is both moderately hopeful and progressive.

From this perspective, discrimination is an historical condition for which appropriate legal remedies have already been enacted. Particularly with respect to race, which forms the model for prohibitions against discrimination on other grounds, the law seeks to correct practices that grew up in an era of customary discrimination and that are no longer publicly endorsed or approved. The law need not reexamine or prohibit a wide range of practices common in contemporary labor markets, but only identify those policies and decisions that are a holdover from an earlier era of widespread discrimination. History, on this view, functions both as the justification for the laws against employment discrimination and as a guide to their enforcement. Our national experience with past discrimination has revealed its dire consequences and has required us to take steps to assure that this experience is not repeated again. For this reason, present claims of discrimination are to be judged by their resemblance to forms of discrimination committed in the past, particularly in their tendency to stigmatize or stereotype victims of discrimination.

In featuring the immediate achievements of the civil rights laws, the historical perspective represents the most widely shared view about the purpose and limits of employment discrimination law. It endorses the familiar ideal of colorblindness with respect to race (and analogous ideals with respect to other grounds of discrimination). This is a wholly negative conception of equality that emphasizes only what cannot be considered in making employment decisions. The virtue of this conception is its simplicity: it prohibits race from being taken into account in employment decisions regardless of any further reasons that an employer might have. In doing

16

so, it abstracts from the need to prove that any particular use of race is stigmatizing or stereotyping and simply presumes, based on past experience, that any use of race is undesirable, whether or not it is accompanied by undesirable motives. Whether an employer is motivated by racial hatred or by racial sympathy, an employer cannot take race into account. Because of its simplicity, this conception of equality also limits legal intervention in the economy. It only tells employers what cannot be considered; it leaves open to them the entire range of other factors that may legitimately play a role in hiring, firing, and a multitude of other personnel decisions. As a matter of legal doctrine, the negative conception of equality figures most prominently in the definition of intentional discrimination, particularly in individual claims of employment discrimination. As Senator Hubert Humphrey, a principal supporter of Title VII, said in arguing for its passage, it "does not limit the employer's freedom to hire, fire, promote or demote for any reasons—or no reasons—so long as his action is not based on race."[2]

This negative conception of equality provides the least controversial rationale for legal prohibitions against employment discrimination because it simply repeats the content of these prohibitions in the language of equality. If the civil rights laws had no further goal than eliminating consideration of characteristics such as race and sex from public life, then this goal was largely achieved as soon as these laws were enacted and effectively enforced, bringing the most obvious forms of past discrimination to an end. Because a negative conception of equality follows the legal prohibitions against discrimination so closely, it attracts the same broad support across the political spectrum as the prohibitions themselves. A strong consensus favors at least this minimal commitment to equality: that advantages and opportunities in public life should be distributed without regard to race, sex, and other prohibited characteristics. Conservatives can endorse this limited conception of equality because it requires only minimal interference with the market and otherwise leaves individuals, whether employers or employees, free to compete on other grounds. Yet liberals can also endorse this limited form of equality because it is a step in the right direction. It provides a precedent for conceptions of equality that justify broader intervention in the market.

If the consensus supporting this view is broad, it is not particularly deep. When questions about extending or limiting analogies to historical forms of discrimination arise, the negative conception of

2. 110 Cong. Rec. 5423 (1964). For one of the many similar statements in judicial decisions, see Loeb v. Textron, Inc., 600 F.2d 1003, 1012 n.6 (1st Cir. 1979).

equality does not offer much in the way of reasons for adding to or subtracting from the existing prohibitions against discrimination. Yet these questions are bound to arise as employers respond to legal prohibitions and as the prohibitions themselves are enlarged, restricted, or otherwise modified. The overt discrimination practiced before enactment of the civil rights laws is not likely to persist unchanged as those laws take effect. Under the threat of legal liability, employers are likely either to abandon discriminatory practices altogether or to engage in discrimination in less obvious ways. Continued litigation raises questions about more subtle forms of discrimination and about the whole procedure, called for by the historical perspective, of seeking analogies to past forms of discrimination. Similar and equally pressing questions arise with respect to discrimination on different grounds, such as age or disability, that have few, if any, similarities to race. The model of racial discrimination, to which the historical perspective inevitably appeals, does not offer much assistance in analyzing these newly recognized grounds of discrimination. The statutes prohibiting such discrimination are framed in much the same terms—often using exactly the same language—as Title VII, but they must be applied to different situations raising different issues. Claims of discrimination in failing to accommodate a disabled employee on the job, for instance, raise very different issues from claims of discrimination on the basis of race.

The historical perspective also has more fundamental limitations, all attributable to its narrow focus on the precise language and surrounding circumstances of the enactment of the civil rights laws. Such a narrow focus is incapable of answering the question why the law prohibits discrimination only on certain grounds and not on others, only on the basis of sex or gender, for instance, but not on the basis of sexual orientation. Nor does the historical perspective offer much insight into the prohibition against racial discrimination itself when it is applied to such controversial issues as affirmative action. To point out that the language of Title VII prohibits any consideration of race in employment is not to settle, but only to begin, an argument over the legality of affirmative action. The historical perspective, consistent with its emphasis on the official documentary record, gives priority to a formal analysis of the language of enacted statutes. Yet most of the debate over affirmative action concerns the question whether a formal approach is appropriate in defining what constitutes prohibited discrimination. The failure to answer such questions would not be so bad if the scope and content of the concept of discrimination were clear—

if "we knew it when we saw it." But, as will become evident, we do not.

Some scholars have turned to recent psychological research to redress these deficiencies in the historical perspective, relying upon empirical studies of "implicit discrimination." This form of discrimination occurs subliminally without an individual necessarily even being aware of it. The studies in this field typically ask subjects to associate members of different groups with desirable or undesirable characteristics. Thus in one kind of experiment, the subject is confronted with faces that appear to be African–American or white and then to decide whether they fit with words like "good" or "bad." The subject usually takes longer to associate African–American with qualities like "good" rather than "bad."[3] The response times, however, are designed to be quite short so that subjects do not conceal their initial reactions. Exactly how to generalize from such rapid responses to more considered decisions, typical of those in the work place, has proved to be a contentious issue. Some scholars conclude that these studies establish the pervasiveness of discrimination in everyday interactions, with an inevitable effect on employment decisions, while others find the evidence for any such link between subliminal and conscious processes to be lacking.[4]

Apart from social scientific questions of validity involved in this debate, further questions of policy also must be asked, and in particular, the extent to which the laws can impose liability based on widely shared attitudes within society. Equality as colorblindness offers a model for decisionmaking free of bias and imposes liability only upon employers who succumb to discriminatory motivation. The argument from implicit discrimination, if accepted and generalized, casts doubt upon whether colorblindness can be achieved at all. It raises the question whether liability can be imposed on other grounds, more realistically limited to only some employers. This question, in turn, requires an appeal to rival conceptions of equality and alternative perspectives on the laws against employment discrimination.

B. The Economic Perspective: Equality as Merit

The economic perspective typically is associated with a conservative position, one that limits legal intervention in the economy in

---

3. Marianne Bertrand, Dolly Chugh & Sendhil Mullainathan, Implicit Discrimination 95 Am. Econ. Ass'n Papers and Proceedings 94 (2005).

4. *Compare* Linda Hamilton Krieger, Behavioral Realism in Employment Discrimination Law: Implicit Bias and Dis-

parate Treatment, 94 Cal. L. Rev. 997, 1027–29 (2006) (finding a connection) *with* Gregory Mitchell & Philip E. Tetlock, Antidiscrimination Law and the Perils of Mindreading, 67 Ohio St. L.J. 1023 (2006) (finding an absence of empirical evidence).

order to foster competition in free markets for employment. In terms of equality, it rests on a view of merit as "careers open to talents," assuring individuals the right to compete based on their existing abilities as determined by their natural endowments as augmented by education and experience. This conception of equality as merit does not guarantee the results of the competition, or indeed, even the opportunity to gain the talents necessary to prevail in the competition. Individuals must compete based solely on the qualifications that they bring to the labor market. Nevertheless, this is a positive conception of equality because, in contrast to the negative conception, it tells employers what to consider, not just what to avoid. Equality as merit in the economic perspective tells employers to consider the productivity of individual employees within the firm.

The force of this command, however, depends upon its source. In the dominant economic view, it comes not from the law but from the market. Employers make judgments about the merit of employees based on competition in the labor market, where those employees are hired; on competition in the product market, where the employer's goods and services are sold; and on the technology of the firm, which determines how an employee's talents are used. All of these factors together determine the employee's overall productivity. Merit, on the economic view, is not required by the legal system but by the market. Unlike the alternative perspectives, the economic view prefers a system of private decisionmaking over legally enforced rules. This distinctive institutional commitment of the economic perspective tends to confer greater discretion upon employers than the alternative perspectives would necessarily allow, with their emphasis on the legal system as the institutional means of achieving equality.

Of course, it is possible to have different views of merit and of the related positive conception of equality, and to endorse different institutional arrangements to ensure that employees are selected according to merit. Merit might be interpreted more broadly, as it has been, for instance, by John Rawls, who would require "full equality of opportunity": providing individuals not only with "careers open to talents," but also with the same opportunity to develop their talents, regardless of differences in social and class background. Methods other than the market might also be used to ensure employment based on merit, as it is in civil service examinations or in internal forms of evaluation used by private firms. These possibilities reveal an ambiguity in the concept of merit that is occasionally exploited in employment discrimination law. Instead of deferring to an employer's assessment of merit and leaving the market to determine whether it is correct, the courts sometimes reassess an employer's decision according to independent standards of merit. The courts tend to take this step when, for one reason or another, an employer's decision is suspected of being discriminatory, for instance, because it conforms to racial or ethnic stereotypes. In contrast to the dominant conception of merit, this conception gives little deference to the business judgment of the employer and instead relies upon the court's own assessment of whether the plaintiff was qualified for the job.

Reliance on such alternative conceptions of merit, however, cannot be regularly invoked in interpreting and enforcing the laws against employment discrimination. These laws have limited aims and limited scope, which impose corresponding limitations on the institutional power of courts. As the term itself implies, the laws against employment discrimination apply only to employment. They do not regulate education, social background, or family upbringing, all of which affect an individual's qualifications for employment. Even if Title VII were to succeed in eliminating all discrimination within its scope, it would still leave great inequalities in wealth and in sources of income other than employment, not to mention many other factors that affect individual ability and motivation. But these laws are limited in another way as well: they prohibit discrimination only on certain specified grounds, such as race and sex. They do not prohibit discrimination based on any of the innumerable factors that might, or might not, affect productivity. These factors are left, with only a few exceptions, to consideration by employers subject to the competitive pressure of the market. This conception of equality as merit, insofar as it defers to the judgment of employers, agrees with the historical conception of equality as colorblindness in leaving these factors outside the scope of legal regulation.

The narrow scope of the economic conception of equality based on merit explains an otherwise puzzling feature of the law: the prominent role of management discretion as a defense to claims of employment discrimination. The courts invoke such discretion so frequently that it has become virtually a countervailing principle of law. For every plaintiff's claim of discrimination, employers can offer an equal and opposite defense of management discretion, which appears routinely in cases of individual discrimination[5] and

---

5. *E.g.*, McDonnell Douglas Corp. v. Green, 411 U.S. 792, 802 (1973).

influences issues as remote as affirmative action.[6] An alternative conception of merit based on independent standards would support broad legal intervention into employment decisions, but the dominant conception of merit has had almost exactly the opposite effect: to confer on employers a degree of immunity from judicial scrutiny of their decisions. The economic perspective has a ready explanation for this seeming anomaly. The law does not neglect merit, but simply assigns it to the market as the institution most capable of assessing the effect of individual qualifications on productivity.

If it were to stop there, however, the economic perspective could offer no justification at all for the laws against employment discrimination. If the market is adequate to assess merit, then it is adequate to prevent discrimination when it is unrelated to merit. And in those cases—perhaps few, perhaps many—in which discrimination is related to merit, then the law detracts from efficiency by prohibiting discrimination. Thus legal prohibitions against discrimination are either redundant or counterproductive, but in any case, unnecessary. Repealing these laws would have the advantages of freeing labor markets from unneeded regulation and eliminating the cost of enforcing the regulations themselves. This conclusion takes the economic perspective and its presumption against regulation to its logical extreme: eliminating all regulation of employment decisions.

Most economists, however, do not go so far. They offer two theories of discrimination that explain the continued existence of discrimination, even in competitive markets. These theories correspond to, and in a sense, elaborate upon the qualities of stigma and stereotype that the historical view finds to be characteristic of past discrimination. The first, devised by Gary S. Becker, explains the different treatment of black and white employees according to a "taste for discrimination," either by coworkers, customers, or the employers themselves.[7] This taste for discrimination increases the cost of employing black workers and so leads to a decrease in their wages or salary, equal in amount to the cost of frustrating the tastes of others who prefer not to associate with blacks. Although this theory was offered as an explanation for the persistence of discrimination in competitive markets, it also provides a justification for the laws against employment discrimination insofar as they prohibit reliance on tastes for discrimination. It offers, in effect, an economic interpretation of the stigma that accompanies many forms of discrimination.

6. *E.g.*, United Steelworkers v. Weber, 443 U.S. 193 (1979).

7. Gary S. Becker, The Economics of Discrimination (2d ed. 1971).

A second economic theory of discrimination, proposed by Edmund S. Phelps, attributes discrimination to statistical differences in measuring the productivity of black and white employees.[8] According to this theory, discrimination against black workers can arise if employers find it more difficult, and therefore more costly, to predict their productivity as compared to the productivity of white workers. Black workers, for instance, might have a greater variance in performance or a lower average performance than white workers, even if they have the same educational credentials or other qualifications as white workers. The greater cost of evaluating black workers or the greater risk of poor performance as compared to white workers, according to this theory, leads employers not to hire black workers or to pay them less if they are hired. Like the theory based on tastes for discrimination, this theory was offered as an explanation for the continued existence of discrimination in competitive markets, and like that theory, it can also be used to justify legal prohibitions against traditional forms of discrimination. This theory, however, appeals to an economic version of stereotyping: asserting that members of racial minorities are either less likely to perform as well as white employees or that their performance is more difficult to predict than the performance of white employees. The statistical theory of discrimination asserts that employers could rationally rely upon the stereotype that members of minority groups are riskier to employ, and therefore more costly, than white employees.

Neither of these theories necessarily leads to a narrow interpretation of the laws against employment discrimination. Reliance on the economic perspective need not lead to a typically conservative view that is skeptical of legal regulation of competitive markets. An economist can—and many do—believe that tastes for discrimination or various forms of statistical discrimination are so deeply embedded in our society that they prevent long-term gains in efficiency that could be achieved through more open labor markets. Pervasive discrimination, even if it is assumed to confer some legitimate benefit on those who engage in it, discourages the victims of discrimination from trying to obtain the qualifications and jobs that would most efficiently use their talents. It is fair to say, however, that most economists would cast the burden of proof on the supporters of regulation and, in particular, the burden of proving that regulation is less costly than the competitive process in the markets themselves in eliminating discrimination. The em-

8. Edmund S. Phelps, The Statistical Theory of Racism and Sexism, 62 Am. Econ. Rev. 659 (1972).

phasis on this question—and not on any particular answer to it—is what identifies the economic perspective, just as the historical perspective emphasizes the question of how present practices resemble past forms of discrimination.

C. The Remedial Perspective and Remedial Equality

The remedial perspective takes the historical perspective and enlarges it to consider the continuing effects of past discrimination. The remedial perspective looks back to consider all of the effects resulting from past discrimination and forward to determine whether these effects persist despite the abolition of past discriminatory practices. From this perspective, the central inquiry is whether present practices, even if they do not repeat the precise forms of past discrimination, continue to perpetuate their unjust effects. This perspective is most frequently invoked to justify programs of affirmative action that seek, in a variety of different ways, to compensate for present disadvantages that can be attributed to past discrimination. It also figures prominently in the justification for imposing liability upon employers for neutral practices with discriminatory effects. Under Title VII, employers are liable for any employment practice with a disparate impact upon minorities or women, subject only to a defense that the disputed practice is "job related for the position in question and consistent with business necessity."[9] Employers are required to take steps to minimize the adverse consequences of their practices upon racial minorities and women.

Both affirmative action and liability for discriminatory effects are characteristically liberal positions and so is the remedial perspective. This perspective would extend the laws against employment discrimination to intervene in labor markets to foster a broader conception of equality: one that ensured the opportunity of previously excluded groups not only to compete for jobs, but to compete free of the debilitating effects of past discrimination. Unlike the economic perspective, the remedial perspective goes beyond a concern solely with equal competition according to present qualifications; it supports a conception of equality that ensures a greater degree of fairness in acquiring the relevant qualifications.

This conception of equality, although broader than merit in the economic sense, stops short of creating "group rights" or "equality of results." It guarantees only a right to compete, not a right to

9. § 703(k), codified as 42 U.S.C. § 2000e2(k) (2000).

succeed. As President Lyndon Johnson said in a famous speech arguing for the passage of civil rights legislation:

> You do not take a person who, for years, has been hobbled by chains and liberate him, bring him up to the starting line of a race and then say, "[Y]ou are free to compete with all the others," and still justly believe you have been completely fair.[10]

The remedial perspective, at least as applied to racial discrimination, remains tied to the past, and it has accordingly become more controversial as the era of open discrimination has faded from memory, making it more difficult to attribute present disadvantages to past wrongs. This trend is apparent in the increasing doubts voiced about affirmative action as a remedy for past discrimination.

Nevertheless, the remedial perspective has been extended in surprising ways and, in particular, to justify compensation for natural disadvantages or, more accurately, disadvantages not resulting from past discrimination. Both with respect to sex discrimination and discrimination on the basis of disability, the law has required employers to accommodate conditions, such as pregnancy and physical or mental impairments, that do not in any way result from past discriminatory practices. To be sure, these laws still speak in terms of prohibiting discrimination, seemingly in the negative sense of not taking account of an individual's sex or disability, yet the obligations imposed upon employers are just the opposite: to consider these characteristics, and to some degree, to compensate for them.

The affirmative nature of this obligation appears most clearly in the Americans with Disabilities Act (ADA), which imposes an explicit duty upon employers to reasonably accommodate disabled individuals who are otherwise qualified for the job.[11] This duty is not an accidental feature of the statute but one that is necessary to achieve a workable version of equal opportunity for disabled individuals. The ADA also prohibits familiar forms of discrimination based on stigmas and stereotypes associated with having a disability, in language borrowed directly from Title VII. These prohibitions are addressed to the social consequences of disabilities and, in particular, to cases in which an employer wrongfully believes that a disability disqualifies an individual from performing a particular job. But a disability necessarily impairs an individual's ability to

---

10. II Public Papers of the Presidents of the United States: Lyndon B. Johnson, 1965 at 636 (1966).

11. § 102(b)(5), codified at 42 U.S.C. § 12112(b)(5) (2000).

perform some tasks and these tasks might be related to the performance of a particular job. When they are, the employer does not act on an erroneous belief in refusing to employ a disabled individual.

In these cases, the employer cannot be told simply to hire the individual regardless of the disability. The costs of doing so would be too great, not just in monetary terms, but often by imposing excessive risks on others. The ADA therefore recognizes various defenses such as "undue hardship" on the employer and "direct threats" to the safety of others.[12] But conversely, to allow an employer to take account of a disability whenever it interfered with good performance on the job would be to allow wholesale exclusion of individuals with disabilities. Even the slightest effect on job performance would result in exclusion of individuals who have the relevant disabilities. Compared to these extreme alternatives, the duty of reasonable accommodation provides a feasible means of increasing the jobs available to the disabled. It does so, however, only by departing from the simple model of racial discrimination and the corresponding prohibition against considering race in Title VII. The duty of reasonable accommodation requires employers to take account of an individual's disability instead of ignoring it, assuring a degree of special treatment based on disability rather than equal treatment regardless of it.

In other respects, the remedial perspective does not explain existing law so much as assume a critical attitude towards it. The status quo seldom conforms to any ideal of equality, and to the extent it falls short, any divergence from the ideal can be attributed to the failure of existing law to fully redress the consequences of past discrimination or natural disadvantages. It is, for instance, difficult to imagine how American society would have developed in the absence of slavery and other forms of pervasive racism. It is correspondingly easy to assume that racial and ethnic minorities would have achieved the same position as the majority in the absence of racism and that they are therefore entitled to compensation for any resulting disadvantage. To take this step, however, would be to embrace "group rights" or "equality of results," in which the economic benefits of employment are divided among groups identified according to otherwise prohibited grounds of discrimination. On this approach, remedial measures would be required until members of each group were employed at every level of income and in each sector in the economy according to their

---

12. §§ 102(b)(5), 103(b), codified as   (2000).
42 U.S.C. §§ 12112(b)(5), 12113(b)

representation in the working age population. Whatever the merits of this conception of equality in the abstract—and it is not without difficulties—it is fundamentally inconsistent both with existing law and with the remedial perspective itself. It would require constant redistribution of jobs in the economy according to the very grounds of discrimination that these laws currently prohibit. A remedial conception of equality cannot, without falling into a vicious circle, collapse the condition to be remedied into the failure simply to implement the proposed remedy. A remedial conception of equality must offer an independent baseline for determining what constitutes past discrimination and its continuing effects that must now be remedied. And even the statutes that prohibit discrimination on the basis of disability, insofar as they remedy natural disadvantages, presuppose different restrictions. They do not cover all disabilities, and even those they do cover receive only partial accommodation.

Legal theorists from a variety of movements have offered different elaborations of the baseline from which the adequacy of different remedial measures can be assessed. These movements tend, at least in recent years, to be focused on specific groups so that, for instance, critical race theorists, feminists, and disability rights advocates offer different accounts of the disadvantages that the law should compensate for. Critical race theorists, on the one hand, emphasize the continuing effects of centuries of slavery and segregation and the persistence of patterns of racism established in earlier eras. Feminists, on the other hand, emphasize the variety of social practices that have confined women to the domestic sphere of home and children under the overall control and authority of men. These differences are multiplied when we look at the differences within these groups themselves. Not all ethnic groups identify the same wrongs and their consequences that need to be remedied and not all women identify the same practices as sexist. And some members of all of these groups do not endorse the remedial perspective in any form.

Such differences are not surprising once we recognize that the model of racial discrimination no longer commands a consensus, either as to other grounds of discrimination or as to racial discrimination itself. Simply eliminating most forms of overt discrimination, which the historical perspective rightly takes to be the great achievement of the Civil Rights Era, does not eliminate all the forms of inequality addressed by the civil rights laws. Exactly what those forms of inequality are remains a matter of controversy and differs from one ground of discrimination to another. The value of the remedial perspective is that it brings these issues out into the open, and in doing so, reveals the gap between what the law seeks to achieve and what it has in fact accomplished.

D. General Theories of Equality

None of these perspectives—historical, economic, or remedial—is entirely freestanding or, indeed, even entirely independent of the alternative perspectives. The differences between them, as I have said, are a matter of emphasis rather than a matter of fundamental principle and comprehensive theory. They are three different ways of looking at the laws against employment discrimination, which would have to be combined and reconciled to develop a fully adequate theory. As will emerge in the subsequent chapters in this book, no single perspective can offer a satisfactory description, let alone a justification or critique, of existing law. For example, Richard Epstein offers a comprehensive argument for repeal of the laws against employment discrimination, mainly from the economic perspective.[13] Yet he also argues from the historical perspective that the civil rights laws were necessary to break down barriers to racial equality created by segregation under state law. In response to the remedial view, he argues at length for the superiority of competitive markets over government regulation in eliminating the consequences of past discrimination. Although his overall position is more critical than descriptive of existing law (because he would drastically limit the degree of legal intervention in employment decisions), he offers a theory broad enough to encompass all three perspectives on employment discrimination law.

Each of these perspectives, and their associated conceptions of equality, must also be related to broader political theories which address issues that go far beyond the field of employment discrimination law. These theories address the distribution of wealth and social status, in addition to employment opportunities, and they define equality in broader terms than the limited grounds on which the law prohibits discrimination. They range across the political spectrum, from libertarian defenses of individual rights to liberal theories of equal opportunity. There is no shortage of different views about equality, whether political, philosophical, or legal.[14]

13. Richard A. Epstein, Forbidden Grounds: The Case Against Employment Discrimination Laws (1992).

14. Ronald Dworkin, Sovereign Virtue 65–119 (2000) (equality of resources); John Finnis, Natural Law and Natural Rights 106–10 (1980) (no arbi- trary preferences among persons); Robert Nozick, Anarchy, State, and Utopia (1974) (equal individual rights); John Rawls, A Theory of Justice 73–78, 86–93 (rev. ed. 1999) (equal opportunity). For an historical survey of different views of equality that have been influential in

Equality with respect to race, for instance, would bear upon only one aspect of a general theory of equality, such as Rawls's theory mentioned earlier. In his theory of justice, Rawls advances two main principles that guarantee both full equality of opportunity and substantial redistribution of resources to those who are worst off, regardless of the opportunities available to them. These principles are broadly consistent with the laws against employment discrimination, but as indicated earlier, they can be transformed into a justification for these laws only with considerable elaboration and qualification.

Prohibitions against discrimination fit into these theories in a variety of different ways: as components of a theory of justice, either incorporated in or logically entailed by the theory itself; or as concrete instances of what satisfies principles of justice, even if alternative social arrangements would also satisfy such principles; or as a means of achieving justice, not in any conceptual manner but empirically, as a means to the desired end of establishing a just society. No doubt other ways of relating abstract theories to specific legal prohibitions could also be devised, and more than one could be invoked to argue for the need to prohibit discrimination on various grounds. There is no inconsistency between arguing that nondiscrimination is an essential element of any just society and that nondiscrimination with respect to one characteristic, such as race, increases the degree of equality with respect to another, such as class.

In an introductory text, a wide-ranging discussion of general theories of equality and their relationship to prohibitions against discrimination would be out of place. The perspectives offered here do not track the essential features of any such theory or its relationship to existing legal doctrine. Instead, these perspectives take only one step in the direction of offering a more general point of view from which to interpret the laws against employment discrimination. They do not answer the question: Are the legal prohibitions against employment discrimination justified as a matter of political morality? Instead, they presume that these prohibitions are justified—indeed, required by any fully developed theory of justice—and that the legislators who enacted these prohibitions acted on this presumption.

The most plausible justifications incorporate one or more of the three perspectives discussed in this chapter–colorblindness, merit,

the United States, see J.R. Pole, The   (2d ed., rev. & enlarged 1993).
Pursuit of Equality in American History

and remedial equality. These perspectives, in turn, allow us to address the question how these laws should be interpreted. On most jurisprudential theories, the justification for a law figures in its interpretation, and the laws against employment discrimination are no exception. This book does not choose among the justifications offered for the laws against employment discrimination, but instead describes the plurality of views that have been offered and how they have influenced the subsequent interpretation and development of these laws. This history of doctrinal refinement and evolution reveals a continuing competition between different perspectives and different conceptions of equality.

Such competition between rival perspectives is only to be expected in a field, such as employment discrimination law, in which statutes predominate as the primary source of law. Nothing is more common than finding competing viewpoints embodied in different statutes, in different provisions of the same statute, or occasionally, within a single provision of the same statute. Compromise lies at the heart of the legislative process and making sense of legislative compromises is essential to sound statutory interpretation. What is surprising about employment discrimination law is the extent to which competing perspectives can be found within different judicial decisions and, again, even within a single decision. Judicial opinions, not just the statutory language, equivocate between different conceptions of equality, invoking one and then another without explicitly acknowledging the differences between them.

Such equivocation cannot be eliminated, only described, in any attempt to give an accurate account of existing law. More comprehensive and more critical theories of equality no doubt would resolve these equivocations one way or another. But these theories can be applied to the law of employment discrimination only after its ambiguities and nuances have been fully explored. The next chapter begins this task with an examination of individual claims of intentional discrimination under Title VII.

Chapter III

INDIVIDUAL CLAIMS OF INTENTIONAL DISCRIMINATION

The great majority of employment discrimination cases involve claims of intentional discrimination asserted by individual plaintiffs.[1] Although large in number, these cases do not usually attract much publicity or attention. They do not involve large classes of employees and they do not challenge affirmative action plans (a topic to be taken up in a subsequent chapter). They are, instead, cases in which an individual plaintiff claims that an adverse personnel decision was based on a prohibited characteristic, of which race is the paradigm and to which others have since been added. Because such claims form so large a part of the caseload, they raise issues of enormous significance in the interpretation and enforcement of the laws against employment discrimination.

The most heavily litigated issue, and the one to which this chapter is devoted, is the definition of intentional discrimination, an issue worked out mainly through allocation of the burden of proof. The opinions on burden of proof have succeeded in formulating a consistent set of doctrinal rules. They have been less successful in achieving the broader goals of assuring the consistent resolution of employment discrimination claims, controlling the allocation of issues between judge and jury, and expediting the overall process of settlement and litigation. The tension between the actual effects of doctrinal rules and what they were designed to accomplish, here as elsewhere in the law, results in continuing litigation and continuing attempts to improve upon existing law.

This chapter begins with an analysis of the statutory prohibitions against intentional discrimination, followed by a detailed discussion of the leading decision on burdens of proof in individual cases of intentional discrimination, *McDonnell Douglas Corp. v. Green*.[2] The discussion then turns to subsequent refinements and limitations on the holding of *McDonnell Douglas*, first in the case law and then through amendments to Title VII. This chapter concludes with an assessment of what the allocation of burdens of

---

1. John J. Donohue III & Peter Siegelman, The Changing Nature of Employment Discrimination, 43 Stan. L. Rev. 983, 1019–21 (1991).

2. 411 U.S. 792 (1973).

proof actually has accomplished in defining intentional discrimination.

A.   Statutory Definitions of Discrimination

Title VII does not contain any definition of intentional discrimination as a technical term of art. Neither do any of the other statutes modeled on Title VII. In this respect, the statutory law of employment discrimination follows constitutional law in leaving the exact nature of what is prohibited without any precise definition. In fact, the phrase "intentional discrimination" is at least partly redundant. All discrimination is intentional in some sense because it requires noticing or acting on some kind of distinction. In ordinary English, outside of civil rights law, the phrase "to discriminate" carries no negative connotations and simply means to "make a distinction," which is an activity that cannot be done inadvertently or accidentally. Exactly what kind of distinction transforms discrimination into a morally disapproved and legally prohibited activity remains controversial, but the most natural answer is found in the main statutory prohibitions against employment discrimination.

In Title VII, these prohibitions are framed in very broad terms that encompass virtually all employment practices, including any form of discrimination or segregation affecting an individual's employment "because of such individual's race, color, religion, sex, or national origin." The language "because of" supports an interpretation of intentional discrimination in terms of reasons for action. An employer cannot use any of the prohibited characteristics as a reason for making any kind of personnel decision. The quoted language focuses on the employer's process of decisionmaking—on what goes into an employer's decision rather than what comes out of it. The intentional aspect of discrimination is simply presumed as part of the process of using a prohibited reason.

The closest that Title VII comes to recognizing the role of intention in discrimination is in two provisions authorizing remedies only for "intentional" violations of the statute. An indication of the difficulties involved in defining intentional discrimination is that the word "intentional" in these provisions has been interpreted in two quite different ways. In one, the action is intentional only insofar as it involves an intent to make a decision with respect to employment. This is the meaning that "intentional" is given in the provision that authorizes general equitable remedies against a defendant who "has intentionally engaged in or is intentionally engaging in an unlawful employment practice."[3] All disputed personnel decisions are intentional in this sense because an employer invariably intends to affect the terms and conditions of employment by making any such decision. Thus general equitable remedies, such as an injunction and back pay, are available for all violations of Title VII.

In the other provision, "intentional discrimination" is given its narrower—and far more common—meaning in employment discrimination law. This meaning refers to the grounds on which an employment decision is discriminatory: an employer intends to discriminate in this sense only by intending to act on the basis of race or some other prohibited characteristic. The provision in question limits damages to cases of "unlawful intentional discrimination (not an employment practice that is unlawful because of its disparate impact)."[4] As the parenthetical phrase indicates, the statute distinguishes between intentional discrimination and disparate impact. The former (sometimes also called disparate treatment) involves consideration of race or some other prohibited characteristic; the latter involves only discriminatory effects. Liability for employment practices that have a disparate impact, discussed in detail in the next chapter, emphasizes the effects of employment decisions, not the process of decisionmaking itself. Only equitable remedies are available for claims of disparate impact. By contrast, intentional discrimination, as it is usually understood in employment discrimination law, refers to consideration of a prohibited characteristic in making an employment decision. Both damages and equitable relief are available for claims of intentional discrimination.

These statutory provisions leave open the possibility of multiple reasons for any single decision. A decision can be "because of such individual's race" and also be because of other factors, such as a lack of experience or other qualifications for the job. Title VII addresses this possibility in a provision, only recently added to the statute, that defines sufficient proof of unlawful discrimination to include proof that a prohibited characteristic "was a motivating factor for any employment practice, even though other factors also motivated the practice."[5] This provision raises two issues, one conceptual and one practical.

The conceptual issue is whether employers can engage in intentional discrimination that they are not entirely aware of. In

3. § 706(g), codified as 42 U.S.C. § 2000e–5(g)(1) (2000).

4. 42 U.S.C. § 1981a(c) (2000).

5. § 703(m), codified as 42 U.S.C. § 2000e–2(m) (2000).

using the phrase "motivating factor," the preceding provision suggests a greater role for purely causal considerations than a definition in terms of reasons for action. Motives, more than intentions, may not be fully appreciated by the employer or the agent who acts on his behalf. And, in fact, many employers are organizations, not individuals, which are capable of acting only through individual agents. For these employers, any employment decision may result from the actions of a variety of different agents, with no agent likely to be aware of all the factors considered by the others. Such factors of which no one is fully conscious figure in disputes over whether the law prohibits "unconscious discrimination": whether an employer is liable for discrimination based on stereotypes and other habitual patterns of thought that are so ingrained that they do not rise to the level of self-conscious discrimination.

"Unconscious discrimination" in this sense is different from simple ignorance of the law, which is an employer's failure to recognize that the law prohibits certain forms of discrimination. The latter is never a complete defense, although it may be a partial defense to recovery of liquidated or punitive damages.[6] In order to establish a violation, the law requires only that a prohibited factor have entered into the employer's decisionmaking process. To require more would open up litigation over the extent of an employer's legal sophistication and would create perverse incentives to remain ignorant of the law.

"Unconscious discrimination" reaches a more subtle form of ignorance, in which an employer discriminates by taking race (or some other prohibited characteristic) into account, but without being aware of having done so. Although of some theoretical interest, actual cases rarely turn on this subtle distinction. It is not a promising defense to a claim of racial discrimination that an employer has treated blacks and whites differently but just wasn't aware of it. As discussed in the next section, the allocation of the burden of proof does not focus on fine distinctions between different states of mind, but on the nondiscriminatory reasons offered by the employer for a decision adverse to the plaintiff. The law turns away from a subjective inquiry in theory—what did the employer or its authorized agent think?—to an objective inquiry in practice—did the employer have some other credible reason for its decision?

This shift in focus makes the multiplicity of reasons that can be offered in defense of any employment decision an issue of great practical significance, so much so that it has been a source of

---

6. *See* 42 U.S.C. § 1981a(b)(1) (2000) (punitive damages can be awarded only if an employer acts "with malice or with reckless indifference to the federally protected rights of an aggrieved individual").

almost unending litigation. On any definition of intentional discrimination that focuses on the decisionmaking process, the presence of one motive or reason for a decision does not exclude the possibility of others. It is this possibility that is addressed by the cases, and more recently the statutory amendments, allocating the burden of proof. These issues arise almost entirely from the tension between rival conceptions of equality.

The prohibition against intentional discrimination is framed according to the negative conception of equality. It is a prohibition upon considering characteristics such as race or sex in making employment decisions. In this respect, it follows the historical perspective in focusing upon previously widespread forms of discrimination. But where these forms of discrimination were open and explicit in the past—simply excluding racial minorities and women from particular jobs—they have become hidden and implicit today. After the passage of Title VII, any employer engaged in overt discrimination on these grounds would face a great risk of liability. Employers have adjusted to the requirements of Title VII by eliminating the most obviously discriminatory employment practices, and even when they cannot succeed in doing so, they have strong reasons to settle claims arising from overt discrimination that can be easily established. It is only the less obvious forms of discrimination that are any longer likely to result in extended litigation. Yet it is in these cases that the historical perspective fails to provide much practical guidance. Almost by definition, the claims of discrimination litigated today are different from the forms of discrimination practiced in the past, before the laws against employment discrimination took effect.

It follows that the historical perspective must be supplemented by alternative perspectives, either the economic perspective with its emphasis on the employer's business judgment in assessing merit or the remedial perspective emphasizing the continuing consequences of past discrimination. A positive conception of merit, as determined by the employer's business judgment in competitive markets, supports the broad range of alternative reasons that an employer can offer for an allegedly discriminatory decision. Any reason, other than a prohibited reason, will do. This follows, not just from a negative conception of equality modeled on past forms of discrimination, but also from the need to give employers the freedom to make personnel decisions to meet the changing demands of the market.

Yet the evaluation of the reasons offered by an employer inevitably introduces a more searching, and more difficult, element into the analysis. Despite judicial decisions and jury instructions

35

that require deference to the employer's judgment, the quality of the reason offered by the employer inevitably affects the determination whether it is merely a pretext for discrimination. The more closely these reasons are tied to the plaintiff's ability (or inability) to perform the job, the more persuasive they are as a defense; and conversely, the weaker the employer's reasons are, the more they support a finding of discrimination. An arbitrary reason, such as a supervisor's distaste for the plaintiff's clothes, is more likely to be found to be a pretext for discrimination than one based on the plaintiff's performance of the job. Legal doctrine does not require employers to offer good reasons for their decisions, but the practicalities of litigation often compel them to do so.

This heightened scrutiny of employers' decisions finds support in the remedial perspective, which gives priority to eliminating the consequences of past discrimination, including continued instances of hidden discrimination. This perspective, more so than the alternatives, emphasizes the need to root out the subtle influence of past discrimination on present decisions. In contrast to the alternative perspectives, it is less concerned about the cost of eliminating hidden discrimination. Overenforcement of the law, according to the remedial perspective, does not lead to undue interference with the employer's business judgment and an unjustified loss in economic efficiency. At most, it results in a misdirected benefit conferred on the wrong individuals—not genuine victims of discrimination, but still members of a group, such as a racial minority, that historically have been denied employment opportunities. Under the remedial perspective, it is the suspicion of hidden discrimination, based on habits of thought resulting from past discrimination, that justifies a closer look at the employer's decisionmaking process. Exactly how close a look is taken, however, depends upon the intricacy of existing law, to which we now turn.

B. McDonnell Douglas Corp. v. Green

No decision in employment discrimination law has been cited more frequently than *McDonnell Douglas Corp. v. Green.* Yet none has had a more ambiguous legacy. This single decision has made shifting burdens of proof a dominant theme in employment discrimination law. Even apart from individual claims of intentional discrimination, most of the substantive law under Title VII concerns who has the burden of proof on a variety of different issues. But despite the proliferation of shifting burdens of proof, fundamental issues have been left unresolved and even the outcome of particular cases has been left to depend upon all the evidence in the record.

36

These failings have led to continued refinements of these burdens, or alternatively, to calls to channel employment discrimination cases to forms of alternative dispute resolution, principally arbitration.

The burden of proof has two different components: the burden of producing evidence and the burden of persuading the trier of fact. The burden of production requires the party with the burden to present evidence from which a reasonable inference can be drawn to a conclusion in its favor. Failure to meet the burden results in entry of summary judgment or a directed verdict (or its equivalents, such as a motion for judgment notwithstanding the verdict, or in current terminology, a motion for judgment as a matter of law). The burden of production is therefore a device for avoiding trial and for controlling the jury by screening out cases in which a party has failed to present sufficient evidence. It can also screen out some issues, but not others, through the partial grant of summary judgment or directed verdict.[7] The jury itself need not be instructed on the burden of production because it operates only to determine which issues go to the jury.[8]

By contrast, the jury must be instructed on the burden of persuasion because that determines what happens once a case gets to the jury. The burden of persuasion (or risk of nonpersuasion) applies to all of those issues on which reasonable inferences can be drawn for either the plaintiff or the defendant. It requires the jury to resolve all issues on which the evidence is evenly balanced against the party with the burden of persuasion. This follows from the fact that in civil cases, the burden of persuasion is proof by a preponderance of the evidence; the party with the burden must only establish more probably than not that the facts are in its favor. This burden is much lighter than the corresponding burden in criminal cases of proof beyond a reasonable doubt. Yet perhaps because of the influence of criminal procedure as a model, the burden of persuasion in civil cases appears to have effects beyond its technical meaning, at least in cases tried to a jury. The jury is instructed on the burden of persuasion and lawyers seek, whenever they can, to have the burden placed upon the opposing party. This common litigation strategy would be inexplicable if the burden only made a difference in the few cases in which the evidence is exactly equally balanced.

---

7. Fed. R. Civ. P. 50(a), 56(d).

8. *E.g.*, Cabrera v. Jakabovitz, 24 F.3d 372, 380 (2d Cir. 1994), *cert. denied*, 513 U.S. 876 (1994) (cautioning against instructing the jury on the shifting burdens of production under *McDonnell Douglas*).

The burden of proof allocated in *McDonnell Douglas* is only the burden of production. The burden of persuasion on the issue of intentional discrimination remains always with the plaintiff. *McDonnell Douglas* itself concerned a fairly unusual case of failure to rehire. Green, a black civil rights activist, had formerly worked for McDonnell Douglas as a mechanic. After he left his job there, he participated in several demonstrations against the company, including acts of civil disobedience that attempted to disrupt the company's operations. When he re-applied for a job with McDonnell Douglas, he was rejected and then filed a claim of racial discrimination.[9]

The Supreme Court held that this claim should be evaluated according to the following framework. A plaintiff may establish a prima facie case of intentional discrimination by showing:

> (i) that he belongs to a racial minority; (ii) that he applied and was qualified for a job for which the employer was seeking applicants; (iii) that, despite his qualifications, he was rejected; and (iv) that, after his rejection, the position remained open and the employer continued to seek applicants from persons of complainant's qualifications.[10]

If the plaintiff carries this burden, then the defendant has the burden "to articulate some legitimate, nondiscriminatory reason for the employee's rejection." And if the defendant carries that burden, the plaintiff has the burden of proving that the stated reason for his rejection was in fact a pretext for discrimination.[11]

On the facts of *McDonnell Douglas*, the Supreme Court held that both the plaintiff's initial burden and the defendant's rebuttal burden had been satisfied, leaving only the issue of pretext. In the plaintiff's prima facie case, Green's qualifications might have been open to dispute, but since he had formerly been employed by McDonnell Douglas and had performed satisfactorily as a mechanic, this requirement was plainly satisfied. Green already had the minimal qualifications for the job, which were all that was required, as a close look at the last element of the plaintiff's prima facie case reveals. This last element is satisfied if the employer seeks applicants of the same qualifications as the plaintiff, even if he would prefer someone with superior qualifications. "Qualifications" in the second element therefore cannot mean best available qualifications. And, indeed, as the Supreme Court subsequently recognized, the

---

9. The Supreme Court did not consider an additional claim of retaliation for opposing discriminatory practices, in violation of § 704(a), codified as 42 U.S.C. § 2000e–3(a) (2000).

10. 411 U.S. at 802 (footnote omitted).

11. *Id.* at 803–04.

selection of a better qualified applicant normally enters into the case as a legitimate, nondiscriminatory reason offered by the defendant.[12]

The actual outcome in *McDonnell Douglas* turned on the issue of pretext: whether the reason offered by the employer—Green's attempt to disrupt its operations—was the real reason for denying him a job, or whether the reason was his race. This issue became decisive, as it has in so many cases, because both the plaintiff and the defendant could easily satisfy their initial burdens of production. The definition of pretext, however, depends heavily on the definition of intentional discrimination, going beyond it only to look behind the legitimate reason offered by the defendant to the real reason for the disputed decision. Was the plaintiff rejected for a legitimate reason or because of his race?

Even without the shifting burdens of production under *McDonnell Douglas*, the ultimate question of intentional discrimination usually would be posed in these terms. The best way for the employer to persuade the judge or jury that the plaintiff was not a victim of discrimination is to offer a reason for rejecting him that makes good business sense. *McDonnell Douglas* succeeds primarily in imposing some structure on this method of proof, which would be used in any event. The opinion itself offers this structure as only one way among others of deciding claims of intentional discrimination.[13]

The opinion also limits the structure of shifting burdens of production in other ways as well. This structure does not affect either the burden of persuasion, which remains always with the plaintiff, or the order of proof, which is subject to the broad discretion of the judge.[14] Plaintiffs still must put on all the favorable evidence available to them in order to meet their burden of persuasion. And to be sure that it is all admitted into evidence, they are well advised to do so in their case-in-chief. Evidence offered in their rebuttal case might be excluded because it does not respond to evidence offered by the defendant. Discovery, if not the pleadings and pretrial orders, should alert plaintiffs to the legitimate reason that the defendant relies on and allow them to present evidence that anticipates it.

In the end, *McDonnell Douglas* succeeds only in devising an uneasy compromise between two fundamentally different interpretations of the statutes prohibiting employment discrimination. One,

---

12. United States Postal Serv. Bd. of Governors v. Aikens, 460 U.S. 711, 713–15 (1983).

13. 411 U.S. at 802 & n.13.

14. Fed. R. Evid. 611(a).

based on the negative conception of equality, emphasizes the subjective intent of the employer: Did the employer consider a prohibited reason in making a decision adverse to the plaintiff? The other, based on a positive conception of equality, emphasizes how objectively reasonable the employer's decision actually was: Did the employer rely on a reason that it should have in rejecting the plaintiff? As the preceding discussion shows, the negative conception of equality has triumphed in the formulation of legal doctrine. Its dominance in the application of legal doctrine to the facts is less clear. Even under a literal application of *McDonnell Douglas*, the persuasiveness of the defendant's offered reason depends inevitably on how good a reason it is. An evaluation of the merits of this reason is tempered only by the deference owed to an employer to manage its business in order to meet the demands of competitive markets.

Another feature of most employment discrimination cases reinforces the tendency to move from a subjective to an objective evaluation of the employer's decisionmaking process. Most employers are institutions, either private organizations or public agencies, rather than single individuals. Although the agents who act on behalf of these institutional employers have intentions, motives, and reasons for action in the ordinary sense, summing up their states of mind to find one to attribute to the institution as a whole can be difficult. A supervisor who makes a recommendation may do so for discriminatory reasons which are then discounted by a higher level manager who makes the final decision. Hence the continued litigation over whether a manager's or supervisor's "stray remarks" are sufficient to establish discriminatory intent. In the search for conclusive evidence of discrimination, plaintiff's lawyers often introduce discriminatory remarks made by authorized agents of the employer. The employer then responds by arguing that the remarks, even if they occurred, were so far removed from the decisionmaking process that they are irrelevant to the issue of discrimination.[15] Although problems in attributing individual intent to an institutional employer do not arise in every case, when they do, they enhance the force of the legitimate nondiscriminatory reasons offered by the employer. The more plausible those reasons are, the less likely the employer's decision was influenced by discriminatory reasons. By remanding the case for consideration of the issue of pretext, *McDonnell Douglas* recognized what was

15. *E.g.*, Shorter v. ICG Holdings, Inc., 188 F.3d 1204, 1209–10 (10th Cir. 1999) (supervisor's racist statements not adequately linked to decision to terminate plaintiff to prove discrimination); EEOC v. Clay Printing Co., 955 F.2d 936, 941–42 (4th Cir. 1992) (manager's comments about age, seniority and cost of work force insufficient to prove age discrimination).

inevitable in any event: that the legitimate reasons offered by an employer for an allegedly discriminatory decision lie at the center of most employment discrimination cases.

An alternative approach, based on a remedial perspective and designed to cure the continuing effects of past discrimination, was rejected by the Supreme Court as soon as it was proposed. In *Furnco Construction Corp. v. Waters*,[16] the plaintiffs alleged that the employer engaged in intentional discrimination in hiring specialized bricklayers who lined the interiors of blast furnaces with "fire brick." The plaintiffs were black and alleged that the employer's reliance entirely on the discretion of a supervisor in contacting and hiring employees resulted in discrimination. The district court found that the plaintiffs had not made out a claim under Title VII, but the court of appeals reversed because of the inadequacy of the employer's offered reasons, based on safety and efficiency, concluding that the "historical inequality of treatment of black workers" required a hiring procedure more accessible to black applicants.[17] The Supreme Court emphatically rejected this appeal to the remedial perspective, because it would have resulted in liability based on a finding "only that different practices would have enabled the employer to at least consider, and perhaps to hire, more minority employees."[18] This falls far short of a finding that the employer's offered reasons were a pretext for discrimination—the conclusion required by the historical perspective and its conception of equality as colorblindness. This minimal finding also runs afoul of the economic perspective because it allows too much judicial intervention in the employer's choice of neutral employment practices. Whatever its force in support of other claims of discrimination— particularly claims of disparate impact not considered in *Furnco*— the remedial perspective must yield to the alternative perspectives in individual claims of intentional discrimination.

C. Subsequent Developments

The limitations on *McDonnell Douglas* are perhaps more important than the decision itself. The Supreme Court has systematically minimized both the scope and the significance of the decision. The analysis in its opinions, however, has been so abstract and formal that much has been left to the discretion of the lower federal courts. They must decide the vast number of routine cases of intentional discrimination, and in trying to do so expeditiously,

16.   438 U.S. 567 (1978).   **18.**   *Id.* at 578.
17.   *Id.* at 573–74.

they have experimented with numerous variations on the shifting burdens of production established in *McDonnell Douglas*. For the most part, these variations have resulted only in modest clarification of the parties' burdens of production.

The limited scope of *McDonnell Douglas* is apparent from the way in which the elements of the plaintiff's prima facie case are defined. The first element, membership in a minority group, simply does not apply to claims of reverse discrimination.[19] Some courts have effectively left this gap open through the simple expedient of identifying whites as a "protected class" equivalent to a minority group.[20] Other courts have tried to fill the gap by requiring evidence of background circumstances supporting an inference of reverse discrimination.[21] Still others have adapted the defendant's rebuttal case to claims of reverse discrimination by allowing evidence of a permissible affirmative action plan to serve as a legitimate, nondiscriminatory reason.[22] This last suggestion has been taken up by the Supreme Court in a little-noticed passage that places on the plaintiff the burden of proving that an affirmative action plan is a pretext for discrimination.[23]

Although proof of intentional discrimination must somehow be reconciled with the scope of permissible affirmative action, this cannot be accomplished simply by modifying the shifting burdens of production in *McDonnell Douglas*. These burdens leave open the possibility of proving intentional discrimination by other means, including direct evidence that the employer relied on a prohibited characteristic.[24] No better direct evidence can be found than proof that the employer relied on an affirmative action plan which, by definition, involves consideration of an otherwise prohibited characteristic. Although the employer must be given the opportunity to present evidence that its affirmative action plan is permissible, this evidence does not easily fit within the framework of *McDonnell Douglas*; affirmative action is better characterized as a legitimate *discriminatory* reason than a legitimate nondiscriminatory reason.

---

19. McDonald v. Santa Fe Trail Transp. Co., 427 U.S. 273, 279 n.6 (1976).

20. *E.g.*, Chaline v. KCOH, Inc., 693 F.2d 477, 480 (5th Cir. 1982).

21. *E.g.*, Lanphear v. Prokop, 703 F.2d 1311, 1315 (D.C. Cir. 1983); *see* Lincoln v. Board of Regents, 697 F.2d 928, 938 (11th Cir. 1983), *cert. denied*, 464 U.S. 826 (1983) (relying on evidence of majority of black teachers at traditionally black college).

22. *E.g.*, Lilly v. City of Beckley, 797 F.2d 191, 194–96 (4th Cir. 1986).

23. Johnson v. Transportation Agency, 480 U.S. 616, 626 (1987).

24. *E.g.*, Trans World Airlines, Inc. v. Thurston, 469 U.S. 111, 121 (1985) (age discrimination case); Ramsey v. City of Denver, 907 F.2d 1004, 1007–08 (10th Cir. 1990), *cert. denied*, 506 U.S. 907 (1992) (sex discrimination case); EEOC v. Alton Packaging Corp., 901 F.2d 920, 923 (11th Cir. 1990) (race discrimination case).

Sensing this, most courts have not relied heavily on *McDonnell Douglas* to resolve claims of reverse discrimination.

Other cases also fall outside the literal terms of *McDonnell Douglas*, including the most common claims of employment discrimination, for wrongful discharge or layoff. Apart from disability claims, a majority of employment discrimination cases are filed by employees who have lost their jobs.[25] Two of the four elements of the plaintiff's prima facie case are largely irrelevant to the disputed issues in most of these cases. The second element, the minimal qualifications for the job, almost always is satisfied; otherwise the plaintiff would not have gotten the job in the first place. Even more so than in hiring cases, in discharge cases the litigation focuses on the plaintiff's failure to perform beyond the minimal qualifications for the job. Likewise, the fourth element, that the position remained open and the employer continued to look for applicants with the plaintiff's qualifications, is irrelevant. As the layoff cases illustrate, the continued existence of the plaintiff's position does not have any bearing at all on whether the plaintiff was discharged for a discriminatory reason.

These deficiencies in *McDonnell Douglas* have not gone unnoticed by the lower federal courts. They have substituted various alternative elements, such as satisfactory performance until the incident giving rise to the discharge,[26] departure from the general policies on discipline or discharge usually followed by the employer,[27] or different treatment compared to someone of another race or other group.[28] This last alternative does not require proof that the plaintiff was replaced by someone from a different group, although that fact might strengthen the plaintiff's claim.[29] It only requires proof that employees like the plaintiff were subject to stricter requirements than were other employees, which is, of course, just another way of stating the ultimate issue of discrimination. This formulation replaces the entire structure of shifting burdens of production, not just a single element of the plaintiff's prima facie case.

Where the lower federal courts have been led to refine *McDonnell Douglas*, the Supreme Court has been more concerned to limit

25. Donohue & Siegelman, *supra*, 43 Stan. L. Rev. at 1015.

26. Crimm v. Missouri Pacific R.R., 750 F.2d 703, 711 (8th Cir. 1984); Flowers v. Crouch–Walker Corp., 552 F.2d 1277, 1282–83 (7th Cir. 1977).

27. Moore v. City of Charlotte, 754 F.2d 1100, 1105–06 (4th Cir. 1985), *cert. denied*, 472 U.S. 1021 (1985); EEOC v. Brown & Root, Inc., 688 F.2d 338, 340–41 (5th Cir. 1982).

28. Perryman v. Johnson Prods. Co., 698 F.2d 1138, 1142–43 (11th Cir. 1983).

29. O'Connor v. Consolidated Coin Caterers Corp., 517 U.S. 308, 311–13 (1996).

its overall significance. The lower federal courts have tried to make more of the burden of proof than the Supreme Court in order to resolve the many cases that come before them. Yet the ease with which each party can satisfy its burden has left them to resolve most cases on the issue of pretext, which is just another way of framing the ultimate issue of discrimination. The Supreme Court, not faced with the need to decide a large number of routine cases, has emphasized the limited significance of all aspects of the burden of production. The Court has said repeatedly that the burden of persuasion always remains with the plaintiff,[30] that the employer's burden of articulating a legitimate nondiscriminatory reason is a light one,[31] and that most cases should be resolved on the factual issue of whether discrimination occurred instead of the legal issue of whether the burden of production has been satisfied.[32] The Court has also held that the plaintiff need not allege the elements of a prima facie case in the complaint, which need only contain "a short and plain statement showing that the pleader is entitled to relief."[33]

A case that summarizes all of these limitations is *St. Mary's Honor Center v. Hicks*,[34] which raised the question whether the plaintiff could prevail simply by discrediting the legitimate nondiscriminatory reason offered by the defendant. Hicks had been a black supervisor of the St. Mary's Honor Center, a halfway house operated by a state prison system. He alleged that he had been discharged because he was black. In its defense, the Honor Center offered as its legitimate, nondiscriminatory reason the fact that the subordinates supervised by Hicks had violated the rules for operation of the center. The district court, which decided the case without a jury, rejected this reason because Hicks was the only supervisor disciplined for violations by his subordinates, but it found for the Honor Center anyway. The district court found that

30. Texas Dep't of Community Affairs v. Burdine, 450 U.S. 248, 253 (1981); Board of Trustees v. Sweeney, 439 U.S. 24, 25 (1978); Furnco Constr. Corp. v. Waters, 438 U.S. 567, 577–78 (1978).

31. *Burdine*, 450 U.S. at 254–55; *Furnco*, 438 U.S. at 579–80.

32. Anderson v. Bessemer City, 470 U.S. 564, 573 (1985); United States Postal Serv. Bd. of Governors v. Aikens, 460 U.S. 711, 715 (1983). The most recent case in this line is Ash v. Tyson Foods, Inc., 546 U.S. 454 (2006) (per curiam), where the Supreme Court reversed a decision allowing an inference of pretext from a disparity in qualifications between the plaintiff and the employee who obtained the job only when "the disparity in qualifications is so apparent as virtually to jump off the page and slap you in the face." The Court held that pretext, instead, must be determined from all the evidence in the record.

33. Swierkiewicz v. Sorema N.A., 534 U.S. 506, 511–14 (2002). The quoted phrase is from Federal Rule of Civil Procedure 8(a)(2).

34. 509 U.S. 502 (1993).

the real reason for Hicks's discharge was not his race, but his supervisor's personal dislike for him.

The Supreme Court ultimately agreed with this decision, holding that the plaintiff only raised an issue of pretext by discrediting the reason offered by the defendant. The trier of fact, in this case the district judge, was free to decide that Hicks had not established pretext based on all the evidence in the record as a whole.[35] This holding accords with previous decisions placing the burden of persuasion always on the plaintiff, as well as with decisions reducing the burden on the defendant to offer a legitimate nondiscriminatory reason and leaving most cases to be decided on the issue of pretext. All of these prior decisions are consistent with allowing the defendant to prevail despite the fact that its offered reason turned out not to be the real reason for its decision.

What was less clear after *St. Mary's Honor Center* was whether the trier of fact was free to decide for the plaintiff based on evidence discrediting the defendant's offered legitimate, nondiscriminatory reason. The opinion plainly stated that a finding of discrimination could be based on such evidence,[36] but the lower courts were divided on the extent to which additional evidence was necessary. This issue was somewhat confusingly stated in terms of the plaintiff's need to present evidence of "pretext plus": evidence in addition to the evidence discrediting the defendant's offered reason. This is plainly the wrong way to pose the question, however. After *St. Mary's Honor Center*, proof of pretext requires more than simply discrediting the defendant's offered reason. It also involves proof that the defendant's motivating reason was discriminatory. There is no "plus" that must be added to the proof of pretext. Nevertheless, some lower courts required such additional evidence, and if it was not forthcoming, entered judgment as a matter of law for the defendant. In *Reeves v. Sanderson Plumbing Products, Inc.*[37] the Supreme Court held that no such evidence was necessary. The plaintiff could rely upon any evidence in the record, including the evidence establishing the prima facie case and the evidence discrediting the defendant's offered reason, to support a finding of discrimination.[38]

Neither of these recent decisions by the Supreme Court, however, gives any help to the lower federal courts in expeditiously deciding the vast bulk of the employment discrimination cases. On the contrary, in *Reeves*, the Supreme Court cautioned against

35. *Id.* at 510–12.

36. *Id.* at 511.

37. 530 U.S. 133 (2000).

38. *Id.* at 147–49.

prematurely resolving these cases without considering all of the evidence favorable to the plaintiff.[39] Following the lead of decisions approving the use of summary judgment,[40] the lower federal courts have closely examined the plaintiff's evidence to determine whether it supports a reasonable inference of intentional discrimination.[41] Nevertheless, the practice in different circuits has been highly variable, with some courts recognizing that these cases should rarely be taken from the jury because they involve questions of intent,[42] while others have allowed judges greater leeway to grant summary judgment or judgment as a matter of law.[43] How much leeway is left after *Reeves* is now an open question.

This question has become all the more significant as the right to jury trial has been extended to the full range of employment discrimination cases. A decision on summary judgment now denies the plaintiff both a trial and a decision by a jury, which can award damages in addition to any back pay awarded by the court.[44] By this means, and by the related practice on motions for judgment as a matter of law, the lower courts have retained control over which employment discrimination cases are submitted to juries. The plaintiff's burden of production must be satisfied before a case can go to the jury. This burden is rarely satisfied simply by making out a prima facie case under *McDonnell Douglas*; the plaintiff must also present sufficient evidence on the issue of pretext. As *St. Mary's Honor Center* and *Reeves* have recognized, this burden can be satisfied by discrediting the reason offered by the defendant. Moreover, the plaintiff gets the benefit of all of the favorable evidence in the record. As Justice Ginsburg observed in her concurring opinion in *Reeves*, the plaintiff will usually meet the burden of producing sufficient evidence to have the case go to the jury,[45] but as the Court made clear, the possibility remains that the plaintiff will fail to meet this burden even after discrediting the defendant's offered reason.

39. *Id.* at 150–54.

40. Celotex Corp. v. Catrett, 477 U.S. 317 (1986); Matsushita Elec. Indus. Co. v. Zenith Radio Corp., 475 U.S. 574, 597–98 (1986).

41. Medina–Munoz v. R.J. Reynolds Tobacco Co., 896 F.2d 5, 8–10 (1st Cir. 1990); Meiri v. Dacon, 759 F.2d 989, 997–98 (2d Cir.), *cert. denied*, 474 U.S. 829 (1985); Merrick v. Farmers Ins. Group, 892 F.2d 1434, 1436–39 (9th Cir. 1990); Weihaupt v. American Med. Ass'n, 874 F.2d 419, 428–30 (7th Cir. 1989).

42. Kerzer v. Kingly Mfg., 156 F.3d 396, 400 (2d Cir. 1998); Sheridan v. E.I. DuPont de Nemours, 100 F.3d 1061, 1071 (3d Cir. 1996) (en banc), *cert. denied*, 521 U.S. 1129 (1997).

43. *E.g.*, Proud v. Stone, 945 F.2d 796 (4th Cir. 1991); Coghlan v. American Seafoods Co., 413 F.3d 1090 (9th Cir. 2005).

44. 42 U.S.C. § 1981a(b), (c) (2000).

45. 530 U.S. at 154 (Ginsburg, J., concurring).

If the plaintiff's burden of production is satisfied, then the case goes to the jury and the jurors need not be instructed that the burden is satisfied. They do need to be instructed on the burden of persuasion, but that rests always with the plaintiff in proving intentional discrimination. The burden of persuasion becomes complicated only at the remedy stage of a case, as discussed in the next section.

D.   Mixed–Motive Cases and Remedies

Both the burden of production and the burden of persuasion shift at the remedy stage of certain cases. This shift was first recognized in class actions and then extended to individual cases and codified by amendments to Title VII.[46] It occurs when the plaintiff carries the burden of persuasion on the issue of intentional discrimination—that a prohibited reason entered into the employer's decision—but the employer then offers evidence that a legitimate reason would have been sufficient for its decision. In sometimes confusing terminology, this allocation of the burden of persuasion is often said to be confined to "mixed-motive" cases. It is probably too late to change this terminology, which has become standard, but the term "mixed-motive" is easily confused with "pretext" under *McDonnell Douglas*. Yet the mixed-motive defense should be available to employers only at the remedy stage of a case. At this point, the plaintiff has already gone beyond the issue of pretext and established that the defendant has engaged in intentional discrimination and, for that reason, the entire burden of proof, including the burden of persuasion, can justifiably be shifted to the defendant.

Wholly apart from when the mixed-motive defense arises, it is analytically distinct from the issue of pretext under *McDonnell Douglas*. It raises the question whether a legitimate reason operated *in addition* to the prohibited reason, not whether it operated *instead* of a prohibited one as in the issue of pretext. A defense of mixed motives, if it is made out, establishes that the plaintiff would have been denied a job for an entirely legitimate reason if the employer had considered it, in addition to the discriminatory reason that the employer actually did consider. Accordingly, a plaintiff in a mixed-motive case has a weaker claim for compensatory relief than a plaintiff who has established pretext alone. Both plaintiffs are

---

46. § 706(g)(2)(B),   42   U.S.C. § 2000e–5(g)(2)(B) (2000); *see* Franks v. Bowman Transp. Co., 424 U.S. 747, 772–73 nn. 31–32 (1976); International Bhd. of Teamsters v. United States, 431 U.S. 324, 361–62 (1977); Price Waterhouse v. Hopkins, 490 U.S. 228, 249–50 (1989) (plurality opinion of Brennan, J.); *id.* at 259–60 (White, J., concurring in the judgment).

victims of discriminatory decisionmaking, but the mixed-motive plaintiff would have been denied a job for a legitimate reason, even in the absence of discrimination, while the pure pretext plaintiff was denied the job only because of discrimination. To be sure, the employer in a mixed-motive case still deserves to be penalized because it has engaged in discrimination, by adding a prohibited reason, such as race, to a legitimate reason in rejecting the plaintiff. But no compensatory remedy is justified because, if the mixed-motive defense is made out, the plaintiff would have been denied employment for an entirely legitimate reason.

This is a forceful argument for recognizing a defense, although one limited in two respects. First, the burden of production and persuasion should be shifted entirely to the defendant because it has already been found to have made a decision based on a prohibited reason. And second, although the cases are not consistent on this issue, the defense should be limited to the remedy stage of litigation and bar only the award of compensatory relief, such as back pay and damages. If these limitations are neglected, the result is an unwieldy and confusing system for allocating the burden of proof and deciding concrete cases. Just defining mixed-motive cases can be difficult, because all decisions based on discriminatory reasons can involve other reasons as well. An employer might refuse to hire the plaintiff both because of his race and because another applicant had better qualifications. Most cases of discrimination, in fact, involve employees whose qualifications are marginal for other reasons. Few employers, even if they harbor discriminatory intent, are inclined to discharge a superstar employee for that reason alone. Such bald-faced discrimination might have been common before enactment of Title VII, but not after enforcement of the statute and public opinion has driven up the cost of blatantly racist or sexist behavior. It follows that most plaintiffs in employment discrimination cases will have some blemishes on their records and that discrimination is most likely to operate in combination with some "legitimate, nondiscriminatory reason" to deny them jobs. Most cases, upon close examination, are likely to be mixed-motive cases; few cases are likely to involve employers who rejected the plaintiff for discriminatory reasons alone. For that reason, it would probably be better to abandon the "mixed-motive" terminology entirely, or if it is used at all, to limit it to the remedy stage of litigation.

Title VII, as amended by the Civil Rights Act of 1991, now takes this approach. The definition of prohibited discrimination, as discussed earlier, requires proof only that a prohibited characteristic, such as race, was "a motivating factor for any employment

48

practice."[47] The plaintiff need not prove that race was the only factor. The term "mixed-motive" usually refers to cases in which the alternative reason would have been sufficient for the employer's decision. These cases are perhaps better called "hypothetical decision" cases: they are cases in which the actual decision was discriminatory, but in which a hypothetical decision, free of the discriminatory reason and based only on the alternative reason, would have come out exactly the same way. Title VII assigns the burden of proof on this issue to the defendant: the defendant must prove that it "would have taken the same action in the absence of the impermissible motivating factor."[48] If the defendant makes this showing, then it is relieved of liability for any compensatory remedy, such as back pay, damages, or reinstatement. It remains liable for injunctive and declaratory relief and for attorney's fees. Read as a whole, Title VII allocates the burden of persuasion to the plaintiff on the issue of violation—involving the defendant's actual decision-making process—and to the defendant on the issue of remedy—involving a hypothetical decision free of discrimination.

As a matter of theory, this allocation of the burden of persuasion may be sound, but as a practical matter, it is difficult to explain to the jury. The plaintiff's burden on the issue of violation follows from the general allocation of the burden of persuasion in civil cases. Because the plaintiff is seeking an alteration in the status quo, she must persuade the court to act on her behalf. The defendant's burden of persuasion on the issue of remedy follows from the need for an exception to this general rule. Because the plaintiff has succeeded in proving that the defendant is a wrongdoer (and has imposed a loss on the plaintiff), the defendant can then be required to prove that, despite its own wrongdoing, no compensation is required. The problem arises not in the abstract realm of justification, but in the concrete realities of explaining such a subtle legal distinction to the jury.

The difficulty of instructing the jury in a comprehensible fashion does not exhaust the complexity of existing law. Despite the amendments to Title VII by the Civil Rights Act of 1991 that clarified the treatment of mixed-motive cases, some decisions still insist on applying the mixed-motive analysis to the liability stage and not to the remedy stage of litigation. These decisions follow the lead of the Supreme Court in *Price Waterhouse v. Hopkins*,[49] a decision rendered before the statutory provision discussed in the

47. § 703(m), codified as 42 U.S.C. § 2000e–2(m) (2000).

48. § 706(g)(2)(B), codified as 42 U.S.C. § 2000e–5(g)(2)(B) (2000).

49. 490 U.S. 228 (1989).

preceding paragraph was added to Title VII. Although this decision did not result in a majority opinion, both the plurality opinion of Justice Brennan and the separate opinions of Justice White and Justice O'Connor placed the mixed-motive issue in the initial stage of the case establishing the defendant's liability. These opinions placed on the plaintiff the burden of proving that a discriminatory reason "played a motivating part" or was "a substantial factor" in the disputed employment decision.[50] If the plaintiff made this showing, then the defendant could entirely escape liability by proving that the same decision adverse to the plaintiff would have been made in the absence of the discriminatory reason.[51] The difference between "motivating" and "substantial" factors in the plurality and separate opinions appears to be slight, so that in this respect *Price Waterhouse* does not differ significantly from the requirement of proof of a "motivating factor" now codified in Title VII. Placing the issue in the liability phase of the case, however, is more significant. Title VII now allows the recovery of injunctive relief and attorney's fees upon the plaintiff's proof that a prohibited reason was a motivating factor regardless of the defendant's proof that it would have reached the same decision entirely for legitimate reasons.

To some extent, returning to *Price Waterhouse* makes sense for claims outside the scope of Title VII, such as those under the Age Discrimination in Employment Act (ADEA). The statutory provisions on mixed-motive cases were added to Title VII by the Civil Rights Act of 1991, but not to statutes like the ADEA (although they were amended in other respects by the act). This pattern of selective amendment yields the inference that mixed-motive cases under the ADEA should be decided according to pre-existing law. Some courts of appeals have drawn this inference,[52] but others went even further, restricting the scope of the amendments in Title VII cases to those in which the plaintiff relied upon "direct evidence" of discrimination.[53]

---

50. *Id.* at 250 (plurality opinion of Brennan, J.); *id.* at 259 (White, J., concurring in the judgment); *id.* at 265 (O'Connor, J., concurring in the judgment).

51. *Id.* at 252 (plurality opinion of Brennan, J.); *id.* at 259–60 (White, J., concurring in the judgment); *id.* at 267–68 (O'Connor, J., concurring in the judgment).

52. *E.g.*, Miller v. CIGNA Corp., 47 F.3d 586, 597 & n.9 (3d Cir. 1995) (en banc). The same inference might also be drawn for individual claims of intentional discrimination under § 1981 and the ADA, which were also amended by the Civil Rights Act of 1991, but not with respect to mixed-motive cases.

53. *E.g.*, Fernandes v. Costa Bros. Masonry, Inc., 199 F.3d 572, 580–83 (1st Cir. 1999) (citing cases).

The Supreme Court eventually rejected these decisions in *Desert Palace, Inc. v. Costa*,[54] holding that a plaintiff can take advantage of a mixed-motive instruction based on circumstantial evidence as well as direct evidence. As the Court framed its holding: "In order to obtain an instruction under § 2000e–2(m), a plaintiff need only present sufficient evidence for a reasonable jury to conclude, by a preponderance of the evidence, that 'race, color, religion, sex, or national origin was a motivating factor for any employment practice.' "[55] Once that finding is made, then the burden of proof switches to the employer to establish that the plaintiff would have been rejected even in the absence of discrimination. Thus the crucial distinction is not between kinds of evidence—whether it is direct or circumstantial—but between findings of fact—whether the judge or jury concludes that race was "a motivating factor." If it wasn't, the defendant wins without more. If it was, the judge or jury goes on to consider the defense that the employer would have made the same decision anyway.

Even after *Desert Palace*, however, complications remain in mixed-motive cases, especially those tried to a jury. When the issue of mixed motives is properly raised, the court must instruct the jury on the niceties of the burden of persuasion on two closely related issues—whether the defendant's decision was motivated by a prohibited reason and whether it would have been the same in the absence of a prohibited reason. A recent decision under the ADEA illustrates how complicated these issues can be. *McKennon v. Nashville Banner Publishing Co.*[56] involved a defense of "after-acquired" evidence, in which an employer discovered, after the plaintiff was discharged and filed a claim of discrimination, that she had misused confidential documents. This conduct would ordinarily have been grounds for discharge, but it was unknown to the employer when the plaintiff was discharged. Despite the employer's concession, for purposes of summary judgment, that it had engaged in age discrimination, the district court granted summary judgment for the employer. The court of appeals affirmed, but the Supreme Court reversed, holding that the "after-acquired" evidence went only to the issue of remedy and limited back pay to the period before such evidence was discovered. The Court's opinion makes clear that reasoning very similar to that under Title VII also applies to claims under other statutes and that it is not limited to the mixed-motive situation, in which the employer's actual decision is motivated by both discriminatory and legitimate reasons. In *McKennon*, the actual decision was based solely on a discriminatory reason and the

54.   539 U.S. 90 (2003).
55.   *Id.* at 101.

56.   513 U.S. 352 (1995).

hypothetical decision solely on a legitimate reason. The technicalities of jury instructions did not arise in *McKennon* because the case came up on summary judgment. Nevertheless, separating the issues into violation and remedy makes a start toward clarifying the law.

E.   Consequences of the Burden of Proof

Any detailed discussion of the burden of proof in employment discrimination cases leaves a strong (and not entirely inaccurate) impression that the complexity of legal doctrine defeats any attempt to achieve efficiency in litigation. The parties dispute the burden of proof in order to gain strategic advantages only distantly related to the reasons for assigning the burden of proof in the first place. They dispute the issue in such detail in order to incline the judge or jury in their favor by any means necessary. The rules on the burden of proof succeed less in clarifying what the law is than in revealing what factual issues the parties believe to be crucial.

Foremost among these is the broad range of "legitimate, nondiscriminatory" reasons that employers seek to insulate from evaluation by judges and juries. The breadth of these reasons finds support in two of the three conceptions of equality prevalent in employment discrimination law. The negative conception of equality restricts the court to an inquiry only into the prohibited grounds for employment decisions, while the positive conception leaves employers free to make their own decisions based on merit, subject only to the competitive pressures of the market. Legal decisions minimizing the defendant's burden of production in its rebuttal case and forcing the plaintiff to persuade the judge or jury of the existence of a discriminatory reason serve both of these limited conceptions of equality. Only the remedial conception of equality would justify a more searching examination of the employer's offered reasons in order to eliminate the effects of past discrimination.

Some courts have seized upon the first two conceptions of equality to emphasize the difference between claims of employment discrimination and claims for wrongful discharge. The latter are available under the law of most states to evaluate a broad or narrow range of reasons for terminating employees.[57] The law of wrongful discharge goes beyond simply prohibiting discrimination on specified grounds; it offers a remedy for an indefinite range of workplace wrongs, from violations of public policy to breach of

---

57. McCoy v. WGN Continental Broad. Co., 957 F.2d 368, 370–73 (7th Cir. 1992); Hanchey v. Energas Co., 925 F.2d 96, 98 (5th Cir. 1990); Lucas v. Dover Corp., Norris Div., 857 F.2d 1397, 1403–04 (10th Cir. 1988).

implied obligations of good faith and fair dealing.[58] As a consequence, the reasons offered by employers receive far less deference on claims of wrongful discharge than on claims of discrimination.

Assigning the burden of proof cannot be wholly successful, however, in distinguishing claims of discrimination from claims of wrongful discharge, or in resolving the tension between different conceptions of equality. Legal rules on the burden of proof cannot close off an examination of the facts. Concrete cases inevitably return to an evaluation of all the evidence in the record, leaving open the defendant's offered reasons for evaluation and second-guessing. Jury instructions and legal doctrine can subordinate, but not eliminate, consideration of merit in the decisions of judges and juries. Cases like *St. Mary's Honor Center*, in which the defendant offers a better reason for its decision than it actually had, illustrate only one of the ways in which the quality of the employer's reasons enter into the decision of actual cases. No employer would like to rely on a weak reason (such as the supervisor's personal vendetta against the plaintiff in *St. Mary's Honor Center*) to explain that it did not engage in discrimination. But offering a better reason, and having it discredited, invariably strengthens the plaintiff's case and often is decisive in the plaintiff's favor. The decision in *St. Mary's Honor Center* leaves open the possibility that the defendant might prevail in these circumstances, but the jury might well decide against the defendant because of the discredited reason that it initially offered.

The inescapable need to examine the facts compromises both the doctrinal rules and the efficiency of litigating claims of employment discrimination, so much so that some authors have seen a tendency for these claims to merge with the law of wrongful discharge.[59] The expansion of the grounds of prohibited discrimination, especially to such characteristics as age and disability, further reinforces this tendency. As the reasons that employers cannot consider continue to multiply, so do the occasions for legal regulation and judicial intervention in employers' decisions. This trend cannot be carried very far, however, without encountering resistance from the economic perspective and its emphasis on employer discretion, as evidenced by the decisions emphasizing the difference

58. Stewart J. Schwab, Life-Cycle Justice: Accommodating Just Cause and Employment at Will, 92 Mich. L. Rev. 8, 32–38 (1993).

59. Robert Post, Prejudicial Appearances: The Logic of Antidiscrimination Law, 88 Calif. L. Rev. 1, 8–16 (2000) (describing the consequences of multi-plying grounds of prohibited discrimination); *see* Richard A. Epstein, Forbidden Grounds: The Case Against Employment Discrimination Laws ch. 8 (1992) (comparing employment discrimination laws against the baseline of employment at will).

between claims of discrimination and claims of wrongful discharge. The balance between this perspective and the opposed remedial perspective, which would justify expanding the scope of employment discrimination law to reach new grounds of discrimination, can only be resolved over the long term.

More immediate problems result from the pattern of litigation over individual claims. The lower federal courts, in particular, have become reluctant to entertain repeated litigation over routine personnel matters. In response to these problems, the Federal Courts Study Committee proposed that claims of employment discrimination be subject to voluntary arbitration sponsored by the Equal Employment Opportunity Commission (EEOC).[60] This proposal to shift cases out of the federal judicial system is a first step toward administrative resolution of claims of employment claims, a system that has been implemented only for federal employees.[61] For all other employees, administrative remedies have been confined to investigation and conciliation of charges as a preliminary to litigation.[62] Indeed, an adjudicative role for the EEOC has been repeatedly rejected, first when Title VII was originally enacted in 1964 and most recently in the Civil Rights Act of 1991, when a damage remedy and the right to jury trial were added to Title VII.[63] The addition of these common law remedies has made the resolution of employment discrimination claims still more elaborate and expensive, exactly the opposite of the proposed benefits of administrative adjudication.

The arguments for reforming procedure and enforcement have met with more success in supporting arbitration of employment discrimination claims. So long as arbitration is authorized by an agreement that gives the employee control over the presentation of his or her claim, it can be used as a substitute for litigation.[64] Recent decisions enforcing agreements to arbitrate employment disputes under the Federal Arbitration Act supports this conclusion.[65] However, arbitration that is under the control of a third party, such as a union, does not bar litigation by an individual

---

60. Report of the Federal Courts Study Committee ch. 3B (1990), reprinted in 22 Conn. L. Rev. 733, 800 (1990) (proposing experimental program of voluntary arbitration sponsored by the EEOC).

61. § 717, codified as 42 U.S.C. § 2000e–16 (2000). Even so, the federal employee can elect to take the case to federal court without first exhausting administrative remedies before the

EEOC. § 717(c), codified as 42 U.S.C. § 2000e–16(c) (2000); 29 C.F.R. § 1614.407 (2006).

62. § 706(b), codified as 42 U.S.C. § 2000e–5(b) (2000).

63. 42 U.S.C. § 1981a(b),(c) (2000).

64. Gilmer v. Interstate/Johnson Lane Corp., 500 U.S. 20, 28 (1991).

65. See Chapter VIII.C. infra.

employee.[66] These principles technically are consistent, but they reflect an overall ambivalence towards arbitration.

In substantive terms, the question is whether allowing employees to bargain away their right to judicial remedies in favor of arbitration confers too great an advantage upon employers. If employers cannot offer contracts of employment that violate the laws against employment discrimination, how can they offer contracts that set the terms for enforcing these laws? Employees cannot waive their protection under these laws because, it is believed, employers would otherwise use their superior bargaining power to obtain agreements that allowed continued discrimination. For the same reason, arbitration agreements cannot be used as a means of weakening enforcement of these laws, for instance, by giving employers effective control over the selection of arbitrators. As a procedural matter, the concern is that the simpler and less costly procedures typical of arbitration will work systematically to the disadvantage of plaintiffs. Unlike employers, plaintiffs need modern procedural devices, such as discovery, to uncover evidence that disputed employment decisions are discriminatory.

Resolving the ambivalence towards arbitration in existing law, like the question of prohibiting discrimination on additional grounds, is a matter for law reform over the long term. But even comprehensive reform cannot hope to eliminate the tensions between different conceptions of equality that underlie this field of law. For the present, the law has settled, no matter how uneasily, on the substantive rules discussed in this chapter.

66. Alexander v. Gardner-Denver Co., 415 U.S. 36, 51 (1974). The results of arbitration in this form are, at most, persuasive in subsequent litigation. *Id.* at 60 n.21.

Chapter IV

CLASS CLAIMS: FROM INTENTIONAL DISCRIMINATION TO DISPARATE IMPACT

Class claims of employment discrimination offer a variety of contrasts with individual claims: the burdens of proof are heavier and therefore more significant; the reliance on statistics and other forms of expert evidence is greater; and the competition between different conceptions of equality is more open and explicit. Procedural structure also makes a bigger difference in class claims than in individual claims, a subject that will be taken up later in the chapters on enforcement and remedies. Class claims, because they immediately affect more employees and applicants, raise the stakes and attract more public interest. This difference in scope also exercises a profound influence over the way in which a violation is proved, beginning with the use of statistical evidence and extending to liability for discriminatory effects under the theory of disparate impact, with important consequences for the controversial issue of affirmative action.

Strictly speaking, the distinction between class and individual claims is one of procedure rather than substance, concerning how individual claims are joined in a single action instead of the theory of liability that the plaintiff pursues in order to establish a violation. The standard procedural form for class claims is either a class action by private plaintiffs under Federal Rule of Civil Procedure 23 or a pattern-or-practice action by public officials under statutory authority. Some of these claims have been litigated as a series of individual claims of intentional discrimination, following the structure of proof in *McDonnell Douglas Corp. v. Green*.[1] And conversely, a few individual cases have been litigated by presenting statistical evidence of intentional discrimination or disparate impact.[2] Yet substantive theories of liability have tended to correspond with the procedural forms of action: individual theories of liability are mostly to be found in individual actions, and class-wide theories of liability, relying mainly on statistics or the theory of disparate impact, have been found mostly in class-wide cases.

---

1. 411 U.S. 792, 802–05 (1973).

2. *E.g.*, Connecticut v. Teal, 457 U.S. 440, 443 (1982).

56

The move from individual to class claims invites—although it does not require—a corresponding move away from the negative conception of equality that predominates in individual cases. Only the clearest cases alleging class-wide liability depend solely on a negative conception of equality and only because the employer has obviously relied on race or some other prohibited characteristic in formulating or applying a general employment practice. These cases were common in the years after Title VII first became effective, but they are now rare. Class claims today focus more on the effects of an employer's decisionmaking process and less on the process itself, with a correspondingly decreased emphasis on the question whether the employer considered a prohibited characteristic in violation of the negative conception of equality. The tendency in group litigation is towards group theories of liability, with evidence of the effects of employment practices upon different groups and the justification, if any, that can be offered for practices with such differential effects. Evidence at this level of generality appeals, even if only implicitly, to a remedial conception of equality focused on compensation for past disadvantages.

Claims brought on behalf of a group of employees come in two varieties: class claims of intentional discrimination (or disparate treatment) and class claims of discriminatory effects (or disparate impact). The difference between these types of claims is significant, so much so that constitutional law only recognizes claims of disparate treatment, not disparate impact.[3] Yet these two kinds of claims resemble one another, especially in the statistical evidence that the plaintiff must present in order to establish liability. This superficial similarity reflects a deeper uniformity in the competing conceptions of equality that animate each of these theories of liability, resulting in different doctrinal formulations, but of the same fundamental issues. At a first approximation, class claims of disparate treatment emphasize the historical perspective and its negative conception of equality as colorblindness, while class claims of disparate impact emphasize the remedial perspective and its goal of eliminating the effects of past discrimination. As the law governing each claim has become more refined, however, the economic perspective has assumed greater prominence in both, yielding the same results in most class-wide cases, regardless of the kind of claim asserted by the plaintiff.

The movement away from a negative conception of equality starts modestly enough with class-wide claims of disparate treatment. The ultimate question of fact is the same as in individual

---

3. Washington v. Davis, 426 U.S. 229, 238–39 (1976).

claims of intentional discrimination—whether the employer relied on a prohibited characteristic—but the method of proof has changed—to focus on statistical evidence of treatment of an entire group instead of a single individual. With the theory of disparate impact, the departure from a negative conception of equality becomes a matter of legal doctrine. It is now codified in the different substantive requirements for proving a violation of Title VII. A finding of intentional discrimination no longer is even necessary. The ultimate questions of fact concern the effect of the disputed employment practice and the business justification offered in support of it, both objective facts distinct from the employer's subjective reasons. This shift in emphasis, in turn, supports a further shift: to affirmative action as a means of securing compliance with the law and remedying the consequences of past discrimination. From the employer's perspective, however, adopting an affirmative action plan is an equally effective means of preventing class-wide claims of all kinds from arising, whether based on a theory of disparate treatment or a theory of disparate impact. The group character of these claims and the statistical evidence used to support them is what becomes decisive, both in determining the outcome of litigation and in causing employers to change their business practices.

A. Class Claims of Disparate Treatment

Class claims of disparate treatment occupy an uncertain middle ground between individual claims of intentional discrimination and class claims of disparate impact. They take a first step toward liability for discriminatory effects by changing the focus of litigation from an individual plaintiff to an entire group, yet they retain the same negative conception of equality as colorblindness that underlies individual claims of intentional discrimination. Class claims of disparate treatment combine statistical evidence of the objective effects of employment practices with the need for a finding of subjective intent to consider a prohibited reason, such as race. This gap between objective evidence and subjective findings has led many courts, following the lead of the Supreme Court, to require proof of individual instances of intentional discrimination that bring "the cold numbers convincingly to life."[4] Apart from relying

---

4. International Bhd. of Teamsters v. United States, 431 U.S. 324, 339 (1977); *see* EEOC v. Chicago Miniature Lamp Works, 947 F.2d 292, 303–04 (7th Cir. 1991) (statistical evidence not strong enough in this case to dispense with the need for individual evidence); American Fed'n of State, County & Mun. Employees v. Washington, 770 F.2d 1401, 1407 (9th Cir. 1985) (same); Garcia v. Rush-Presbyterian-St. Luke's Med. Ctr., 660 F.2d 1217, 1225 (7th Cir. 1981) (same).

upon such familiar forms of anecdotal evidence, the courts have had to develop standards for evaluating statistical evidence to determine when it yields an inference of intentional discrimination. Technical issues of statistics and labor economics, and legal issues of burden of proof, have done little to simplify the litigation of class claims of disparate treatment. Just as much as individual claims, these claims must be resolved on the evidence presented in each case. As the Supreme Court has said, "statistics are not irrefutable; they come in infinite variety and, like any other kind of evidence, they may be rebutted."[5]

Statistical evidence raises the seeming paradox of objective evidence used to prove subjective intent. Yet the same paradox can be found in the use of evidence on the issue of qualifications to perform the job in individual cases. The problem common to both class and individual claims is the absence in most cases of a "smoking gun": a statement by a supervisor or manager revealing that the employer actually relied upon a prohibited characteristic in making the disputed personnel decision. In both kinds of cases, the law must reason backwards from the effects of disputed decisions to the question whether they were discriminatory. Statistical evidence introduces complexities in class cases because of the various ways in which the body of relevant evidence can be defined and then analyzed.

The desire to back up statistical evidence with anecdotal evidence is natural, and to some extent defensible. A general pattern of discrimination should yield at least a few examples of discrimination against individuals who can come forward to testify about their experiences. Where statistical evidence is abstract and a matter for expert testimony, anecdotal evidence is concrete and can be analyzed as a matter of common sense. Statistical evidence also is open to sharply different interpretations, best summarized in the aphorism that there are "lies, damn lies, and statistics." Although the same might be said of the selective use of anecdotal evidence, each form of evidence might usefully serve as a check on manipulation of the other. Anecdotal evidence is certainly more familiar to judges and juries, and for that reason, provides a useful contrast to statistical evidence and the arcane disputes that it often generates between competing experts. It is not necessary to decide whether evidence of individual instances of discrimination is required as a matter of black-letter legal doctrine. Plaintiffs' lawyers will invariably seek to present such evidence, and if they fail to do so, its absence can very damaging to any claim of class-wide intentional

5. *Teamsters*, 431 U.S. at 340.

discrimination.[6] If it exists at all, a pattern of class-wide discrimination is likely to reveal itself in at least a few instances of discrimination against identifiable individuals.

The variety of statistical evidence poses more immediate choices for legal doctrine. Judges and juries cannot be left entirely on their own in evaluating such evidence, yet they also must not be hemmed in by simplistic rules of statistical inference. The Supreme Court has offered two models of analysis and the lower federal courts have endorsed several variations on these models, some unfortunately that confuse judicial pronouncements on statistical inference with judicial statements of rules of law. Judges can only be authoritative about the latter. Statistical inference must remain the province of experts in other professions. The Supreme Court has clearly recognized this point and has refused to offer any definitive method of analyzing statistical evidence. As it has said, in cautioning that statistical evidence comes in many forms and is always rebuttable, the force of such evidence "depends on all of the surrounding facts and circumstances."[7] The methods the Supreme Court has endorsed are suggestive and instructive; they should not be taken to exclude the use of alternative methods of evaluating statistical evidence upon a proper showing.

1. The Simple Model

The simpler of the two models of statistical analysis endorsed by the Supreme Court concerns extreme disparities in the treatment of workers from different groups, "the inexorable zero," as it was called by the court of appeals in the case recognizing this model, *International Brotherhood of Teamsters v. United States*.[8] That was a "pattern-or-practice" case, so called because the government alleged that the Teamsters Union and various trucking companies had engaged in a systematic practice of denying better-paying jobs to blacks and Hispanics. These were "over-the-road" jobs involving driving between major cities, in which the defendants employed few, if any, members of minority groups. Almost all the blacks and Hispanics were employed instead as "city drivers" and "servicemen," who worked within a single metropolitan area. Although the opinion compared the proportion of minority employees in these different positions, the decisive comparison was between

---

6. For instance, in the well-known case of EEOC v. Sears, Roebuck & Co., 839 F.2d 302 (7th Cir. 1988), the court held that evidence of individual instances of discrimination was not legally required to prove class-wide intentional discrimination, but that the absence of such evidence undermined any inference of discrimination generated by the plaintiff's statistical evidence. *Id.* at 310–11.

7. *Teamsters*, 431 U.S. at 340.

8. *Id.* at 342 n. 23.

the proportion of minorities employed as over-the-road drivers and the proportion of minorities in the general population. The latter figure, the Court made clear, was relevant only because it was an adequate approximation of the proportion of minorities in the relevant labor market.[9]

Such a rough approximation, and the general common sense approach taken by the Supreme Court, are the distinguishing features of the simple model of statistical inference. Everything depends upon the disparity in treatment being large enough to dispel any lingering doubts from imprecise estimates. The Court simply assumed that the proportion of minorities in the general population would approximate the proportion in the labor market, an assumption only partly confirmed by the statistics on hiring for city driver and serviceman positions.[10] Any remaining doubts about this assumption were overcome by the enormous disparity represented by "the inexorable zero" of minorities among over-the-road drivers. Accordingly, the Court found no need to rely on even elementary tests of statistical significance.

2.   The Complex Model

Few cases from recent years present the stark disparities found in *Teamsters*. Under the influence of Title VII, most employers have entirely abandoned explicit discriminatory practices with obvious effects on large numbers of employees. Consequently, the disparities revealed by statistical evidence have become narrower and the assessment of the evidence has become subject to greater and more technical disputes. Expert witnesses are essential for the plaintiffs in most of these cases, and often for the defendant as well. Although *Teamsters* was decided without the benefit of expert testimony, its simple model of statistical inference presumed a more sophisticated model, which consists of three separate steps: first, an examination of the presence or treatment of a minority in the relevant labor market; second, a determination of how the same group is treated by the defendant employer; and third, a comparison between the figures generated by the first two steps to determine whether they support an inference of intentional discrimination.

The leading case on this more complex model for evaluating statistical evidence is *Hazelwood School District v. United States*.[11] That case concerned a claim of racial discrimination in hiring teachers by a public school district in the suburbs of St. Louis,

---

9. *Id.* at 337 n. 17.

10. *Id.* at 339 n.20, 342 n.23.

11. 433 U.S. 299 (1977).

Missouri. In analyzing this claim, the district court erroneously compared the proportion of blacks among the teachers employed by the school district with the proportion of blacks among students in the district, both about 2%, and found no discrimination. These numbers have little to do with one another and the court of appeals reversed on this ground and ordered judgment to be entered for the plaintiff based on figures showing that 15% of teachers in the greater metropolitan area were black. The Supreme Court agreed with the court of appeals that the proportion of blacks in the relevant labor market provided the appropriate baseline for evaluating the school district's hiring practices. According to the Supreme Court, the appropriate statistics compared the racial composition of participants in the labor market with the racial composition of those hired by the school district, for the period after the effective date of Title VII, and by means of tests for statistical significance.

As the facts of *Hazelwood* illustrate, the labor market must be defined according to the job allegedly involving discrimination. As an initial matter, it must include only persons with undisputed qualifications for the job—in *Hazelwood* those with state teaching certificates. Whether a qualification is necessary for the job, of course, is often a matter of dispute, so that the appropriate definition of the labor market depends upon the employment practices in dispute and the qualifications, like the state teaching certificate in *Hazelwood*, that remain undisputed. If no qualifications are required for the job, or only qualifications that are easily acquired, then general population figures provide an adequate approximation to the racial composition of the labor market.[12]

The labor market must be defined in geographical terms, most often limiting it to the area surrounding the place of employment. In *Hazelwood*, the labor market was limited to all or part of the St. Louis metropolitan area. The St. Louis city school district had attempted to maintain a ratio of 50% blacks among its teachers. The United States, as the plaintiff, argued that teachers in the St. Louis city schools should be included in the labor market in the greater metropolitan area, thereby increasing the proportion of blacks in that market, because they could quit their jobs in the city and commute to the Hazelwood schools in the suburbs. The school district argued that these teachers should be excluded from the labor market because the affirmative action policy of the St. Louis city school district had depleted the pool of black applicants from which suburban school districts could hire teachers. The Court did

---

12. *Id.* at 308 & n.13.

not resolve this issue in *Hazelwood* but left it for consideration on remand.

A final issue involved in defining the relevant labor market—and also left unresolved in *Hazelwood*—was the use of applicant-flow statistics. Applicant-flow statistics can be used instead of population statistics to identify more precisely those who are interested in the particular job offered by the employer. Population statistics for a given geographical area, whether for the population as a whole or for those with the qualifications sought by the employer, include individuals who are not interested in the job in question. They also exclude individuals outside the geographical area who are interested. The racial composition of the group actually interested in the job may differ significantly from the racial composition of the general or qualified population. The disadvantage of applicant-flow statistics is that they may reflect distortions in the proportion of minority applicants, arising either from the deterrent effect of the disputed employment practice or from the employer's general reputation for discrimination, or from the opposite effect of an employer's affirmative action efforts to recruit minority employees. In *Hazelwood*, the Supreme Court left the need for applicant-flow statistics to be determined on the facts of each case.[13]

After the racial composition of the labor market has been determined, it must be compared with the racial composition of those actually hired by the employer during the relevant time period, determined by the effective date of Title VII or, more commonly, by the statute of limitations. Under Title VII, the latter is usually 300 days,[14] so that a charge filed with the Equal Employment Opportunity Commission (EEOC) can properly seek relief only for discrimination occurring within the preceding 300 days. Only discrimination that occurred during this period and after the effective date of Title VII constitutes an actionable violation of Title VII. Discrimination that occurred earlier can no longer be the subject of a timely claim, if it ever could have. The existence of such discrimination can still support an inference of discrimination within the appropriate period,[15] but it is only evidence, not the fact that must be proved. For the same reason, the appropriate comparison is not with the racial composition of the employer's current work force, which may reflect the cumulative effect of discrimination

---

13. *Id.*

14. § 706(e)(1), codified as 42 U.S.C. § 2000e–5(e)(1) (2000). The precise statute of limitations is a complex subject taken up in Chapter VIII.

15. Bazemore v. Friday, 478 U.S. 385, 401–02 (1986).

outside the relevant period determined by the statute of limitations. The correct figure is limited to the pool of employees actually hired over the relevant period defined by the statute of limitations.[16] Employees hired earlier provide direct evidence only of discrimination that itself can no longer be the subject of a timely claim. Evidence of such earlier discrimination can still be relevant, but only indirectly—by establishing the discriminatory effects of employment practices which, if unchanged, have continued into the limitations period. Only the latter can support a finding of liability under Title VII.

The comparison between the racial composition of the labor market and the racial composition of those hired should be made by statistical methods, at least in the absence of extreme disparities like those found in *Teamsters*.[17] It is another question whether the particular statistical method mentioned in *Hazelwood* is appropriate in other complex cases.[18] This is a question for labor economists and statisticians. The important point is that statistical methods are needed to take account of the possibility that differences in the racial composition of the labor market and of those hired arose solely by chance, for instance, through the hiring of only a small number of employees. Statistical measurements of this effect, however, have their limitations. In particular, they cannot be used to determine whether the difference in selection rates is large enough to justify a finding of intentional discrimination. This is a matter for the judge or the jury, not for statistical experts.

Statistical significance itself has received undue attention, undoubtedly because of its technical difficulty. Despite the variety of mathematical devices that can be used to quantify statistical significance, its basic meaning is clear enough: to determine the effect of chance on the difference between any two statistics, such as the proportion of blacks in the labor market and among those actually hired. The most commonly used measures of statistical significance concern one kind of error: false positives or Type I errors. This error concerns false rejection of the null hypothesis, which in discrimination cases almost always is an absence of discrimination. In terms of litigation, it is the risk of making a mistake in favor of the plaintiff by finding discrimination when none actually exists. Statistics that estimate false positives give the probability that such an error has occurred. So, for instance, if the labor market is 20%

---

16. 433 U.S. at 309 & n.15.

17. *Id.* at 307.

18. *Hazelwood*, 433 U.S. at 310–12 & n.17; *see* Paul Meier, Jerome Sacks & Sandy L. Zabell, What Happened in *Hazelwood*: Statistics, Employment Discrimination and the 80% Rule, 1984 Am. B. Found. Res. J. 139.

black and 80% white and an employer hires 5 employees, all of whom are white, the initial comparison of statistics yields a difference between a 20% black labor market and a 0% black labor force. Unlike in *Teamsters*, however, this zero is hardly inexorable. Using a common measure of statistical significance, no black employees would be hired in this situation 33% of the time.[19] As a matter of common sense, this probability is so high because of the small number of employees, only five, who were hired. Entirely in the absence of discrimination, there was a one-third chance that no blacks would have ended up in the employer's work force.

In the complicated cases that actually arise in litigation, exactly how to quantify the probability of false positives is a subject for statisticians, and more importantly, for labor economists. Some scholars also have argued that the probability of false negatives, or Type II errors, should also be calculated. This is the probability of a mistake in favor of the defendant by finding no discrimination when it actually is present.[20] The lower federal courts have not accepted this suggestion and instead have emphasized the risk of false positives in their opinions. Even so, there are a variety of different methods for measuring Type I errors.

A greater problem, however, is the focus on statistical significance alone. Even assuming that the evidence reveals a statistically significant disparity, in the narrow sense of one not likely to have arisen by chance, the disparity still must be practically significant: large enough to justify an inference of intentional discrimination. An employer might, for instance, hire enough employees so that any difference between the percentage of blacks among those hired and the percentage of blacks in the labor force is likely to be statistically significant. To modify the preceding example, suppose that the employer hires 5,000 employees, instead of only five, and suppose that 950 of these employees are black. Assuming that the labor market remains 20% black, the disparity between the percentage of blacks in the labor market and the percentage of blacks hired, 19%, appears to be small. It is nevertheless statistically significant because of the large number of employees hired. Using the same measure of statistical significance as in the earlier example, there is only a 4% probability that it could have arisen by chance. Yet it remains difficult to draw an inference of intentional discrimination from such a small disparity in percentages. It is

19. This computation is based on a binomial probability for a one-sample model assuming random selection of employees from the labor market. *See* Meier, Sacks & Zabell, *supra*, 1984 Am. B. Found. Res. J. at 176–77.

20. David H. Kaye, Apples and Oranges: Confidence Coefficients and the Burden of Persuasion, 73 Cornell L. Rev. 54, 71–73 (1987).

difficult to believe that a discriminatory employer would hire a work force that contained almost, but not quite, the same percentage of black employees as the labor market. In the absence of further evidence of discrimination, such a small disparity does not support a convincing inference of intentional discrimination.

This example, like the earlier one, is deliberately simplified, in order to isolate the effect of purely numerical comparisons. In actual cases, most of the controversy concerns the analysis of the labor market and the analysis of the disputed employment practice which together yield those figures. Concentrating on statistical significance, or even on practical significance, obscures the overriding importance of the assumptions and evidence that make one model of the labor market and hiring more persuasive and appropriate than another. Simply as a matter of litigation tactics, the assumptions and evidence can usually be manipulated to generate results in favor of either party. The statistical evidence, as the saying goes, can be "tortured until it confesses." A statistically significant result can be produced from almost any set of data by relying on an unrealistic economic model. An obsessive fascination with statistical significance can obscure a more realistic assessment of the economic models used to prove or disprove discrimination. Stripped of the fascination with statistical significance, *Hazelwood* is largely concerned with these issues.

Another decision of the Supreme Court, *Bazemore v. Friday*,[21] illustrates how the same general approach to statistical evidence can be applied to a claim of discrimination in pay. The plaintiffs in *Bazemore* were a group of black employees who alleged that their pay was set lower than that of similarly situated white employees. They used a statistical technique, regression analysis, to ascertain the effect of race on pay. A regression analysis determines the effect of various factors, called independent variables, on a particular outcome, called the dependent variable. In employment discrimination cases, the dependent variable is a term or condition of employment, like pay, or a decision related to employment, like hiring, firing or promotion. The independent variables include factors that can legitimately affect the dependent variable, such as education and experience, and a discriminatory factor, such as race, that cannot. In *Bazemore*, the regression equations contained independent variables for the factors legitimately related to pay, based on an economic model of how employers actually set pay. This economic model is fully as important to the regression analysis in *Bazemore* as the definition of the labor market was in *Hazelwood*. The

21. 478 U.S. 385 (1986).

independent variables in *Bazemore* provided a statistical means of comparing the pay of similarly situated employees. In technical terms, these variables allowed a measurement of the correlation between the factors that can legitimately affect pay and actual pay. A separate variable in the equations took account of race, enabling the equations to isolate the correlation between race and pay. Taken as a whole, the regression equations provided a statistical means of comparing the pay of black and white employees who were otherwise similarly situated.

In *Bazemore*, the correlation between race and pay turned out to be both statistically and practically significant.[22] Nevertheless, because of limitations in the available evidence and because of theoretical disputes over what factors legitimately affect compensation, the regression analysis did not take account of all the factors that might conceivably be relevant to setting salary. In *Bazemore*, the Court recognized that a regression analysis may omit some measurable variables, particularly when the record as a whole supports an inference of discrimination. In *Bazemore* itself, the plaintiffs submitted evidence that an omitted factor, the county where employees worked, did not account for the difference in salary between black and white employees.[23] The Court's decision may have been in response to the overly skeptical attitude of the lower courts towards statistical evidence, holding, as they did, that the plaintiffs' regression analysis was " 'unacceptable as evidence of discrimination.' " In its turn, the Supreme Court remanded the case with instructions to consider the regression analysis as evidence of discrimination, stopping just short of rejecting the district court's finding of no discrimination and entering a contrary finding itself.[24] If the message of *Hazelwood* is that statistical evidence usually requires expert analysis, the message of *Bazemore* is that statistical evidence need not be perfect.

3.   The "Prima Facie" Case

These technical issues about the proper use of statistical evidence are embedded in a legal structure that allocates the burden of proof, just as in individual cases. At some stage in the litigation, the plaintiff either succeeds or fails in making out a "prima facie" case of class-wide intentional discrimination, with consequences that are often decisive. Unfortunately, the Supreme Court has not been clear about exactly what stage of the litigation is identified by the "prima facie" case. We have already seen how this term has led to

22. *Id.* at 398–401.   **24.** *Id.* at 403–04 & n.14.
23. *Id.* at 402–03.

confusion in individual cases. The same problem, arising from the same ambiguity, also appears in class-wide cases. The phrase can have at least three different meanings, only the first of which is appropriate for class claims of intentional discrimination. This first meaning is simply that the plaintiff has submitted sufficient evidence to support a reasonable inference of class-wide intentional discrimination. In this sense, a prima facie case does not shift any aspect of the burden of proof—either the burden of production or the burden of persuasion—to the defendant. In *Teamsters* (and *Hazelwood* as well),[25] all that follows from the plaintiff's success in making out a prima facie case in the first sense is that the trier of fact can find class-wide intentional discrimination, but only after considering the evidence presented by the defendant in rebuttal. This is, of course, a completely unexceptionable conclusion that holds for all forms of civil litigation. If the plaintiff makes out a prima facie case in this sense, the trier of fact may find in the plaintiff's favor, but is not required to do so.

Unfortunately, in *Teamsters*, the Supreme Court used the phrase in two other senses. In one, it described the prima facie case as "shifting to the employer the burden of rebutting the inference raised by the figures."[26] This burden appears to be a burden of production, requiring the defendant to come forward with evidence to dispel a presumption in favor of the plaintiff. If that is what the phrase means in this passage, then the nature of the defendant's burden should have been spelled out later in the opinion. But it was not, beyond the general admonition, quoted earlier, that the usefulness of statistical evidence "depends on all of the surrounding facts and circumstances."[27] It is more likely that the passage refers to the overwhelming evidence of intentional discrimination—"the inexorable zero"—in this particular case. Perhaps the evidence was so overwhelming that the only reasonable inference was that the defendants had engaged in intentional discrimination. If so, *Teamsters* would have been one of the very few cases in which a directed verdict, or perhaps even summary judgment, should have been entered for the plaintiff. No such issue was presented to the Supreme Court, however, which simply affirmed findings of discrimination made by the district court.

Another sense of "prima facie" also appears in the opinion, in the section on remedies, where it seemingly refers to a shift in the entire burden of proof, both of production and persuasion. In this passage, it refers to the effect of finding class-wide intentional

---

25. *Teamsters*, 431 U.S. at 342–43;   **27.** *Id.* at 340.
Hazelwood, 433 U.S. at 309.

26. 431 U.S. at 339.

discrimination: "By 'demonstrating the existence of a discriminatory hiring pattern and practice,' the plaintiffs had made out a prima facie case of discrimination against individual class members."[28] This use of "prima facie" must be clearly distinguished from either of the first two, since it refers to the effect of a finding of discrimination. Any such finding occurs later in the litigation—and has far greater consequences—than any inference or presumption arising only from evidence of discrimination. A "prima facie" entitlement to relief is not prima facie at all with respect to a violation of the statute, which already must have been found to support any entitlement to relief. Statistical evidence itself bears only on the issue whether discrimination can be found, and in most cases, only by generating a reasonable inference on this issue.

The Supreme Court did not clearly distinguish the other senses of the term "prima facie," leaving unsettled exactly which use of the term it intended. In particular, its silence on the consequences of a prima facie case leaves open the possibility that the burden of production shifts to the defendant, under the second sense of "prima facie," requiring the defendant to present evidence from which a reasonable inference of no disparate treatment may be drawn and, if the defendant fails to do so, requiring the court to enter a finding of intentional discrimination.[29] On the other hand, because it failed to specify the content of the defendant's rebuttal case, it is not clear what burden, if any, shifted to the defendant. In the absence of any specific showing that the defendant must make, the safest conclusion is that the defendant has to do only what all defendants in civil litigation have to do: convince the trier of fact not to draw an inference in the plaintiff's favor. On this interpretation, the Court invoked only the first, unexceptionable, sense of the term "prima facie."

Whether or not this interpretation is accepted, class claims of disparate treatment differ dramatically from class claims of disparate impact in shifting at most a poorly defined and uncertain burden of proof onto the defendant. Class claims of disparate impact, as we shall see later in this chapter, clearly impose a heavier burden of proof upon the defendant.

4. Colorblindness and Class Claims of Disparate Treatment

Much more might be added to the discussion of statistical evidence and its relationship to the plaintiff's prima facie case.

---

28. *Id.* at 359 (quoting Franks v. Bowman Transp. Co., 424 U.S. 747, 772 (1976)).

29. *Hazelwood*, 433 U.S. at 309.

Disputes over statistical techniques, labor market analysis, the reliability of underlying data and whether all these considerations, taken together, permit a finding of intentional discrimination, can be found throughout the cases on proof of class-wide disparate treatment. What is remarkable about these issues, however, is how they stand at one remove from a purely negative conception of equality, with its emphasis on "colorblindness" and on what cannot be considered in making employment decisions. Disputes over statistical evidence look only to the effects of an employer's personnel practices, not its decisionmaking process in adopting or applying those practices. Of course, inferences from effects to intent have long been recognized in the common law. And conversely, individual instances of discrimination have routinely been used as anecdotal evidence of class-wide discrimination. Nevertheless, the emphasis on statistical evidence in class cases inevitably causes the focus to shift away from a purely negative conception of equality.

Aspects of a remedial conception of equality enter into the necessarily judgmental decision of whether statistical disparities are practically significant: whether any given disparity in the treatment of different groups is large enough to support an inference of intentional discrimination. This issue is framed more naturally as one of equality of opportunity rather than colorblindness, invoking the remedial rather than the negative conception of equality. Equality of opportunity can be denied by means other than consideration of race or some other prohibited characteristic. It can also be caused by inequality in pre-existing conditions, and in particular, by the continuing effects of past discrimination.

A positive conception of equality based on merit also enters into the analysis of class-wide claims of intentional discrimination. As with individual claims, it does so in the employer's attempt to rebut an inference of intentional discrimination. The justification for a disputed employment practice, just like the statistical evidence of its discriminatory effects, inevitably takes on a more objective cast in class cases than in individual cases. In addition to attacking the plaintiff's statistical evidence or offering additional statistical evidence, an employer can offer a justification for the disputed employment practice based on its own business judgment. Yet even more so than in individual cases, it is not a promising strategy for an employer to offer any reason, no matter how unsound, so long as it is not a discriminatory reason. Courts are more inclined to inquire into an employer's business judgment in class cases than in individual cases. The unequal consequences of hiring, promotion, or compensation decisions, established by objective statistical evidence, require a similarly objective justification to be persuasively rebutted. In theory, perhaps, an employer remains free to offer its own idiosyncratic preferences to explain away any such unequal consequences, but in order to persuade a judge or jury, a credible appeal to merit or ability to perform the job is necessary.

In class claims of disparate treatment, the negative conception of equality is dominant in the formulation of legal doctrine. Nevertheless, it yields to competing conceptions of equality at crucial and controversial points of implementation and enforcement. In proving class-wide intentional discrimination, the role of these competing conceptions remains largely implicit. With class-wide claims of disparate impact, however, these rival conceptions exercise an explicit influence on the framing of legal doctrine.

B.   Class Claims of Disparate Impact

The defining characteristic of claims of disparate impact is that they do not require proof of intentional discrimination, but only of discriminatory effects. Exactly what "disparate impact" means— how it is proved by the plaintiff and how it is rebutted by the defendant—has been a source of controversy since this theory of liability was first recognized in *Griggs v. Duke Power Co.*[30] Indeed, this theory of liability lies at the center of doctrinal disputes over Title VII. It brings together the contrast between proof of intent and proof of effects, the justification for affirmative action, the relationship between statutory interpretation and constitutional law, and the underlying tension between different conceptions of equality.

In *Griggs*, the Supreme Court held that Title VII does not require proof of intentional discrimination. A plaintiff can recover by proving that an employment practice has a disparate impact on persons of a particular race, national origin, sex, or religion. If the plaintiff proves disparate impact, then the burden of proof shifts to the defendant to prove that the disputed practice is justified by "business necessity" or is "related to job performance." The Supreme Court soon added a third stage to cases of disparate impact. If the defendant carries its burden of proof, then the burden of proof shifts back to the plaintiff to prove that the offered justification is a pretext for discrimination.[31]

---

30.   401 U.S. 424 (1971).

31.   Albemarle Paper Co. v. Moody, 422 U.S. 405, 425 (1975).

Several later decisions elaborated on the theory, but left the elements of the plaintiff's case and the defendant's rebuttal uncertain. The Supreme Court resolved these uncertainties in favor of defendants in *Wards Cove Packing Co. v. Atonio*,[32] only to have its decision largely overruled by the Civil Rights Act of 1991. The act clarified several uncertainties surrounding the theory, and in particular, it made clear that the full burden of proof—both the burden of production and the burden of persuasion—shifted to the defendant to justify practices that have a disparate impact. Nevertheless, doubts still remain about exactly what this theory of liability requires and the purposes that it serves.

These doubts have been aggravated by the diminished role of class actions in enforcing Title VII in recent decades. Ironically enough, the theory of disparate impact was codified only after the procedural means for asserting class claims, whether of disparate treatment or disparate impact, had fallen into relative neglect. For over two decades, most claims of employment discrimination have been individual claims of intentional discrimination, not class claims of disparate impact.[33] In the late 1970's, the number of class actions fell dramatically, and with them, the most promising procedural form for asserting liability for disparate impact. Despite amendments to Title VII designed to make these claims easier to prove, there has been no significant increase in the proportion of Title VII claims brought as class actions. Neither has this theory of liability been widely used under other statutes or under the Constitution, either because it has been explicitly rejected,[34] or because doubts have been expressed about its validity,[35] or because other statutory provisions have been the focus of litigation.[36]

Perhaps the theory of disparate impact has been a victim of its own success and few such claims have recently been brought because employers have eliminated personnel policies with obvious adverse effects on minorities and women. Employers might have either eliminated tests and qualifications that had a disparate

---

32. 490 U.S. 642 (1989).

33. John J. Donohue III & Peter Siegelman, The Changing Nature of Employment Discrimination Litigation, 43 Stan. L. Rev. 983, 1019–21 (1991).

34. General Bldg. Contractors Ass'n v. Pennsylvania, 458 U.S. 375, 382–91 (1982) (no liability for disparate impact under 42 U.S.C. § 1981 (2000)); Washington v. Davis, 426 U.S. 229, 238–39 (1976) (none under the Constitution).

35. Smith v. City of Jackson, 544 U.S. 228 (2005) (liability for disparate impact not available under the Age Discrimination in Employment Act on terms as favorable to plaintiffs as under Title VII).

36. The most notable example is the Americans with Disabilities Act, which codifies the theory of disparate impact, yet has given rise mainly to litigation over its coverage provisions and the requirement of reasonable accommodation. *See* 42 U.S.C. §§ 12111(8)–(10), 12112(b)(5), 12113(a) (2000).

impact or eliminated the disparate impact itself through compensatory programs of affirmative action. At the same time, the burden of bringing class claims has also increased. The procedural requirements for class actions have become more demanding and the substantive requirements for the use of statistical evidence more onerous, as discussed earlier in this chapter. Most of the doctrinal dispute over the theory of disparate impact has concerned the nature and magnitude of the defendant's burden of proof after a finding of disparate impact. Yet the plaintiff's initial burden of proving disparate impact in the first place has also grown heavier and more complicated. All of these developments make claims of disparate impact less promising, particularly for attorneys, who are likely to obtain a full recovery of their fees only in successful cases.

None of these trends diminishes the doctrinal significance of the theory of disparate impact. And, indeed, in order to understand how significant the theory is in litigation, it is first necessary to understand its doctrinal complexity, all of which can be traced back to fundamental arguments over the purposes that it serves. Is it only a modest addition to class claims of disparate treatment, departing from the historical perspective and its conception of equality as colorblindness only by placing upon employers some of the burden of eliminating hidden discrimination? Or is it an entirely independent theory, following the remedial perspective and its goal of eliminating the continuing effects of past discrimination? On the latter view, its purpose is to discourage employers from using employment practices that have an adverse impact upon previously disadvantaged groups.

If the theory of disparate impact is designed only to prevent hidden discrimination, then it would result in liability only when there is evidence of disparate treatment (evidence not strong enough, however, to justify a finding of intentional discrimination), and it would impose a significant, but not overwhelming, burden on the employer to show that a disputed employment practice is related to performance on the job. The theory would ease the plaintiff's burden of proving intentional discrimination, but only to a degree. By contrast, if the theory of disparate impact is designed to discourage employment practices that disproportionately exclude members of minority groups and women, then it would result in liability in the absence of evidence of disparate treatment and it would impose a heavy burden of justification on the employer. The theory would serve the independent purpose of eliminating neutral employment practices that imposed systematic disadvantages upon racial minorities and women.

73

The ambiguity in the theory results not only from the competition between the historical and remedial perspectives in the law of employment discrimination. It also results from the ambiguity latent in the economic perspective between merit as determined by the employer, supporting management discretion, and merit as determined by some objective standard, resulting in judicial reexamination of management decisions. In individual claims of intentional discrimination, merit appears in the first sense, allowing employers a wide range of choices among "legitimate, nondiscriminatory reasons" for disputed employment decisions. In class claims of disparate impact, employers must advance a stronger justification for practices that have a disparate impact. Exactly how much stronger has been a matter of continuous dispute dating back to the original decision in *Griggs*. It is therefore necessary to examine the development of the theory of disparate impact in detail in order to understand the ambiguities that lie at the foundation of the theory.

1. From Griggs to Wards Cove

Until its decision in *Wards Cove*, the Supreme Court did not choose between a narrow or a broad interpretation of the theory of disparate impact, sometimes endorsing both interpretations in one and the same opinion. Thus, in *Griggs*, the Court first seemed to adopt a narrow interpretation of the theory when it stated, "Discriminatory preference for any group, minority or majority, is precisely and only what Congress has proscribed." A few paragraphs later, however, the Court appeared to adopt a broad interpretation of the theory: "But Congress directed the thrust of the act to the consequences of employment practices, not simply the motivation." Likewise, on the issue of the defendant's burden of justification, the Court first appeared to place a heavy burden on the defendant, consistent with a broad interpretation of the theory: "The touchstone is business necessity." But in the very next sentence, it seemed to impose only a light burden on the employer, consistent with the narrow interpretation: "If an employment practice which operates to exclude Negroes cannot be shown to be related to job performance, the practice is prohibited."[37] What does the theory of disparate impact require—a difficult showing of business necessity or an easy showing of relationship to job performance?

These ambiguities in *Griggs* cannot be resolved by examining the facts of the case. The evidence before the Court was equally consistent with a finding of liability based on a narrow or a broad

---

37. *Griggs*, 401 U.S. at 431–32.

interpretation of the theory. The disputed employment practices in *Griggs* were the requirement of a high school diploma and passing scores on two general intelligence tests for hiring or promotion to higher-level departments, from which blacks had formerly been excluded entirely. The evidence before the Court was that 34% of white males in North Carolina, but only 12% of black males, had completed high school and that 58% of whites, but only 6% of blacks, had passed a similar battery of tests, although in an unrelated case.[38] More striking was the fact that the employer had required a high school diploma for more jobs and imposed the testing requirement for the first time when it abandoned segregation just before the effective date of Title VII.[39] Moreover, no black worker had been employed in the higher-level departments until administrative proceedings were commenced in *Griggs* itself,[40] and the employer offered no justification for the disputed requirements beyond a desire to improve the overall quality of its work force.[41] The principal obstacle to application of the theory of disparate treatment was not absence of evidence, but the findings of the district court that the employer had not engaged in intentional discrimination.[42] The record in *Griggs* may have required application of the theory of disparate impact, but it did not require a choice between a narrow or a broad version of that theory.

Subsequent decisions of the Supreme Court were equally ambiguous on the choice between a narrow or a broad version of the theory. Most of these decisions concerned the defendant's burden of justifying an employment practice that has a disparate impact. The decisions are discussed in detail later in this chapter, but broadly speaking, the decisions divide into two groups. One group is consistent with the guidelines on testing and qualifications adopted by the EEOC; the other is not. These guidelines impose exacting requirements upon defendants to justify practices that have a disparate impact, although the current version of the guidelines, the Uniform Guidelines on Employee Selection Procedures,[43] have relaxed these requirements slightly. The cases following the guidelines generally endorsed a broad interpretation of the theory of disparate impact.[44] The other group of cases imposed less stringent requirements upon the employer than the guidelines and, to that extent, favored a narrow interpretation of the theory.[45] These cases

---

38. *Id.* at 430 n.6.

39. *Id.* at 427–28.

40. *Id.* at 427 & n.2.

41. *Id.* at 431.

42. *Id.* at 428.

43. 29 C.F.R. pt. 1607 (2006).

44. *E.g.*, Albemarle Paper Co. v. Moody, 422 U.S. 405, 425–436 (1975); Dothard v. Rawlinson, 433 U.S. 321, 328–33 (1977).

45. *E.g.*, Washington v. Davis, 426 U.S. 229, 249–52 (1976); New York City Transit Authority v. Beazer, 440 U.S.

also raised the further issue of the authority of the guidelines themselves. The EEOC does not have authority to promulgate substantive regulations with the force of law,[46] so that its guidelines constitute only interpretative regulations. Because the Supreme Court has sometimes given "great deference" to guidelines issued by the EEOC[47] and sometimes not given them any deference at all,[48] it is difficult to determine what authority they actually possess.

The continued ambivalence of the Supreme Court towards the theory of disparate impact is perfectly illustrated by the case that immediately preceded *Wards Cove, Watson v. Fort Worth Bank & Trust*.[49] In that case, the Court both expanded the scope of the theory of disparate impact and divided exactly evenly over the burden of proof that it placed upon employers. The first part of the opinion resolved a question that had generated a conflict among the circuits: whether the theory of disparate impact applied to subjective employment practices, which require the exercise of discretion and judgment in evaluating any individual employee, as opposed to standardized tests and qualifications, which do not. In *Watson*, the challenged employment practice was the employer's reliance upon the subjective judgment of supervisors in making promotions. The Court held that this practice could be challenged under the theory of disparate impact because otherwise employers could avoid application of the theory simply by replacing objective employment practices with subjective decisionmaking, which could equally well be tainted by subconscious stereotypes and prejudices.[50] While the Court was unanimous on expanding the scope of the theory of disparate impact, it divided evenly on what the theory required the defendant to prove after disparate impact had been shown. Writing for a plurality of four, Justice O'Connor would have limited the defendant's burden of proof to a burden of production and only to justifying the disputed employment practice by reference to "legitimate business purposes" and "business reasons." Four justices dissented from this part of the opinion, and because one justice did not participate, the statements of Justice O'Connor on the defendant's burden of proof represent the views of only four justices and

---

568, 587 & n.31 (1979); *cf.* Connecticut v. Teal, 457 U.S. 440, 453 n. 12 (1982) (refusing to follow the Uniform Guidelines on the issue of proof of disparate impact).

46. § 713(a), codified as 42 U.S.C. § 2000e–12(a) (2000).

47. *Albemarle Paper*, 422 U.S.at 431; *Griggs*, 401 U.S. at 433–34.

48. General Electric Co. v. Gilbert, 429 U.S. 125, 140–45 (1976); City of Los Angeles, Dep't of Water & Power v. Manhart, 435 U.S. 702, 719 n.36 (1978).

49. 487 U.S. 977 (1988).

50. *Id.* at 989–91

so have no precedential effect.[51] The failure of the Court to resolve these issues in *Watson* led directly to *Wards Cove* and ultimately to the Civil Rights Act of 1991.

2. Wards Cove and the Civil Rights Act of 1991

The decision in *Wards Cove* was largely, but not entirely, overruled by the Civil Rights Act of 1991. On the issue of the plaintiff's initial burden of proving disparate impact, the act does not overrule the decision and may go further than the decision in requiring the plaintiff to identify the employment practices that caused the disparate impact. It is only on the issues of the defendant's burden of proof and the plaintiff's burden of proving pretext that the act overruled the decision. Although all of these issues are of theoretical interest, the first issue may have the greatest practical significance, because the burden of proof switches to the defendant only after the plaintiff has proved disparate impact.

The claims in *Wards Cove* concerned discrimination in hiring workers in two salmon canneries that operated in Alaska over the summer. The jobs in the canneries were divided into cannery jobs, which did not require any skills, and noncannery jobs, which did. The noncannery jobs paid more than the cannery jobs and were filled predominantly by white workers. The cannery jobs were filled predominantly by minority workers: Filipinos and Alaska Natives. The cannery and noncannery workers also lived in separate dormitories and ate in separate mess halls. The Court held that the plaintiffs could not establish disparate impact simply by proving a racial imbalance in the composition of the work force for cannery and noncannery jobs. The plaintiffs, instead, had to establish a disparity between the proportion of minority workers in noncannery jobs and the proportion of those workers in the labor market for such jobs.[52] Moreover, the plaintiffs also had to identify the particular employment practices that caused this disparity.[53]

The Court's analysis of this issue follows the treatment of statistical evidence in *Hazelwood School District v. United States*,[54] where such evidence was used to prove disparate treatment. *Wards Cove* went beyond *Hazelwood* in requiring the plaintiff to identify the particular employment practices that caused the disparate impact. This holding was codified—not overruled—by the Civil

---

51. *Id.* at 996–99 (opinion of O'Connor, J.); *id.* at 1000–11 (Blackmun, J., concurring in part and concurring in the judgment); *id.* at 1011 (Stevens, J., concurring in the judgment). Justice Kennedy did not participate in the decision.

52. 490 U.S. 642, 653–54 (1989).

53. *Id.* at 656.

54. 433 U.S. 299 (1977).

Rights Act of 1991, which imposed the same requirement in nearly identical terms.[55] Since the act did not address the use of statistical evidence in any other respect, the entire treatment of this issue in *Wards Cove* remains good law, and is discussed more fully in the next section of this chapter.

The controversial holdings in *Wards Cove* concerned the defendant's burden of proof and the plaintiff's burden of proving pretext. The Court held that if the plaintiff succeeds in establishing disparate impact, only the burden of production switches to the defendant and that the court's examination of the employer's evidence is limited to "a reasoned review of the employer's justification for his use of the challenged practice."[56] If the defendant then succeeds in carrying this lighter burden of proof, the plaintiff is required to show that an alternative employment practice with a smaller disparate impact is equally effective in meeting the same business purposes.

In the Civil Rights Act of 1991, Congress rejected both of these holdings,[57] and indeed, identified *Wards Cove* as one of the decisions overruled by the act.[58] In particular, Congress defined "demonstrate" to mean "meets the burden of production and persuasion" and required the defendant to "demonstrate that the challenged practice is job related for the position in question and consistent with business necessity." Congress also required that the plaintiff's proof of an alternative employment practice with lesser adverse impact meet the standards existing on the day before *Wards Cove* was decided.[59] In the preamble to the act and in the single interpretive memorandum identified as authoritative on these issues, Congress stated that the terms "business necessity" and "job related" are intended to follow the law as it existed before *Wards Cove*.[60]

Despite the clarity with which Congress rejected these holdings in *Wards Cove*, the ultimate effect of its legislation remains ambiguous. In rejecting these holdings, Congress clearly rejected a narrow interpretation of the theory of disparate impact. What it accepted is not quite so clear. In the crucial provision defining the

55. § 703(k)(1)(A)(i), (B)(i), codified as 42 U.S.C. § 2000e–2(k)(1)(A)(i), (B)(i) (2000).

56. 490 U.S. at 659.

57. §§ 701(m), 703(k)(1)(A)(i), codified as 42 U.S.C. §§ 2000e(m),–2(k)(1)(A)(i) (2000).

58. Pub. L. No. 102–166, §§ 2(2), 3(2), 105 Stat. 1071 (1991), reproduced at 42 U.S.C. § 1981 note (2000).

59. § 703(k)(1)(C), codified as 42 U.S.C. § 2000e–2(k)(1)(C) (2000).

60. Pub. L. No. 102–166, §§ 3(2), 105(b), 105 Stat. 1071, 1075 (1991), reproduced at 42 U.S.C. § 1981 note (2000). The interpretive memorandum appears at 137 Cong. Rec. S15276 (daily ed. Oct. 25, 1991), 137 Cong. Rec. 28,623 (permanent ed. 1991).

defendant's burden of proof, Congress did not choose between the terms "business necessity" and "related to job performance," first used in *Griggs* to characterize the defendant's burden of proof. Instead, it used both phrases, by requiring the defendant to prove "that the challenged practice is job related for the position in question and consistent with business necessity."[61] Reading this provision with the authorized legislative history, Congress plainly meant to turn the clock back to before *Wards Cove*. Nevertheless, as we have seen, and as the section on the defendant's burden of proof discusses in detail, the decisions before *Wards Cove* were ambiguous on exactly what was required of the defendant. The Civil Rights Act of 1991 did not eliminate this ambiguity.

On the issue of proof of an "alternative employment practice," it is even less clear what Congress accomplished because it is doubtful that *Wards Cove* made any change in the law at all. In *Albemarle Paper*, the Supreme Court had already placed on the plaintiff the burden of proving pretext after the defendant carried its burden of proof. That decision, like *Wards Cove*, simply mentioned, as one way to prove pretext, evidence that the employer could have adopted an equally effective employment practice with less disparate impact.[62] The entire issue of pretext, however, does not make much difference in class claims of disparate impact. Contrary to what happens in individual cases alleging intentional discrimination, few of these claims ever get as far as the issue of pretext. It is the earlier stages of disparate impact cases—the plaintiff's initial proof of disparate impact and the defendant's rebuttal on job relationship and business necessity—that usually prove to be dispositive. Each of these stages deserves separate discussion.

3. Proof of Disparate Impact

The surviving holding in *Wards Cove* makes clear that the plaintiff's burden of proving disparate impact should be analyzed along the same lines as in *Hazelwood School District v. United States*.[63] Yet because *Hazelwood* involved a claim of disparate treat-

---

61. §§ 701(m), 703(k)(1)(A)(i), codified as 42 U.S.C. §§ 2000e(m),–2(k)(1)(A)(i) (2000).

62. *Albemarle Paper*, 422 U.S. at 425. By contrast, the Uniform Guidelines impose upon the employer the burden of proving that a validated employment practice has the least disparate impact among available alternatives. 29 C.F.R. § 1607.3B (2006). Even if this provision of the guidelines could have been reconciled with *Albemarle Paper*, it is now plainly superseded by the Civil Rights Act of 1991, which places the burden of proof on this issue explicitly on the plaintiff. § 703(k)(1)(A)(ii), codified as 42 U.S.C. § 2000e–2(k)(1)(A)(ii) (2000).

63. *Wards Cove*, 490 U.S. at 650–55.

ment, the ultimate fact to be proved, and therefore the burden of proof on the plaintiff, must differ in claims of disparate impact. The cases are surprisingly silent on exactly what this difference is. On a narrow view of the theory of disparate impact, invoking the historical perspective of colorblindness, the difference should be minimal. Proof of disparate impact should differ from proof of intentional discrimination only in moving the ultimate question of fact from a subjective inquiry into the defendant's intention to an objective inquiry into the effects of the defendant's employment practices. The disparity revealed by statistical evidence should be statistically and practically significant, large enough by itself to support an inference of intentional discrimination, but not so large that the trier of fact actually has to draw the inference. Under the theory of disparate impact, the trier of fact need not find intentional discrimination in order to shift the burden of proof to the defendant. On a broad view of the theory, a much smaller disparity should be sufficient, one that leads the trier of fact to conclude that significant opportunities have been denied to members of the plaintiff's group.

Beyond these qualified generalizations, it is impossible to specify more precisely what the plaintiff must prove. This impasse results partly from the similar treatment of statistics to prove disparate impact and disparate treatment. In both kinds of claims, the statistical evidence must be analyzed according to the same three-step process. First, the labor market for the jobs at issue must be defined and the proportion of a particular group among those in the labor market must be established. Second, the proportion of the same group among those who possess the disputed qualification must be established. And third, the two proportions must be compared for statistical and practical significance. Failure at any one of these steps is likely to undermine the statistical evidence entirely, leaving no inference to be drawn from it, either of intentional discrimination or disparate impact. Moreover, in close cases, in which the plaintiff presents evidence establishing a significant disparity in the treatment of different groups, the crucial issue is not likely to be how strong the evidence of disparate impact is, but how convincing the defendant's justification is. Courts that find only a minimal disparity are likely to require the defendant only to come forward with a correspondingly diminished justification.

The complications added by the Civil Rights Act of 1991 to proof of disparate impact have only reinforced the all-or-nothing quality of the evidence required of the plaintiff. In addition to meeting the general requirements of *Hazelwood*, the plaintiff must also establish that "a particular employment practice" resulted in disparate impact.[64] In this respect, the act codified a holding of *Wards Cove* instead of superseding it. Alternatively, the plaintiff can prove that elements of the defendant's decisionmaking process cannot be separated for analysis, in which case they are treated as a single employment practice.[65] The defendant can rebut either of these showings by demonstrating that the particular employment practice identified by the plaintiff did not cause the disparate impact.[66] These provisions add another layer of complexity, and another layer of shifting burdens of proof, to claims of disparate impact. Such added complexity may be dismaying, but it serves the useful purpose of focusing the inquiry onto specific employment practices that the defendant must then justify.

The decision in *Connecticut v. Teal*,[67] which preceded the Civil Rights Act of 1991, served a similar purpose. *Teal* rejected the "bottom line" rule of the Uniform Guidelines for determining disparate impact. The "bottom line" rule examines the net effect of all of the employer's tests and qualifications on the ultimate selection of members of a particular group for a particular job.[68] The Court held that the disparate impact of a test or qualification was to be determined without regard to the effect of the employer's selection process as a whole. In *Teal*, the employer used a test that had a disparate impact upon blacks, but instead of proving that the test was justified, it instituted an affirmative action plan after the litigation had begun. The Court allowed the plaintiff to decide whether to attack the test alone or to attack the overall effect of the employer's selection process. That option has now been eliminated by the act: each selection device must be evaluated separately. After *Teal*, and even more so after the Civil Rights Act of 1991, the disparate impact of each component of a selection process must be established separately.

The Uniform Guidelines therefore depart from existing law in adopting the "bottom line" rule for determining disparate impact, although the extent of this departure should not be exaggerated. The Uniform Guidelines purport only to establish rules for the guidance of federal agencies in exercising their discretion to enforce the law. Thus, the Uniform Guidelines explicitly state that the "bottom line" rule is subject to exceptions and that it is not put

---

64. § 703(k)(1)(B)(i), codified as 42 U.S.C. § 2000e–2(k)(1)(B)(i) (2000).

65. *Id.*

66. § 703(k)(1)(B)(ii), codified as 42 U.S.C. § 2000e–2(k)(1)(B)(ii) (2000).

67. 457 U.S. 440 (1982).

68. *Id.* at 452–53; 29 C.F.R. § 1607.4C (2006).

forward as a rule of law but only as guidance for the exercise of prosecutorial discretion.[69]

Nevertheless, other provisions of the Uniform Guidelines depart strikingly from the analysis of statistical evidence in *Hazelwood* and in the Civil Rights Act of 1991. The Uniform Guidelines do not require an analysis of the relevant labor market in each case, but establish the general rule that an employer should examine applicant-flow statistics to determine disparate impact and, in particular, that the pass rate for any group cannot be less than four-fifths of the pass rate of the most successful group. Unlike the analysis in *Hazelwood*, the four-fifths rule of the Uniform Guidelines does not require a statistically significant disparity between pass rates, although it allows an exception for statistically insignificant disparities based on small numbers.[70] The Uniform Guidelines provide a simpler method of determining disparate impact than does *Hazelwood*, apparently in order to make it easier to identify particular employers who are likely to have violated Title VII. Nevertheless, the guidelines acknowledge the possibility of a more accurate analysis of statistical evidence only in recognizing limited exceptions and qualifications.

The overall approach of the Uniform Guidelines generally favors plaintiffs by decreasing their burden of proof and increasing the defendants' burden of proof. This approach has limited consequences for the plaintiffs' proof of disparate impact, but depending on how literally it is taken, dramatic implications for the defendants' proof of job relationship and business necessity, as we shall see in the next section. The guidelines' lenience towards plaintiffs can be taken as favoritism towards the minority groups and women from which plaintiffs typically are drawn, so much so that in *Teal* the Supreme Court made a point of insisting that Title VII protects only individuals, not groups. As the dissent in that case correctly pointed out, however, this is not the real question posed by the theory of disparate impact.[71] Title VII confers rights only on individuals, not on groups. The real question is how it protects individuals and, in particular, how the theory of disparate impact uses evidence of group effects to protect individual rights.[72] That question has come up most forcefully in disputes over the defendant's burden of justifying practices that have a disparate impact.

4. Defendant's Burden of Proof

The defendant's burden of proof has been the focus of disputes over the purpose and interpretation of the theory of disparate

69. 29 C.F.R. § 1607.4C (2006).

70. *Id.* § 1607.4D.

71. *Teal*, 457 U.S. at 458 (Powell, J., dissenting).

72. *Id.* at 458–59 (Powell, J., dissenting).

impact for several different reasons. First, any shift in the burden of proof away from the plaintiff identifies an issue as one on which the defendant is particularly vulnerable. Any significant uncertainty on such issues is resolved against the defendant. Second, the content of what the defendant must prove is inherently uncertain. The issue whether a disputed practice is "job related for the position in question and consistent with business necessity" raises all of the ambiguities surrounding the conception of equality as merit. Is merit to be determined according to the discretion of the employer, as a straightforward application of the economic perspective would imply? Or is it to be determined according to some external standard of merit to be ascertained and applied by the courts? These alternative interpretations result, respectively, in a narrow or a broad interpretation of the theory of disparate impact, invoking still other perspectives on the law of employment discrimination: either the historical perspective with its emphasis on equality as colorblindness or the remedial perspective with its emphasis on eliminating the consequences of past discrimination. And third, purely as a matter of legal doctrine, the content of the defendant's burden is systematically ambiguous, using both the phrase "job related for the position in question," which implies that any relationship between the disputed practice and the job is sufficient, and the phrase "consistent with business necessity," which suggests that only a strong relationship is sufficient.

This doctrinal ambiguity is the easiest to explain, even if, in the end, it is the most difficult to resolve. Several crucial provisions of the Civil Rights Act of 1991 addressed the defendant's burden of proof, beginning with the definition of the word "demonstrate" to refer specifically to meeting "the burden of production and persuasion." The statutory formulation of the defendant's burden, quoted in the preceding paragraph, then requires the defendant "to demonstrate" both job relationship and business necessity. The statutory language, however, qualifies the second element by requiring proof only that the disputed practice is "consistent with business necessity," not that it is "required by business necessity." These changes in the text of Title VII are explained by both the preamble to the statute and the authorized legislative history as an attempt to restore the law to where it was just before *Wards Cove*.[73] Yet

---

73. Pub. L. No. 102–166, §§ 3(2), 105(b), 105 Stat. 1071, 1075 (1991), reproduced at 42 U.S.C. § 1981 note (2000). The second of these provisions identified the only authorized legislative history of the provisions on the theory of disparate impact as an interpretive memorandum appearing at 137 Cong.

turning the clock back to this point in the development of the theory of disparate impact leaves intact all of the ambiguity that has surrounded it from its inception.

This ambiguity is most apparent in the differing attitudes that the Supreme Court has taken towards the analysis of these issues in the Uniform Guidelines and their predecessors. The Uniform Guidelines allow three forms of justification (or "validation" in their terminology) for employment practices that have a disparate impact: content validation, criterion validation, and construct validation. These forms of validation can be applied to any employment practice, either a subjective process of evaluation or an objective test or qualification.[74] It is simplest, however, to discuss these forms of validation as they apply to objective employment tests.

In content validation, a test is shown to be related to the job by proving that the content of the test is "representative of important aspects of performance on the job for which the candidates are to be evaluated."[75] The most important requirements for content validity are that the content of the test contain all important aspects of the job and that performance of those aspects of the job be readily observable. The latter requirement is necessary to distinguish content validation from construct validation, in which abstract abilities and characteristics are related to performance on the job. The standard example of a content-valid test is a typing test for the position of typist. Note, however, that a typing test would not be content valid for a secretary's job that required significant work other than typing, such as taking dictation, making appointments, answering phone calls, and filing. Note also that a typing test is content valid for the position of typist because it directly incorporates actual components of the job, not because it measures some abstract ability or characteristic, such as manual dexterity, which could be related to the job only through construct validation.

Criterion validation is the most general and acceptable form of validation under the Uniform Guidelines. It requires that a test be shown to be related to performance on the job according to some criterion, such as error rate, output, or supervisors' evaluations.

Rec. S15276 (daily ed. Oct. 25, 1991), 137 Cong. Rec. 28,632 (permanent ed. 1991). In discussing the defendant's burden of proof, this memorandum states:

> The terms "business necessity" and "job related" are intended to reflect the concepts enunciated by the Supreme Court in *Griggs v. Duke Power Co.*, 401 U.S. 424 (1971), and in the other Supreme

Court decisions prior to *Wards Cove Packing Co. v. Atonio*, 490 U.S. 642 (1989).

The statement in section 3(2) of purposes of the act says the same thing in almost exactly the same words.

74.   29 C.F.R. § 1607.2B (2006).

75.   *Id.* § 1607.5B.

The crucial steps in criterion validation are proving that the chosen criterion in fact measures performance on the job and establishing a statistically significant correlation between good scores on the test and good performance on the job according to the chosen criterion.[76] An example of criterion validation is a showing that a test for manual dexterity is related to performance on an assembly-line job, as measured by the criteria of speed and error rate. Validation requires that the criteria of speed and error rate be established as appropriate measures of job performance and that a statistically significant correlation be established between good test scores and good performance on the job according to these criteria. Note that the process of validating this test, like the process of validating the typing test discussed earlier, does not make any appeal to the abstract ability or construct of manual dexterity. Even a test that purported to measure some other construct, for instance, intelligence, would be criterion valid if it were shown to have a statistically significant correlation with good performance on the job according to the specified criteria. Unlike content validation, criterion validation is not limited to tests that reproduce important components of the job, and unlike construct validation, its acceptability is not openly doubted by the Uniform Guidelines. The requirements of criterion validation, however, are difficult and costly to satisfy. In many complicated jobs, the only appropriate criterion of good performance is some form of supervisors' evaluations, which cannot easily be checked for lack of bias and uniformity.[77] Establishing a statistically significant correlation between the good test scores and good performance on the job is even more difficult and costly.[78] Consequently, some decisions have applied the requirements for criterion validation with a degree of leniency not found in the Uniform Guidelines.[79]

Construct validation is the least favored form of validation under the Uniform Guidelines. Employers using construct validation must show that a test or qualification measures a "construct," an abstract ability or characteristic such as intelligence or manual dexterity, and that possessing the construct is correlated with good performance on the job. The notorious problems with intelligence tests illustrate the problems posed by construct validation. First, any construct like intelligence is difficult to define,

---

76. *Id.* § 1607.14B(2), (5).

77. *Id.* § 1607.14B(2), (3). *See also* Albemarle Paper Co. v. Moody, 422 U.S. 405, 432–33 (1975).

78. Barbara Lindemann Schlei & Paul Grossman, Employment Discrimi-nation Law 113 n.106 (2d ed. 1983) (criterion validation costs estimated at between $100,000 and $400,000 in 1978).

79. *E.g.,* Washington v. Davis, 426 U.S. 229, 248–52 (1976).

precisely because it is an abstract ability or characteristic. Does intelligence include ability in higher mathematics, but not shrewdness in business deals? If it includes both, how is good performance in these separate activities to be weighted? Second, constructs that are difficult to define are also difficult to measure. How do we know that an intelligence test measures the forms of intelligence relevant to both higher mathematics and business deals? Third, constructs are difficult to relate to good performance on the job. How can a statistically significant correlation be established between intelligence and good performance on any particular job? The Uniform Guidelines impose exacting standards for construct validation in order to avoid these problems. The most exacting standard is a preliminary requirement that the construct itself have been related to good performance on the job by criterion validation.[80] Since few such criterion validations of constructs have been performed for particular jobs, an employer is better off directly relying on criterion validation of the test at issue. It is easier to validate an intelligence test directly by criterion validation than by first showing that it measures intelligence and then showing that intelligence is related to good performance on the job.

The Supreme Court's reaction to the Uniform Guidelines has been mixed. In *Albemarle Paper Co. v. Moody*,[81] the Court strongly endorsed an earlier version of the guidelines that imposed even more stringent requirements on validation than the Uniform Guidelines. Quoting *Griggs*, the Court stated that these guidelines were " 'entitled to great deference.' "[82] Like *Griggs*, however, *Albemarle Paper* was a case in which there was independent evidence of intentional discrimination and in which the employer's attempt to justify its use of employment tests was obviously flawed. Although the employer's validation study was superficially in compliance with the guidelines, it was hastily conceived and poorly executed, and failed to yield statistically significant results.[83] Likewise, in *Dothard v. Rawlinson*,[84] the Court held that an employer had offered an inadequate justification for height and weight requirements with a disparate impact upon women. The employer, however, had offered only an unsupported correlation between height and weight, on the one hand, and strength, on the other, as requirements for the job.

In cases in which the employer has offered some plausible justification for a practice that has a disparate impact, the Court

---

80. 29 C.F.R. § 1607.15D(7) (2006).

81. 422 U.S. 405 (1975).

82. *Id.* at 431.

83. *Id.* at 431–36.

84. 433 U.S. 321 (1977).

has been much more lenient than the Uniform Guidelines. In *Washington v. Davis*,[85] the Court went out of its way, in a case not directly concerned with Title VII, to hold that the earlier version of the guidelines endorsed in *Albemarle Paper* had been satisfied. The disputed employment practice was a test of verbal and writing ability used to screen applicants for jobs as police officers. The plaintiffs alleged that the test had a disparate impact upon blacks. The defendants tried to justify use of the test by showing that scores on the test were correlated with scores on a test administered to newly hired police officers after a seventeen-week training course. The Court held that the requirements of the earlier guidelines were satisfied despite the existence of a correlation only between scores on the two written tests. There was also no proven relationship between scores on the training test and performance in training or between performance in training and performance as a police officer.[86] The Court reasoned that it was "apparent" that some minimal level of verbal ability was necessary for completion of the training program and that establishing only a relationship between the test and the training program was "the much more sensible construction of the job-relatedness requirement."[87] In a later case, decided after the Uniform Guidelines took effect, the Court was even more summary in finding a justification for an employment practice that had an alleged disparate impact. In *New York City Transit Authority v. Beazer*,[88] the Court held that the exclusion of methadone users from jobs in a transit system, despite the possible disparate impact upon blacks and Hispanics, was justified by a showing that it served the employer's legitimate goals of safety and efficiency.[89]

A possible explanation for the lenient standards applied by the Supreme Court to the attempts at validation in both *Washington v. Davis* and *New York City Transit Authority v. Beazer* is the absence of evidence of intentional discrimination and, at least in the latter case, the weakness of the evidence of disparate impact.[90] These facts support the conclusion that the Court has adopted only a narrow version of the theory of disparate impact, one designed to ease the plaintiff's burden of proving a violation of Title VII, but not to force employers to abandon employment practices that have a disparate impact. This conclusion also fits the facts of *Griggs* and *Albemarle Paper*, which both involved employers who adopted tests and quali-

---

85. 426 U.S. 229 (1976).

86. *Id.* at 250–52.

87. *Id.* at 251.

88. 440 U.S. 568 (1979).

89. *Id.* at 587 & n.31.

90. *Id.* at 584–87.

fications as thinly veiled substitutes for recently abandoned forms of racial segregation.

Yet to focus exclusively on a narrow interpretation of the theory of disparate impact is to miss its complexity and its manifestation of the fundamentally different perspectives that can be brought to bear on Title VII. Appeals to a narrow interpretation of the theory do not take account of the remedial goals of the statute and the ways in which they have been invoked by the Supreme Court. The opinion in *Griggs*, for instance, attributes to Congress the intent "to achieve equality of employment opportunities and remove barriers that have operated in the past to favor an identifiable group of white employees over other employees."[91] Statements like these are not simply dicta added to the rhetoric of the opinion, but departures from the model of colorblindness that underlies any narrow view of Title VII. Colorblindness, and the historical view that supports it, only look backward to identify practices that Title VII was intended to abolish, not forward to any further goals that it was intended to achieve. These goals must include standards for determining equal opportunity in the competition for jobs, particularly as applied to practices whose effects in perpetuating past discrimination were not fully appreciated when Title VII was first enacted. The codification of the theory of disparate impact by the Civil Rights Act of 1991 assures the remedial perspective a significant role in any interpretation of the theory.

This role, however, does not require rigid adherence to the Uniform Guidelines. The decisions of the lower courts interpreting the Uniform Guidelines have taken a flexible approach, particularly in evaluating attempts at criterion and content validation, citing their character as guidelines rather than as regulations with the force of law.[92] The cases that have addressed these issues after the Civil Rights Act of 1991 have applied the guidelines in the same flexible way.[93] Nothing in the act requires a different conclusion. The meaning of the present statutory language—"job related for the position in question and consistent with business necessity"— was not determined by the decisions before *Wards Cove*. Nor was it

91. 401 U.S. at 429–30.

92. Contreras v. City of Los Angeles, 656 F.2d 1267, 1281 (9th Cir. 1981), *cert. denied*, 455 U.S. 1021 (1982); Guardians Ass'n of the New York City Police Dep't v. Civil Serv. Comm'n, 630 F.2d 79, 90–91 (2d Cir. 1980), *cert. denied*, 452 U.S. 940 (1981).

93. Officers for Justice v. Civil Serv. Comm'n, 979 F.2d 721, 726–27 (9th Cir.

1992), *cert. denied*, 507 U.S. 1004 (1993); Legault v. aRusso, 842 F.Supp. 1479, 1488–89 (D.N.H. 1994); *cf.* Bradley v. Pizzaco of Nebraska, Inc., 7 F.3d 795, 797 (8th Cir. 1993) (defendant must prove "compelling need" for disputed practice based on prior circuit decisions instead of the Uniform Guidelines).

determined by Congress in using this language to amend Title VII. It will have to be worked out by decisions in the future.

5. The Theory of Disparate Impact and Affirmative Action

Before the Civil Rights Act of 1991, doubts about the theory of disparate impact focused on two issues: first, its source in the statutory language, which in Title VII as originally enacted was addressed mainly to prohibiting practices with discriminatory intent, not those with discriminatory effects; and second, the relationship of the theory of disparate impact to affirmative action. These two issues are closely related because liability for practices with discriminatory effects, if defined broadly enough and not subject to employer defenses, is equivalent to requiring affirmative action. In section 703(j), a provision that dates from the original enactment of Title VII, Congress explicitly disclaimed any intent to require affirmative action. That section provides that "[n]othing in this title shall be interpreted to require any employer, employment agency, labor organization, or joint labor-management committee subject to this title to grant preferential treatment to any individual or to any group because of the race, color, religion, sex, or national origin of such individual or group...." The force and effect of this provision will be considered in detail in the next chapter, but its bearing on the theory of disparate impact deserves separate discussion.

The Civil Rights Act of 1991 settled the question of whether Title VII prohibits practices with discriminatory effects by codifying the theory of disparate impact in section 703(k). It did not settle the question of the theory's relationship to affirmative action. Opponents of the act characterized it as a "quota bill." Their objections led Congress to adopt a studied silence in the act on the issue of affirmative action, with only two exceptions. First, the act included a strict prohibition against "group norming" of test scores: the practice of altering scores on employment-related tests based on race, national origin, sex or religion.[94] This constitutes a direct prohibition against a specific form of affirmative action. Second, in an uncodified section of the act, Congress disclaimed any effect on "court-ordered remedies, affirmative action, or conciliation agreements, that are in accordance with the law."[95] The effect of these provisions, like the other provisions on the theory of disparate impact, is intertwined with the decision in *Wards Cove*.

---

94. § 703(*l*), codified as 42 U.S.C. § 2000e–2(*l*) (2000).

95. Pub.L.No. 102–166, § 116, 105 Stat. 1079 (1991).

One of the reasons offered in *Wards Cove* for adopting a narrow interpretation of the theory of disparate impact was that a broad interpretation of the theory would effectively require employers to engage in affirmative action.[96] Any such requirement would be inconsistent with section 703(j) and its disclaimer of any form of required affirmative action.[97] Whether the Civil Rights Act of 1991 endorsed this reasoning in *Wards Cove* is an open question. On the one hand, this passage appears in a part of the opinion concerned with proof of disparate impact. On this issue, as we have seen, the Civil Rights Acts of 1991 followed *Wards Cove*. Moreover, the act added a new prohibition against "group norming" test scores, which had been one way of adjusting test scores to compensate for disparate impact on the basis of race or national origin.

On the other hand, the act overruled *Wards Cove* on the issue of the defendant's burden of proof. The act imposed a heavier burden on the defendant, which might well lead employers to engage in affirmative action. If they can eliminate the disparate impact of questionable employment practices through affirmative action, then they can avoid the burden of proving that such practices are justified. Voluntary affirmative action itself is not problematic, as we shall in the next chapter. As the defendant's burden of proof becomes heavier, however, affirmative action becomes less and less a voluntary option and more and more a mandatory requirement. It becomes the only realistic way of avoiding liability under the theory of disparate impact.

Whatever doubts were entertained by Congress on this issue, they are not shared by the Uniform Guidelines. The guidelines explicitly provide that affirmative action plans that eliminate disparate impact are an alternative to validation[98] and that an employer's affirmative action policies shall be taken into account in determining disparate impact.[99] The guidelines also contain a policy statement on affirmative action approving the use of affirmative action plans,[100] and as the next chapter also discusses, the EEOC has adopted separate guidelines approving a wide range of affirmative action plans.[101] All of these guidelines must now be qualified in light of the prohibition against group norming of test scores. Whether these regulations require more extensive revision remains

---

96. 490 U.S. at 652.

97. § 703(j), codified as 42 U.S.C. § 2000e–2(j) (2000).

98. 29 C.F.R. § 1607.6A (2006).

99. *Id.* § 1607.4E.

100. *Id.* § 1607.17.

101. Affirmative Action Appropriate Under Title VII of the Civil Rights Act of 1964, as amended, 29 C.F.R. pt. 1608 (2006).

to be seen. This question, too, was raised but not resolved by the Civil Rights Act of 1991.

Apart from the political controversy that surrounds the subject of affirmative action, Congress failed to resolve these questions because they bring out in the sharpest possible form the contrasts among the different perspectives on employment discrimination law, and in particular, between the historical perspective with its conception of equality as colorblindness and the remedial perspective with its emphasis on compensating for the continuing effects of past discrimination. As will become apparent in the next chapter, even the Supreme Court has been unable to choose definitively among these perspectives, either under the Constitution or under Title VII.

Chapter V

AFFIRMATIVE ACTION

Affirmative action raises questions at every level of civil rights law. It is ultimately a subject for constitutional law, but it also raises issues of statutory interpretation and regulatory authority. Under Title VII, the controversy concerns the relationship between scattered and incomplete provisions on affirmative action and the main substantive and remedial provisions of the statute. Congress has not stated in so many words either that affirmative action is generally permitted or that it is generally prohibited, but instead has maintained a studied ambiguity. This has left the statutory issues mainly to be resolved by the courts. Title VII also raises constitutional questions, but only insofar as government is involved in affirmative action plans. The Fifth Amendment applies only to action by the federal government and the Fourteenth Amendment applies only to state action. Purely private forms of affirmative action fall entirely outside these constitutional provisions. All of these issues, both statutory and constitutional, are made more complicated by the presence of two sets of regulations on affirmative action: guidelines issued by the EEOC and a comprehensive set of regulations governing federal contractors issued by the Office of Federal Contract Compliance Programs (OFCCP) in the Department of Labor.

Beneath all of the doctrinal complexity of these different sources of law lies a fundamental question about affirmative action: how far to follow each of the different perspectives on employment discrimination law and, in particular, how far to take the remedial perspective in compensating for past discrimination in the absence of proof that the beneficiaries of affirmative action have actually suffered from past discrimination, no matter how remote it may be. Limiting remedies only to proven victims of discrimination—as is done routinely for all other claims of discrimination—would leave many instances of discrimination entirely without any remedy. The small amount of any possible recovery, procedural obstacles such as the statute of limitations, or simple inadequacy of evidence prevent many otherwise meritorious claims from being successfully prosecuted. The remedial perspective seeks to fill this gap in ordinary enforcement of the civil rights laws by prescribing broader prohibitions, such as the theory of disparate impact, or permitting broader remedies, such as affirmative action. Yet the remedial perspective cannot be carried so far as to allow affirmative action without any connection to past discrimination (or, in the case of disabilities, natural disadvantage). Absent such a connection, a remedial purpose would then be wholly lacking, resulting in violation of the principle of equality as colorblindness without any justification whatsoever. Preserving the appropriate balance between a remedial conception of equality and the conception of equality as colorblindness turns out to be a difficult task even when it is undertaken without the heated rhetoric that usually accompanies political debates over affirmative action.

A. Statutory Issues

As originally enacted, Title VII contained two provisions on affirmative action: one, a narrow provision that allows preferences in favor of Native Americans on or near a reservation,[1] and the other, a general disclaimer of any form of required affirmative action. The former has given rise only to limited litigation, mainly over constitutional issues discussed later in this chapter. Nevertheless, it is remarkable that affirmative action in favor of Native Americans has gone virtually unnoticed. Evidently, this form of affirmative action remains on such a small scale that, in most parts of the country, it does not create the appearance of any significant advantage conferred on a racially defined group. The reaction to affirmative action in favor of larger racial and ethnic groups, and in favor of women, of course, has been quite different.

The other provision in Title VII as originally enacted, section 703(j), addressed this more significant and more volatile issue. Section 703(j) was one of several important exceptions and qualifications to Title VII that were added on the floor of the Senate without consideration by committee, as part of an overall compromise to assure passage of the statute. This parliamentary strategy was necessary to prevent Title VII from being referred to committee and killed there by powerful southern senators, while at the same time permitting amendments so as to gain the two-thirds majority then required to end debate on the floor of the Senate. For this reason, section 703(j) is both crucial to understanding the application of Title VII to affirmative action and somewhat difficult to understand itself. It states that "[n]othing contained in this title shall be interpreted to require any employer, employment agency, labor organization, or joint labor-management committee subject to this title to grant preferential treatment to any individual or to any

---

1. § 703(i), codified as 42 U.S.C. § 2000e–2(i) (2000).

group because of the race, color, religion, sex, or national origin of such individual or group. . . .''[2]

In addition to the questions raised by the theory of disparate impact, discussed in the previous chapter, two questions have arisen about the language of section 703(j): first, whether "require" should be read as "require or permit," thus making section 703(j) a prohibition against all forms of preferential treatment, either undertaken voluntarily by an employer or required by the government; and second, whether "[n]othing in this title" should refer only to the prohibitions against discrimination in Title VII or also to the provisions for remedying violations of Title VII. The first question was resolved by the Supreme Court in favor of a literal interpretation of the word "require." Title VII does not prohibit preferential treatment voluntarily undertaken by an employer. The second question was resolved in favor of a nonliteral interpretation of the phrase "[n]othing in this title." Title VII does not prohibit courts from ordering preferential treatment as a remedy for employment discrimination, although it authorizes such orders only in extremely limited circumstances.

The Supreme Court decided that Title VII does not prohibit voluntary preferential treatment in *United Steelworkers v. Weber*.[3] Kaiser Aluminum & Chemical Corporation and the United Steelworkers had entered into a collective bargaining agreement that established a preference for black employees for admission to on-the-job training programs for craft positions. In particular, one-half of the openings in these programs were reserved for black employees. The Court characterized this preference as a wholly voluntary and private effort to eliminate the racial imbalance in Kaiser's work force of craft employees.[4] But as Justice Rehnquist emphasized in his dissent,[5] evidence in the record suggested that the preference was adopted after an investigation by the OFCCP, which enforces the nondiscrimination and affirmative action obligations of federal contractors. Because the Court found no government involvement in the preference, it avoided any constitutional question about federal power to establish or to require preferences in employment.[6] The Court's holding was limited to Title VII and to private preferences. These were permitted, the Court held, because both the statute and its legislative history reflect a policy of leaving management and labor free to devise remedies for discrimination

---

2. § 703(j), codified as 42 U.S.C. § 2000e–2(j) (2000).

3. 443 U.S. 193 (1979).

4. *Id.* at 201.

5. *Id.* at 222–23 (Rehnquist, J., dissenting).

6. *Id.* at 200.

without government interference.[7] Consequently, wholly voluntary, private preferences violate neither section 703(j) nor the prohibitions against discrimination in section 703(a) and (d).

The Court's holding was further limited to the characteristics of the Kaiser preference. This preference was a permissible racial classification under Title VII because it was "designed to break down old patterns of racial segregation and hierarchy" and because it did "not unnecessarily trammel the interests of the white employees."[8] On the first point, the Court relied on the nearly complete absence of blacks from craft positions in Kaiser's work force and the long history of exclusion of blacks from craft positions generally.[9] On the second point, the Court emphasized that the preference did not require the discharge of white workers, that it did not prevent them from receiving training or promotions, and that it was a temporary measure designed to end as soon as the racial imbalance in craft positions ended.[10]

In merging these specific points into a single standard for privately initiated affirmative action, the Court combined the economic and remedial perspectives in a surprising and illuminating way. From the economic perspective, it took the principle of management discretion to adopt private affirmative action plans (augmented in this case by union participation), and from the remedial perspective, the need to remedy past discrimination without a finding of any past violation of Title VII. Preserving management discretion supplied a plausible explanation for why Congress had limited section 703(j) to a disclaimer of any required form of affirmative action. As the legislative history revealed, despite some passages to the contrary cited by the dissent, Congress was mainly worried about overly broad regulation of employment practices, not overly narrow regulation. Privately initiated affirmative action would serve as an effective remedy for past discrimination, as Justice Blackmun emphasized in his concurring opinion, only if employers could undertake such programs without conceding that they had not already incurred liability under Title VII.[11]

In *Johnson v. Transportation Agency*,[12] the Supreme Court upheld a preference in favor of women. The case involved a public employer, but it was decided entirely under Title VII because the plaintiff failed to assert any claim under the Constitution.[13] Over

---

7. *Id.* at 204–07.

8. *Id.* at 208.

9. *Id.* at 198 & n.1.

10. *Id.* at 208–09.

11. *Id.* at 210–11 (Blackmun, J., concurring).

12. 480 U.S. 616 (1987).

13. *Id.* at 620 n.2.

two bitter dissents,[14] the Court continued to adhere to the decision and reasoning in *Weber*, modifying its analysis in only one significant respect: by suggesting that a preference would be upheld only if it were flexibly applied according to the proportion of the favored group—here women—who possessed the qualifications for the job.[15] Justice O'Connor, in a separate opinion, would have taken this reasoning a step further and required evidence sufficient to make out a prima facie case of past discrimination against women, equating "manifest imbalance" under *Weber* with proof of disparate impact.[16] This reasoning reveals the systematic connection between the theory of disparate impact and affirmative action, since both are concerned with the effects of employment practices. Nevertheless, this reasoning was not strictly necessary to the decision because the imbalance in *Johnson*, as in *Weber*, was substantial. No woman had ever been employed in the position in dispute, or even in the same department.[17]

The Supreme Court extended the same approach in a different direction, to judicially approved preferences negotiated by the parties in settlement of litigation, in *Local No. 93, International Association of Firefighters v. City of Cleveland*.[18] That case concerned a consent decree that settled claims of racial discrimination in promotions in the Cleveland Fire Department. The plaintiffs, a group of black firefighters, and the city had reached agreement on the consent decree, but the union representing the firefighters as a whole, most of whom were white, had intervened in the action and objected to the decree because it established a preference in promotions. The only question presented to the Supreme Court was whether Title VII authorized the district court's approval of the consent decree. The Court held that it did, even if it would not have authorized the district court to impose the same preference on its own.[19] Instead, the same standards governing purely private preferences under *Weber* also governed judicial approval of consent decrees under Title VII.[20] The Court held, however, that the consent decree was binding only on the plaintiffs and the city, not on the union or on white firefighters disadvantaged by the preference. The latter were not precluded from raising constitutional objections to the preference on remand, although the union might have waived

---

14. *Id.* at 657 (White, J., dissenting); *id.* at 657–77 (Scalia, J., dissenting).

15. *Id.* at 636–37.

16. *Id.* at 649–53 (O'Connor, J., concurring in the judgment). The majority explicitly refused to take this step. *Id.* at 632–33 & n.10.

17. *Id.* at 636.

18. 478 U.S. 501 (1986).

19. *Id.* at 517–18, 522–23.

20. *Id.* at 518.

such objections by attacking the consent decree only on statutory grounds.[21]

The Supreme Court's only decision on modification, as opposed to approval, of consent decrees strikes a much different note, but principally because it concerned a preference that the parties had not agreed to. In *Firefighters Local Union No. 1784 v. Stotts*,[22] the Court held that a district court could not unilaterally modify a consent decree to add a preference protecting blacks from layoffs. The consent decree settled claims of racial discrimination in hiring and promotion in the Memphis Fire Department and it established long-term and interim goals for hiring and promotion of blacks, but it did not provide for any preferences with respect to layoffs. After the city announced that firefighters would be laid off in reverse order of seniority (beginning with those having least seniority, according to the rule of "last hired, first fired"), the plaintiffs obtained an injunction against layoffs that would reduce the proportion of blacks employed as firefighters. On appeal by the union and the city, the court of appeals affirmed the injunction issued by the district court, but the Supreme Court reversed.

The Court found no basis for modifying the consent decree in the terms of the decree itself. In particular, the consent decree did not require the city to abandon its practice, confirmed in a collective-bargaining "memorandum of understanding" with the union, of laying off firefighters in reverse order of seniority.[23] The purposes of the decree did not extend beyond the remedies that it explicitly provided for. The Court also emphasized the importance of union participation in matters affecting seniority, relying on the provision in Title VII that protects seniority systems from claims of disparate impact.[24]

In the most controversial part of its opinion, the Court also relied on more general limits on judicial remedies under section 706(g), similar to those that now apply in mixed-motive cases. These limits prohibit awards of compensatory relief to any individual who "was refused admission, suspended, or expelled, or was refused employment or advancement or was suspended or discharged for any reason other than discrimination" in violation of Title VII.[25] The Court quoted statements by prominent supporters of Title VII in the House and Senate who interpreted this provision

---

21. *Id.* at 529–30.

22. 467 U.S. 561 (1984).

23. *Id.* at 574–75.

24. § 703(h), codified as 42 U.S.C. § 2000e–2(h) (2000). For further discus-

sion of this provision, see Chapter VII. E *infra.*

25. § 706(g)(2)(A), codified as 42 U.S.C. § 2000e–5(g)(2)(A) (2000).

to limit remedies under Title VII to actual victims of discrimination. Three of the statements equated this limitation with a prohibition against "racial quotas."[26] Taken at face value, these statements apply to all forms of preferential relief ordered by a district court, whether or not they affect seniority.

This last part of the opinion simply made clear what was implicit in the opinion as a whole: that affirmative action that results from government coercion, in this case in the form of judicial modification of a consent decree, must be judged by completely different standards from those applicable to privately initiated affirmative action plans. This conclusion follows from the skeptical view that the economic perspective takes of government action that interferes with management discretion. Judicially ordered preferences override the decisions of employers and constrain their response to market pressure. Where privately adopted preferences are supported by economic considerations, judicially ordered preferences are opposed by the same considerations and are therefore subject to correspondingly stricter standards.

A literal reading of the opinion in *Stotts*, in fact, would completely bar judicially ordered preferences, but subsequent decisions have taken a different course, approving such preferences in exceptional circumstances. Coercion in these cases can be justified as a necessary means of preventing future discrimination. This was the conclusion in the Supreme Court's decision in *Local 28, Sheet Metal Workers' International Association v. EEOC*,[27] holding that a district court could impose a goal of minority membership upon a union that had engaged in a pattern of longstanding racial discrimination in the construction industry. The union had persisted in this practice despite repeated judicial and administrative findings of past discrimination and repeated injunctions against future discrimination. As a remedy for violations of these previously issued injunctions, the district court ordered the disputed membership goal, along with the creation of a fund primarily for the benefit of minority apprentices. The Supreme Court affirmed the imposition of these race-conscious remedies, but by a divided vote. Justice Brennan wrote for a plurality of four justices and Justice Powell wrote a separate opinion concurring in part and concurring in the judgment.[28]

26. 467 U.S. at 579–83 (internal quotation marks omitted).

27. 478 U.S. 421 (1986).

28. Justice Powell joined the opinion of Justice Brennan, thereby creating an opinion for the Court, only on a few collateral issues. *See id.* at 440–44, 481–82 (opinion of Brennan, J.).

Both Justice Brennan and Justice Powell felt compelled to interpret the membership goal with a degree of flexibility, so that it would not cause white employees to lose their jobs if its schedule for admissions were not met.[29] They reached this conclusion despite statements by the district judge that he intended to enforce the goal according to its literal terms, requiring 29.23% minority membership. Such statements led Justice O'Connor and Justice White to conclude that the membership goal was a rigid quota,[30] but as flexibly interpreted by the majority, the goal would not have caused any whites to lose their jobs, thus apparently distinguishing this case from *Stotts*.

On the general question whether preferential remedies are authorized by Title VII, Justice Brennan identified three circumstances in which they are appropriate: when a defendant has engaged in "particularly longstanding or egregious discrimination"; "when informal mechanisms may obstruct equal employment opportunities" (for instance, when an employer has a reputation for discrimination); and when interim goals are necessary "pending the development of nondiscriminatory hiring or promotion procedures."[31] He also emphasized, however, that other remedies were adequate in most cases and he approved the cautious approach to judicially ordered preferences taken by the courts of appeals.[32] Justice Powell agreed with the need for preferences only in "cases involving particularly egregious conduct."[33] Surprisingly, Justice White also expressed general agreement with the approach of Justice Brennan, despite his conclusion that the membership goal in this case was invalid because it operated as a rigid quota.

The studied silence of the Civil Rights Act of 1991 does not appear to have affected the holding in *Sheet Metal Workers*. The only provision explicitly addressed to affirmative action is uncodified and states, somewhat cryptically, that "[n]othing in the amendments made by this title shall be construed to affect court-ordered remedies, affirmative action, or conciliation agreements, that are in accordance with the law."[34] The immediate purpose of this provision appears to have been to preserve existing affirmative action plans, despite the addition to Title VII of the definition of "an unlawful employment practice" as one in which "race, color,

---

29. *Id.* at 477–78 & n.49 (opinion of Brennan, J.); *id.* at 487–88 (Powell, J., concurring in part and concurring in the judgment).

30. *Id.* at 497–98 (O'Connor, J., concurring in part and dissenting in part); *id.* at 499–500 (White, J., dissenting).

31. *Id.* at 448–50 (opinion of Brennan, J.).

32. *Id.* at 475–76 & n.48.

33. *Id.* at 483 (Powell, J., concurring in part and concurring in the judgment).

34. Pub. L. No. 102–166, § 116, 105 Stat. 1079 (1991).

religion, sex, or national origin was a motivating factor."[35] It is doubtful that this provision goes any further and ratifies pre-existing decisions on affirmative action, although it does nothing to undermine them either.[36]

As the preceding chapter explains, the Civil Rights Act of 1991 did more to endorse affirmative action indirectly by codifying the theory of disparate impact than it did directly. By erasing the doubts and limitations that had accumulated around the theory of disparate impact, the act gave employers a reason to adopt affirmative action plans: to avoid liability for neutral practices that have discriminatory effects. The act limited this use of affirmative action only by imposing an explicit prohibition against "group norming" of employment tests by adjusting test scores on the basis of race, national origin, sex, or religion.[37] This provision eliminated a form of preferential treatment that was particularly inflexible and likely to be perceived as conferring an unjustifiable advantage on the basis of race. It did not impose any general limits on affirmative action plans. A further provision limited collateral attacks upon judicially approved or ordered affirmative action plans, principally by requiring those opposed to such plans to object at the first available opportunity.[38] As this provision itself recognizes, its effect necessarily is limited by the constitutional right to notice and opportunity to be heard. No statute can restrict this right beyond the minimum procedures required by the Due Process Clause.

B. Constitutional Issues

The constitutionality of affirmative action raises controversial issues of constitutional doctrine and theory, not to mention political and civil rights. These have concentrated on the standard of review for affirmative action plans by government, not just in employment, but in higher education, housing, and government contracts. After a series of inconsistent and fragmented decisions, the Supreme Court eventually settled on a standard of "strict scrutiny" for all government decisions based on race, whether or not connected to affirmative action. These decisions are even more variable than those under Title VII, so much so that they make the latter look relatively stable.

35. § 703(m), codified as 42 U.S.C. § 2000e–2(m) (2000).

36. Officers for Justice v. Civil Service Comm'n, 979 F.2d 721, 725 (9th Cir. 1992), *cert. denied*, 507 U.S. 1004 (1993).

37. § 703(*l*), codified as 42 U.S.C. § 2000e–2(*l*) (2000).

38. § 703(n)(1), codified as 42 U.S.C. § 2000e–2(n)(1) (2000). This provision is discussed further in Chapter VIII. E *infra.*

Perhaps this difference in relative stability of legal doctrine is attributable to the possibility of congressional revision of decisions interpreting Title VII, in contrast to the near impossibility of amending the Constitution to overrule a decision of the Supreme Court. In adhering to its previous decisions under Title VII, the Court may be content to let Congress amend the statute to make any changes in existing law that ultimately prove to be necessary. The greater stability of the law under Title VII may also result from the narrower range of affirmative action plans within its scope, as compared to the Constitution which covers the entire range of government action. This last point may account for the absence of any consideration of diversity under the statutory standards as a justification for affirmative action, an argument that has figured prominently in the debate over racial preferences in higher education.

The constitutional and statutory standards diverge in other respects as well, illustrating how employment discrimination law has developed and changed from its origins in constitutional law. First, as was emphasized in *Weber*, the constitutional standards do not reach all forms of affirmative action in employment, only those involving sufficient government action to trigger the application of the Fifth Amendment (to the federal government) or the Fourteenth Amendment (to the states). Government action in employment discrimination cases can take two different forms: court-ordered remedies, such as injunctions, or action taken by the government as an employer itself. Second, even when the Constitution does apply to an affirmative action plan through these means, different standards of judicial review apply to affirmative action on different grounds. In particular, classifications on the basis of sex are not subject to strict scrutiny, but judged by the slightly weaker requirement of an "exceedingly persuasive" justification.[39] By contrast, as *Johnson v. Transportation Agency* illustrates, preferences in favor of women are treated the same under Title VII as preferences on the basis of race.

In its recent constitutional decisions taking a critical view of affirmative action, the Supreme Court has mainly considered claims arising outside of employment. In *City of Richmond v. J. A. Croson Co.*,[40] a majority of justices held that benign preferences on the basis of race are subject to "strict scrutiny" and so, presumably, are more difficult to justify than other remedies for discrimination.[41] That case held unconstitutional a local ordinance setting

---

39. United States v. Virginia, 518 U.S. 515, 531 (1996).

40. 488 U.S. 469 (1989).

41. *Id.* at 493–98 (opinion of O'Connor, J.); *id.* at 520–21 (Scalia, J., concurring in the judgment).

aside a fixed proportion of government contracts for minority-owned businesses. The same principles were extended to federal statutes creating similar preferences in *Adarand Constructors, Inc. v. Pena*,[42] although only after prior decisions had reached contrary results.[43] It is now clear that all racial classifications by government—whether federal, state, or local—must meet the same standard of "strict scrutiny" under the Constitution.[44] *Adarand* overruled prior decisions to the extent that they applied a more lenient standard,[45] remanding only the question whether the preference at issue met the demanding standard of being narrowly tailored to serve a compelling government interest.[46]

Exactly what that standard means, however, remains a matter of dispute, as the decisions on affirmative action in higher education illustrate. These decisions begin with *Regents of the University of California v. Bakke*,[47] in which Justice Powell provided the decisive fifth vote. Four justices would have upheld the affirmative action plan at issue in that case, reserving a specified number of places in medical school for designated minorities, and four justices would have struck it down. Justice Powell held that the particular plan at issue was unconstitutional because it considered race in too rigid a fashion, but that a plan that allowed race to be considered as one factor among others would have served a compelling government interest in diversity in higher education.[48] Some decades later, his position was eventually adopted by a majority of the Court in *Grutter v. Bollinger*.[49] That case upheld an affirmative action plan by the University of Michigan Law School which, as Justice Powell had held in *Bakke*, considered race as only one factor among others in the individual evaluation of each applicant. In her opinion for the Court, Justice O'Connor emphasized a position that she had taken in her plurality opinion in *Adarand*: "Strict scrutiny is not 'strict in theory, but fatal in fact.' "[50] Diversity provided a sufficient justifica-

---

42. 515 U.S. 200, 235–36 (1995) (opinion of O'Connor, J.). Justice Scalia provided the crucial fifth vote for the decision in this case. He would have gone further and simply prohibited all government classifications on the basis of race. *Id.* at 239 (Scalia, J., concurring in part and concurring in the judgment).

43. Metro Broadcasting, Inc. v. FCC, 497 U.S. 547 (1990) (upholding a preference for minority-owned businesses in the award of broadcast licenses by the FCC); Fullilove v. Klutznick, 448 U.S. 448 (1980) (upholding a set-aside for minority-owned contractors in local public works financed with federal funds).

44. 515 U.S. at 235.

45. *Id.*

46. *Id.* at 237–38 (opinion of O'Connor, J.). In the parts of her opinion for a plurality, but not a majority, Justice O'Connor went out of her way to reject the position that strict scrutiny is "strict in theory, but fatal in fact." *Id.* at 237.

47. 438 U.S. 265 (1978).

48. *Id.* at 291 (opinion of Powell, J.).

49. 539 U.S. 306 (2003).

50. *Id.* at 326.

tion for affirmative action, provided that race was used flexibly in the admissions process, because of the importance of universities and law schools in training the nation's leaders: "In order to cultivate a set of leaders with legitimacy in the eyes of the citizenry, it is necessary that the path to leadership be visibly open to talented and qualified individuals of every race and ethnicity."[51] By contrast, the companion case of *Gratz v. Bollinger,*[52] struck down the affirmative action plan for admissions to the undergraduate college at the University of Michigan. That plan awarded a fixed number of points in the admissions process to applicants from specified minority groups and, because it considered race in this mechanical fashion, was not narrowly tailored to serve the compelling interest in diversity.

One form of affirmative action, however, stands on an entirely different constitutional footing from programs generally in favor of minority groups. In *Morton v. Mancari,*[53] the Supreme Court held that a preference for employment of Native Americans in the Bureau of Indian Affairs (BIA) violated neither Title VII nor the Fifth Amendment. The Court reasoned that the preference was not prohibited by Title VII, although it fell outside a statutory exception for preferences in favor of Native Americans living on or near reservations,[54] because Title VII was not intended to disturb the longstanding federal policy of preferential employment of Native Americans in the BIA.[55] The preference also did not violate the Fifth Amendment because it was "reasonably designed to further the cause of Indian self-government and to make the BIA more responsive to the needs of its constituent groups."[56] The Court characterized the preference as one not involving race, despite the fact that it only applied to persons of "one-fourth or more degree Indian blood."[57] Based on this reasoning, the decision might be limited to the special situation of Indian tribes, as suggested in a recent decision invalidating a racial classification by the state of Hawaii that favored citizens of Hawaiian ancestry.[58] It remains difficult, however, to distinguish Native Americans from other racial and ethnic groups, such as Hawaiians, without begging the very question at issue. Favorable treatment of Native Americans at the level of constitutional standards cannot be used to justify

---

51. *Id.* at 332.

52. 539 U.S. 244 (2003).

53. 417 U.S. 535 (1974).

54. § 703(i), codified as 42 U.S.C. § 2000e–2(i) (2000). Congress also exempted Native American tribes from the coverage of the statute. § 701(b), codified as 42 U.S.C. § 2000e(b)(1) (2000).

55. 417 U.S. at 541–45.

56. *Id.* at 554.

57. *Id.* at 553 n.24.

58. Rice v. Cayetano, 528 U.S. 495, 518–19 (2000).

favorable treatment of Native Americans at the concrete level of particular programs of affirmative action. The constitutional decisions on affirmative action have not yet developed a satisfactory solution to this problem.

When the Supreme Court has actually applied strict scrutiny to affirmative action in employment, its decisions have been surprisingly free of controversy. For instance, in *Sheet Metal Workers,* after holding that Title VII authorized judicially ordered preferences to remedy egregious discrimination, the Court also held that this remedy survived strict scrutiny. For a plurality of four justices, Justice Brennan found a race-conscious remedy to be justified by the overwhelming evidence of past discrimination in the record in that case. He also found it to be narrowly tailored to the goal of eliminating past discrimination, both because it had only minimal effects on white workers and because other remedies had proved to be ineffective.[59] Justice Powell essentially followed the same analysis, although he undertook a more searching examination of the remedy to determine whether it was narrowly tailored to the goals of eliminating past discrimination.[60] One year later, the Supreme Court again reached the same conclusion, upholding a judicially ordered preference to remedy egregious discrimination in *United States v. Paradise,*[61] a case alleging longstanding violations of the Constitution by the Alabama Department of Public Safety in hiring and promoting state troopers.[62]

The Supreme Court addressed the constitutional question more fully in *Wygant v. Jackson Board of Education,*[63] a case concerned with a preference in layoffs established by agreement between a union and a public employer. The preference required teachers to be laid off in reverse order of seniority unless doing so would reduce the percentage of minority teachers, in which case white teachers with greater seniority would be laid off instead of minority teachers with less seniority. Because the employer was a public school district, unlike the private employer in *Weber,* the case raised the constitutional question whether the preference violated the Fourteenth Amendment. The Court held that it did, in a combination of separate opinions. Justice Powell, writing on behalf of three jus-

---

59. 478 U.S. at 481 (opinion of Brennan, J.).

60. *Id.* at 485–89 (Powell, J., concurring in part and concurring in the judgment).

61. 480 U.S. 149 (1987).

62. Justice Brennan wrote for a plurality of four justices and found egregious discrimination a sufficient ground for judicially ordered preferences. *Id.* at 166–71. Justice Stevens concurred in the judgment based on the broad remedial authority of federal courts to remedy constitutional violations. *Id.* at 189–95.

63. 476 U.S. 267 (1986).

tices, and in part, on behalf of Justice O'Connor, applied strict scrutiny.[64] He reasoned that the preference was defective because it was not based on evidence of past employment discrimination by the school district, but on the need to provide minority students with role models and on the existence of general societal discrimination.[65] Although he would not have required findings of discrimination to be made when the preference was adopted, he found insufficient evidence of past discrimination by the school district in the record before the Court.[66] He also found that the preference was not narrowly tailored to remedy past discrimination because it imposed too great a burden upon laid-off white employees.[67] Justice O'Connor agreed with Justice Powell on the absence of evidence of past discrimination, but she found the preference to be unrelated to remedying any form of employment discrimination since it was designed to match the percentage of minority teachers with the percentage of minority students.[68] Justice White concurred in the judgment solely on the ground that the preference effectively required whites to be discharged and minorities to be hired until the school district achieved a suitable racial balance.[69]

The net effect of these opinions, and the opinions in *Sheet Metal Workers*, is to emphasize the difference between private preferences—adopted voluntarily by a private employer—and public preferences—ordered by a court or adopted by a public employer. The former are governed by the comparatively lenient standards of *Weber*. The latter are governed by the stricter constitutional standards of *Wygant*. The one significant question, still unanswered, is the scope of *Wygant*, and in particular, whether it applies beyond affirmative action in layoffs, which has always been a particularly sensitive issue. Even *Weber* casts doubt on affirmative action plans that "require the discharge of white workers and their replacement with new black hirees."[70] Outside the area of layoffs and seniority, the Court might be more likely to find that the requirements of strict scrutiny have been satisfied by evidence of past discrimination by a public employer, and in particular, by evidence that would support a finding of disparate impact of other employment practices on the minority favored by the preference. Along the lines suggest-

---

64. *Id.* at 273–74 (opinion of Powell, J.).

65. Id. at 274–76.

66. *Id.* at 277–78.

67. *Id.* at 279–84.

68. *Id.* at 294 (O'Connor, J., concurring in part and concurring in the judgment).

69. *Id.* at 294–95 (White, J., concurring in the judgment).

70. 443 U.S. at 208; *see* Firefighters Local Union No. 1784 v. Stotts, 467 U.S. 561, 578–83 (1984) (judicial modification of consent decree to create preferences in layoffs not authorized by Title VII).

ed by Justice O'Connor in her separate opinion in *Johnson v. Transportation Agency*,[71] evidence sufficient to support a finding of disparate impact may also support a finding that an affirmative action plan serves the compelling government interest of preventing a violation of Title VII. This point of constitutional doctrine, however it is resolved, illustrates the fundamental connection between the theory of disparate impact and affirmative action.

C.   Federal Regulations

Two sets of regulations, both familiar only to specialists in employment law, deal with affirmative action in employment. One set, promulgated by the EEOC, attempts to prescribe standards for permissible preferences under Title VII. The other, far more comprehensive and far more significant, has been promulgated by the OFCCP in the Department of Labor. The OFCCP regulations implement executive orders that prohibit discrimination and require affirmative action by federal contractors. Both sets of regulations have been cited by the Supreme Court in its decisions on affirmative action, but in a telling omission, not on points of any significance. The Court has neither held the regulations invalid nor attempted to offer a limiting interpretation of their provisions. Consequently, both sets of regulations have an uncertain degree of authority, enough so that employers cannot ignore them, but not so much that courts are bound by their literal terms.

1.   The EEOC Guidelines on Affirmative Action

In its Guidelines on Affirmative Action, the EEOC has tried to establish a safe harbor for preferences under Title VII. It has not attempted to set forth the necessary conditions that all permissible preferences must meet, but only the conditions sufficient to guarantee favorable treatment under Title VII. Whether this attempt has been successful remains an open question, even though the guidelines were first promulgated in 1979, because so few judicial opinions rely upon their provisions. Yet the guidelines set forth three requirements for favorable treatment of affirmative action plans under Title VII: that such plans are supported by a "reasonable self analysis"; by a "reasonable basis for concluding action is appropriate"; and that they prescribe "reasonable action."[72]

A "reasonable self analysis" determines whether an employer's personnel practices have resulted in a disparate impact or disparate

---

71.   480 U.S. at 649–53 (O'Connor, J., concurring in the judgment).

72.   29 C.F.R. § 1608.4 (2006). The full set of guidelines appears at 29 C.F.R. pt. 1608 (2006).

treatment and whether such practices leave uncorrected the effects of prior discrimination.[73] Any finding of disparate impact, disparate treatment, or uncorrected effects of prior discrimination provides a reasonable basis for establishing a preference, but it does not constitute an admission that Title VII has been violated.[74] The resulting preference, in turn, must be a reasonable means of remedying the problems revealed by the self-analysis.[75] Affirmative action plans that comply with these requirements and that are dated and in writing constitute a complete defense to claims of reverse discrimination.[76] They do not provide any defense, however, to claims of discrimination that arise from the conditions they were designed to correct. Similar consequences follow from preferences implemented in various enforcement proceedings under Title VII (and similar laws), and in some circumstances, from unwritten plans.[77]

The availability of a defense to reverse discrimination claims is the most important consequence of complying with the guidelines. Section 713(b) of Title VII provides that action "in good faith, in conformity with, and in reliance on any written interpretation or opinion of the Commission" constitutes a complete defense to claims based on such action.[78] By its own regulations, the EEOC has narrowly defined which of its statements give rise to a defense under section 713(b),[79] but the Guidelines on Affirmative Action explicitly declare themselves to be such a statement.[80] Nevertheless, the binding effect of the guidelines remains uncertain. Section 713(a) only authorizes the EEOC to issue procedural regulations,[81] a limited grant of rulemaking authority which implies that substantive regulations issued by the EEOC do not have the force of law.[82]

The only decision of the Supreme Court to cite the guidelines, *Local No. 93, International Association of Firefighters v. City of Cleveland,*[83] expressed a similar ambivalence to regulations issued by the EEOC. In that case, the Court upheld an affirmative action

---

73. *Id.* § 1608.4(a).

74. *Id.* § 1608.4(b).

75. *Id.* § 1608.4(c).

76. *Id.* §§ 1608.4(d), 1608.10(b).

77. *Id.* §§ 1608.4–.9.

78. § 713(b), codified as 42 U.S.C. § 2000e–12(b)(1) (2000).

79. 29 C.F.R. § 1601.93 (2006).

80. *Id.* § 1608.2.

81. § 713(a), codified as 42 U.S.C. § 2000e–12(a) (2000).

82. Both the original enactment of Title VII and its amendment by the Equal Employment Opportunity Act of 1972, Pub. L. No. 92–261, 86 Stat. 103 (1972), depended on compromises limiting the power of the EEOC and expanding the power of the federal courts. *See* Francis J. Vaas, Title VII: Legislative History, 7 B.C. Indus. & Com. L. Rev. 431, 435–37, 439, 450–52 (1966); George P. Sape & Thomas J. Hart, Title VII Reconsidered: The Equal Employment Opportunity Act of 1972, 40 Geo. Wash. L. Rev. 824, 830–45 (1972).

83. 478 U.S. 501 (1986).

plan established by a consent decree settling claims of racial discrimination against black firefighters. The Court cited the Guidelines on Affirmative Action, but only for the general policy in favor of settlement of Title VII claims, not for the permissibility of affirmative action plans under the guidelines and section 713(b). Instead, the Court said that the guidelines were entitled to some deference as a source of experience and informed judgment, pointedly adding that they "do not have the force of law."[84] Thus, to take an obvious case, the guidelines do not immunize employers from liability for "group norming" of employment tests, a form of affirmative action that is now prohibited by the Civil Rights Act of 1991.[85] Whether the guidelines offer employers any protection for affirmative action plans that are less clearly illegal remains an open question. The implication from the Supreme Court's limited citation of the guidelines, although only suggestive, is that the issue of affirmative action is too important to be resolved by administrative regulations.

2. OFCCP Regulations

The OFCCP regulations on affirmative action, although equally arcane as the EEOC guidelines, have exercised far greater influence over the development of affirmative action plans. Enforcement of these regulations, for instance, led to the adoption of the affirmative action plan upheld in *United Steelworkers v. Weber.*[86] The OFCCP regulations on affirmative action are part of a comprehensive scheme of regulations of federal contractors based on Executive Order 11246. This executive order, issued by the President on the basis of his statutory authority over federal contracts, prohibits discrimination and requires affirmative action by federal contractors on the basis of race, national origin, sex, and religion.[87] These obligations are stated in only the most general terms in the executive order itself, but they are spelled out in great detail in the OFCCP regulations.

The resulting scheme of regulations is as elaborate as the statutory law under Title VII, but differs from it in several crucial respects. First, the executive order requires affirmative action rather than simply prohibiting discrimination. Second, it is enforced

---

84. *Id.* at 518. In earlier cases concerned with other guidelines of the EEOC, the Court's attitude has varied from "great deference," in Griggs v. Duke Power Co., 401 U.S. 424, 433–34 (1971), to almost no deference at all in General Elec. Co. v. Gilbert, 429 U.S. 125, 140–45 (1976).

85. § 703(*l*), codified as 42 U.S.C. § 2000e–2(*l*) (2000).

86. 443 U.S. 193, 222–23 & n.2 (1979) (Rehnquist, J., dissenting).

87. Exec. Order No. 11246, 3 C.F.R. 339 (1964–65), *reprinted as amended in* 42 U.S.C. § 2000e note (2000).

mainly through administrative procedures instead of private litigation. Third, the executive order has been interpreted and implemented primarily through administrative regulations rather than judicial opinions. And fourth, the executive order and its implementing regulations have never been explicitly approved or authorized by Congress. A full account of the employment obligations of federal contractors would go into each of these features in great detail. This section can only examine them briefly as they bear on the issue of affirmative action.

The OFCCP regulations apply to all employers who have contracts with the federal government in excess of $10,000, with increased compliance and reporting requirements for employers with 50 or more employees and contracts in excess of $50,000.[88] Employers in the latter category must prepare written affirmative action plans containing a "work force analysis," a determination whether any racial or ethnic minority group or women have been "underutilized" by the employer, and "goals and timetables" to remedy any underutilization found.[89] These requirements resemble those for reasonable self-analysis, a reasonable basis for action, and reasonable action under the EEOC guidelines, but the OFCCP regulations are both more detailed and more demanding. The regulations elaborate on each of the three requirements and add further requirements as well, and compliance is enforced by sanctions instead of simply by withholding favorable treatment as under the EEOC guidelines.[90] Moreover, special provisions apply to employers with federal construction contracts in excess of $10,000, with goals set by the OFCCP for employment of minority groups and women in most major geographical areas.[91]

All of these various requirements are enforced almost entirely through administrative decisions of the OFCCP to terminate contracts or to suspend or debar contractors, but public actions may be brought against contractors to enforce their obligations under the order.[92] The OFCCP can also seek awards of back pay in administrative enforcement proceedings.[93] Private individuals cannot sue under the executive order, although in limited circumstances, they can sue to require the OFCCP to take enforcement action.[94]

---

88. 41 C.F.R. §§ 60–1.5(a)(1), –1.40(a) (2006).

89. *Id.* §§ 60–2.11, –2.12.

90. *Id.* §§ 60–1.26, –1.27, –2.13, –2.14, –2.20 to –2.26.

91. *Id.* pt. 60–4.

92. *Id.* § 60–1.26.

93. *Id.* § 60–1.26(a)(2).

94. *See* Legal Aid Soc'y v. Brennan, 608 F.2d 1319 (9th Cir. 1979), *cert. denied*, 447 U.S. 921 (1980).

The process of administrative enforcement lends a degree of flexibility to the OFCCP regulations on affirmative action, thereby reducing the incentives of federal contractors to challenge their validity. The OFCCP enforces these regulations along with the prohibition against discrimination by federal contractors, saving the most severe sanctions for the employers found to have engaged in outright discrimination. As a practical matter, most enforcement proceedings result in negotiated settlements in which the employer retains its eligibility for federal contracts in exchange for changes in its personnel practices to meet the demands of the OFCCP. Because a settlement cuts off any further proceedings, the OFCCP usually has the last word on the implementation of the executive order, either formally through its regulations or informally through its administrative enforcement policy. The opportunities for judicial review of a case that is settled are minimal, and when sanctions are actually imposed, they are usually based on clear evidence of discrimination. For these reasons, few challenges have been brought in recent years to the validity of the OFCCP regulations on affirmative action.

Several such challenges were brought, however, soon after the regulations were issued in substantially their present form. All of these challenges were rejected on the ground that the regulations served the government interest in eliminating past discrimination, particularly in the construction industry.[95] It is doubtful that similar challenges today would be resolved in precisely the same way, after the subsequent decisions of the Supreme Court requiring strict scrutiny of all racial classifications by government. Nevertheless, this question is not likely to be resolved so long as the OFCCP moderates the literal requirements of its regulations through its enforcement policy.

An independent basis for challenging the OFCCP regulations relies on the limited congressional authority on which they are based. The only statute that explicitly confers authority on the President to issue the executive order concerns general policies for procuring goods and services for the federal government; it does not address the employment practices of federal contractors.[96] The closest that Congress has come to specifically endorsing the executive order is a provision, added to Title VII in 1972, that specifies the procedures that must be followed before any sanctions may be

---

95. *E.g.*, Northeast Constr. Co. v. Romney, 485 F.2d 752, 757–58 (D.C. Cir. 1973); Contractors Ass'n v. Secretary of Labor, 442 F.2d 159, 171 (3d Cir.), *cert. denied*, 404 U.S. 854 (1971).

96. 40 U.S.C. § 486(a) (2000).

imposed on federal contractors.[97] This provision presupposes the validity of the executive order and their implementing regulations without, however, explicitly authorizing or endorsing it. The Supreme Court openly doubted whether this degree of congressional support was sufficient in *Chrysler Corp. v. Brown*,[98] a complicated action to enjoin disclosure of an affirmative action plan under the Freedom of Information Act. A few lower federal courts have followed up on these doubts and have restricted the scope of the executive order to employment practices closely connected with federal procurement.[99] No court, however, has rejected the overall validity of the executive order and the regulations based on it.

With the prominence given to constitutional litigation over affirmative action, the validity of the OFCCP regulations, like the EEOC regulations on the same subject, is likely to be determined only after the constitutional question is settled. On this issue, more than any other in employment discrimination law, the influence of constitutional law goes far beyond its immediate doctrinal implications. It provides the framework and much of the content for narrower arguments over statutes and regulations on the same subject. The interpretation of these nonconstitutional sources of law depends in large part on how the ultimate constitutional question is resolved.

97. § 718, codified as 42 U.S.C. § 2000e–17 (2000). *See* Robert P. Schuwerk, Comment, The Philadelphia Plan: A Study in the Dynamics of Executive Power, 39 U. Chi. L. Rev. 723 (1972).

98. 441 U.S. 281, 303–08 (1979).

99. *E.g.*, Liberty Mut. Ins. Co. v. Friedman, 639 F.2d 164 (4th Cir. 1981).

Chapter VI

SEX DISCRIMINATION UNDER TITLE VII AND THE EQUAL PAY ACT

Title VII is the most important federal prohibition against sex discrimination in employment, but it was not the first. It was preceded by the Equal Pay Act of 1963,[1] which was enacted by the same Congress that enacted the Civil Rights Act of 1964. In contrast to Title VII, the Equal Pay Act prohibits only sex discrimination, only in compensation, and only when women and men perform equal work. The interpretation and enforcement of both Title VII and the Equal Pay Act have been complicated by the history of their enactment. As noted in Chapter I, constitutional law did not develop a general prohibition against sex discrimination until several years after the enactment of Title VII. This sequence of constitutional law following statutory law was the reverse of that for racial discrimination, in which constitutional decisions came first. The statutory prohibitions against sex discrimination, however, had no pre-existing basis in constitutional law, raising persistent questions which have endured to this day: How is the prohibition against sex discrimination related to the prohibition against racial discrimination? Is it narrower, or broader, or simply different? Is the continued existence of sex discrimination as great a problem as continued racial discrimination? Should the conceptions of equality that apply to racial discrimination also apply to sex discrimination? These questions arise most forcefully in interpreting distinctive statutory provisions that apply only to sex discrimination.

The most apparent of these provisions are in the Equal Pay Act, with its narrow prohibition against sex discrimination in pay in jobs involving equal work. The substantive and procedural provisions of this act are discussed in the first section of this chapter. Proceeding in chronological order, the next section takes up the consequences of the enactment of Title VII, and in particular, the relationship between its broad prohibition against sex discrimination and the narrow prohibition of the Equal Pay Act. The uncertain relationship between these prohibitions derives from the unusual way in which sex was added to Title VII, as an amendment on the floor of the House of Representatives without any previous consideration by committee. A third section then considers the general nature of the prohibition against sex discrimi-

---

1. 29 U.S.C. § 206(d) (2000).

nation in Title VII and its interpretation according to the model of colorblindness in the law of racial discrimination. A formal interpretation according to this model, barring the consideration of sex in any decision related to employment, has proved to be surprisingly influential under Title VII. Nevertheless, the model of colorblindness cannot be applied literally to sex discrimination, as made clear by the different treatment of race and sex under Title VII, discussed in the following sections of this chapter. The first of these discusses the special provision on discrimination on the basis of pregnancy. The second examines the exception for "bona fide occupational qualifications" (or BFOQ) on the basis of sex. A final section discusses the law of sexual harassment.

In analyzing each of these specific topics, much depends upon the perspective and conception of equality that is applied to sex discrimination. Feminist legal theorists began by articulating the difference between a "sex-blind" conception of equality and a remedial conception in terms of "difference" rather than "sameness."[2] Should the goal of sex discrimination law be to achieve the same treatment of women and men, or as nearly the same as can possibly be achieved? Or should the goal be to take account of the differences between women and men and alter the conditions applicable to women accordingly? Each approach has something to be said for it. "Sameness" has all the force of the model of racial discrimination and the consensus in favor of colorblindness as a conception of equality. If the law prohibits discrimination on the basis of sex, it must require blindness with respect to sex, just as it does with respect to race. "Difference," however, has the advantage of recognizing the significant biological differences between the sexes and the social differences constructed upon them—which are perhaps even more important. A perspective based on difference also recognizes the limitations, discussed in previous chapters, of a purely colorblind conception of equality. Simply prohibiting further consideration of sex threatens to leave women with the disadvantages they have always had because of their past exclusion from employment.

More recent discussions in feminist theory have sought to go beyond the debate between "sameness" and "difference," inquiring more closely into the reasons why women have not participated fully in public life, including employment. Advocates of "dominance" explanations for the subordinate place of women, led by

2. The range of feminist theories has been summarized in various ways. For a representative sample, see Deborah L. Rhode, Justice and Gender: Sex Discrim- ination and the Law 305–17 (1989); Cass Sunstein, Introduction: Notes on Feminist Political Thought, 99 Ethics 219 (1989).

Catharine MacKinnon, argue that the categories of sameness and difference both have resulted from the dominant status of men and that adopting either category as the basis for reform only reinforces the current status of women.[3] Either women are held to the same standards as men, despite the fact that these standards were set with only men in mind, or they are held to different standards, which leave them with jobs carrying less prestige and lower pay. Other advocates of an alternative approach have relied on the psychological theories of Carol Gilligan, arguing that the unique experiences and attitudes of women support a greater emphasis on responsibility and less on rights and legal rules.[4] Sometimes this approach is framed in terms of women's stronger connections to other people, through experiences such as motherhood. It is the characteristic attitudes of women, on this view, that current employment practices fail to take into account, leaving women at a systematic disadvantage in an individualistic and competitive market for jobs. In the terms used in Chapter II, all of these approaches expand upon a remedial perspective and seek to give a stronger foundation for women's claims than a "difference" viewpoint that seems to take biological and cultural differences at face value.

Feminist theories have concentrated on adapting the remedial perspective to the distinctive situation of women. The only similar debate with respect to race has concerned affirmative action, an issue that has not stood out, either on the agenda of women's groups or in the law of sex discrimination. In part, this difference is attributable to the relative ease with which women have gained access to higher education under neutral standards of admission. The academic success of women, comprising now a majority of students enrolled in colleges and universities, has greatly increased their opportunities for employment. Other impediments to full equality of opportunity still persist, such as the concentration of women in some occupations, their exclusion from others, and the "glass ceiling" on their promotion to higher level jobs, but proposals to remedy these problems have not emphasized affirmative action as the solution. A more profound difference between race and sex concerns the role that women have traditionally taken in family life, beginning with pregnancy and childbirth and extending through childrearing and housekeeping. Adjusting the demands of employment to these aspects of family life requires alteration of the remedial conception of equality developed for race.

3. Catharine A. MacKinnon, Feminism Unmodified: Discourses on Life and Law 42 (1987).

4. For a discussion of these views, see Mary Becker, Patriarchy and Inequality: Towards a Substantive Feminism, 1999 U. Chi. Legal F. 21, 40–49.

In contrast to the debates over how the remedial perspective applies to sex discrimination, the economic perspective remains largely unchanged when it is applied to sex. In its usual formulation, the economic perspective emphasizes merit as determined by the employer and subject to the constraints of the market. Like race discrimination, sex discrimination is likely to have reduced the efficiency of the economy over the long run by deterring women from gaining the education and experience necessary to hold high-level jobs.[5] Discrimination reduces both the opportunities available to individual women and the overall welfare of society as a whole, by reducing the pool of qualified workers who can add to the total productivity of the economy.

Theoretical disputes over the various perspectives on employment discrimination law seldom make an immediate difference in concrete cases. Yet when they do, the differences are profound and enduring. Abstract differences in theory yield competing arguments that affect the overall direction and scope of the law. Interpretation of the prohibitions against sex discrimination in Title VII and the Equal Pay Act has settled on an uneasy reliance upon a formal approach, although one not quite equivalent to the conception of equality as colorblindness. Where enforcing an absolute prohibition upon considering sex increases the employment opportunities of women, the courts have been content to follow the model of colorblindness. Where exceptions and qualifications are necessary, as in the law of sexual harassment, alternative conceptions of equality have come into play. These leave room for arguments based on the entire range of theories about the nature of sex discrimination and how best to remedy it.

A.   The Equal Pay Act

The Equal Pay Act contains provisions that are distinctive both as a matter of substantive law and as a matter of procedure. Substantively, the act requires employers to give equal pay to men and women "for equal work on jobs the performance of which requires equal skill, effort, and responsibility, and which are performed under similar working conditions."[6] This requirement, in turn, is subject to exceptions "where such payment is made pursuant to (i) a seniority system; (ii) a merit system; (iii) a system which measures earnings by quantity or quality of production; or (iv) a

---

5. John J. Donohue III, Prohibiting Sex Discrimination in the Workplace: An Economic Perspective, 56 U. Chi. L. Rev. 1337 (1989).

6. 29 U.S.C. § 206(d)(1) (2000).

differential based on any other factor other than sex."[7] As under Title VII, much of the substantive law under the Equal Pay Act is devoted to allocating the burden of proof. The plaintiff has the burden of proving that the work performed by members of both sexes is "substantially equal" according to the four factors listed in the statute: equal skill, effort, and responsibility, and similar working conditions.[8] If the plaintiff carries the burden of production and persuasion on these issues, then both burdens shift to the defendant to prove that one of the four exceptions justifies the difference in pay.[9]

A leading case, *Corning Glass Works v. Brennan*,[10] illustrates how the burden of proof operates under the Equal Pay Act. That case concerned a claim of unequal pay asserted by women who worked in the same position as men, as product inspectors, but during the day shift instead of the night shift. The men were paid more ostensibly because they worked at night, but the record also indicated that the original difference in pay, established in the 1920s, was based partly on the fact that only women worked during the day and only men worked at night. The Supreme Court held that time of work was not a matter of "similar working conditions," which Congress intended to define according to technical standards that included only the surroundings and hazards of employment. Since these standards excluded time of work, the plaintiff could establish that women performed the same work as men even though they worked on different shifts. The burden of proving that the difference in shifts justified the difference in pay was then placed on the defendant, who had to prove that it fell within the catch-all exception for "any other factor other than sex." Because of the evidence that the shift differential was related to sex, the defendant lost on this issue and was held to have violated the act. Moreover, the employer's violation was continuing even though women had long since been admitted to the night shift. Another substantive provision of the act requires employers to cure any difference in pay by raising the pay of the lower-paid sex, almost invariably women.[11] Because the employer had never raised the pay of female inspectors on the day shift to eliminate the original differential with male inspectors on the night shift, the employer remained in violation of the statute.

7. *Id.*

8. Shultz v. Wheaton Glass Co., 421 F.2d 259, 265 (3d Cir.), *cert. denied*, 398 U.S. 905 (1970).

9. Corning Glass Works v. Brennan, 417 U.S. 188, 196–97, 204–05 (1974).

10. *Id.* at 197–205.

11. 29 U.S.C. § 206(d)(1) (2000).

The narrowness of the Equal Pay Act is evident in several of its provisions. As a preliminary matter, its requirement of equal pay applies only "within any establishment," so that differences in pay among employees in different locations operated by the same employer are not covered by the act at all.[12] The requirement of equal pay itself, as already noted, applies only if the prerequisite of equal work is met. Thus, outright discrimination against women in setting rates of pay does not violate the act if they perform different work from men, for instance, if women perform secretarial work and men perform janitorial work. This conclusion holds even if women are paid less than men for doing work that is more valuable. The plaintiff, however, need not prove that women perform exactly the same work as men, only that they perform "substantially equal" work.[13] The Equal Pay Act does not go any further in authorizing courts to evaluate the worth of different jobs or to reexamine employers' decisions about different levels of pay.

In enacting the requirement of equal pay for equal work, Congress explicitly considered and rejected a broader requirement of equal pay for "comparable work." In doing so, Congress adopted an economic perspective, endorsing management discretion and the market as the best means of setting pay.[14] This cautious approach might well have been justified in the first federal legislation concerned with sex discrimination in employment. Before the passage of the Equal Pay Act, only two states had general laws against sex discrimination in employment and no more than half the states had laws requiring equal pay for equal work. Without widespread experience with these laws, Congress framed its initial effort at regulation narrowly. The great irony, of course, is that the very same Congress, only a year later, would enact the very broad prohibition against sex discrimination in Title VII.

Whatever the cause, the narrow prohibition in the Equal Pay Act has led to equally narrow litigation, requiring a detailed comparison of the jobs held by women and jobs held by men in order to determine whether the work performed by one sex is "substantially equal" to that performed by the other. This inquiry resembles in many ways the inquiry into "pretext" in individual claims of intentional discrimination under Title VII. It must be conducted on the facts of each case. The defendant typically relies on objective differences between the work of men and women. And the plaintiff typically seeks to discredit the significance of these differences in

---

12. *Id.*

13. *Shultz*, 421 F.2d at 265.

14. *Id.* For a further review of the legislative history, see County of Wash-

ington v. Gunther, 452 U.S. 161, 184–97 (1981) (Rehnquist, J., dissenting).

order to establish that any difference in pay is discriminatory.[15] More ambitious litigation to restructure pay scales must be brought under Title VII, but as we shall see in the next section, even under Title VII the narrow prohibition of the Equal Pay Act continues to exert a restraining influence.

The distinctive procedures and remedies under the Equal Pay Act offer another explanation for the continued influence of the act. It is enforced according to the provisions of the federal minimum-wage law, the Fair Labor Standards Act (FLSA).[16] In fact, in its codified form, the Equal Pay Act is embedded in the FLSA as a separate subsection and it therefore applies only to employers already covered by the FLSA, although it extends to some employees exempt from coverage of that act.[17] The procedural and remedial provisions of the FLSA authorize criminal actions for "willful" violations by employers. The FLSA also authorizes civil actions, both public and private, against employers.[18] Although the Equal Pay Act prohibits unions from causing employers to violate the statute, it provides no civil remedies against unions for doing so, presumably because it was enacted at the behest of the labor movement.[19]

The FLSA authorizes the Secretary of Labor to bring civil enforcement actions, but an executive reorganization plan transferred this authority to the EEOC.[20] Public actions come in two varieties. Under section 216(c),[21] the EEOC can sue for back pay and an equal amount in liquidated damages to be awarded in the discretion of the district court. Under section 217,[22] the EEOC can sue for injunctive relief, including an order for back pay, but not for liquidated damages.[23] The difference between actions under the two sections is largely a result of parallel judicial interpretations and statutory amendments that have not yet been integrated in a

---

15. *See, e.g.,* Horner v. Mary Institute, 613 F.2d 706, 709–12 (8th Cir. 1980) (comparing jobs of male and female physical education teachers in great detail).

16. Codified as 29 U.S.C. §§ 201–19 (2000).

17. 29 U.S.C. §§ 203, 213, 216–17 (2000). The application of the FLSA to commercial enterprises operated by a religious organization does not violate the religion clauses of the First Amendment. Tony & Susan Alamo Found. v. Secretary of Labor, 471 U.S. 290, 303–06 (1985).

18. 29 U.S.C. § 215–17 (2000).

19. *Id.* §§ 206(d)(2), 216–17 (2000). *But see* Hodgson v. Sagner, Inc., 326 F.Supp. 371 (D. Md. 1971), *aff'd sub nom.* Hodgson v. Baltimore Regional Jt. Bd., 462 F.2d 180 (4th Cir. 1972) (per curiam) (injunction awarded against union).

20. 29 U.S.C. § 216 (2000); Reorg. Plan No. 1 of 1978, 3 C.F.R. 321 (1979), *reprinted in* § 1, 5 U.S.C. app. at 1574 (2000).

21. 29 U.S.C. § 216(c) (2000).

22. *Id.* § 217.

23. *E.g.,* Brennan v. Board of Education, 374 F.Supp. 817 (D.N.J. 1974).

comprehensive revision of the FLSA. Private individuals can sue under section 216(b), but only if they have not previously accepted relief awarded in a public action and if a public action has not yet been filed on their behalf.[24]

The expanded remedies and simplified procedures under the Equal Pay Act explain its continued attractiveness to private plaintiffs. If they establish a violation of the act, they are entitled to back pay and, in the discretion of the district court, an equal amount in liquidated damages.[25] They are also entitled to an award of attorney's fees.[26] Employees can be brought into a private action only with their written consent, a requirement that has been interpreted to allow only opt-in class actions.[27] Nevertheless, in contrast to Title VII, exhaustion of administrative remedies is not required. Plaintiffs need only sue within a limitation period of two years for ordinary violations and three years for "willful" violations, where "willful" is defined as knowing or reckless disregard of the fact that the disputed action is in violation of the law.[28] Unreasonable conduct alone is not enough to support the longer limitation period.[29] The FLSA also provides for a complete defense of reliance on written policy[30] and a partial defense of good faith, or reasonable belief in compliance with the act, which may reduce liquidated damages in the discretion of the district court.[31]

Unlike these highly specialized provisions, the issues of greatest continuing significance under the Equal Pay Act concern its relationship to Title VII, the subject of the following section.

B. Sex Discrimination in Pay: The Relationship Between the Equal Pay Act and Title VII

The contrast between Title VII and the Equal Pay Act is most striking where these two statutes overlap: on claims of sex discrimination in pay. It is on these claims that Congress attempted to reconcile the broad prohibition of Title VII with the narrow prohibition of the Equal Pay Act. The reconciling provision in Title VII, called the "Bennett Amendment," allows an employer to "differen-

24. 29 U.S.C. § 216(b)–(c) (2000).

25. *Id.* §§ 216(b), 260.

26. *Id.* § 216(b).

27. *Id. See* Hoffmann-LaRoche Inc. v. Sperling, 493 U.S. 165, 169 (1989) (federal district court has discretion to facilitate notice to class members in ADEA action); LaChappelle v. Owens-Illinois, Inc., 513 F.2d 286 (5th Cir. 1975) (opt-in class action allowed on ADEA claim under same provision as in FLSA).

28. McLaughlin v. Richland Shoe Co., 486 U.S. 128, 131–35 (1988).

29. *Id.* at 135 n.13.

30. 29 U.S.C. § 259 (2000).

31. *Id.* § 260.

tiate upon the basis of sex" in compensating its employees "if such differentiation is authorized by" the Equal Pay Act.[32] The Bennett Amendment was one of several provisions added to Title VII to limit or qualify the prohibition against sex discrimination, which had been added to the statute on the floor of the House of Representatives. The Bennett Amendment was also added to Title VII without any consideration by committee. This procedure was necessary because the Civil Rights Act of 1964 was never referred to committee in the Senate, for fear that it would be bottled up by conservative Southern senators who controlled several committees to which it would have been referred. As a result, neither the prohibition against sex discrimination nor this limitation upon it received close examination in either house of Congress.

The language of the Bennett Amendment reflects this lack of sustained consideration. It presupposes that some differences in compensation on the basis of sex are "authorized" by the Equal Pay Act, when the Equal Pay Act does not explicitly authorize any such differences. Indeed, it does not even permit differences on the basis of sex for any jobs within its scope. The text of the Equal Pay Act only permits differences in pay based on "(i) a seniority system; (ii) a merit system; (iii) a system which measures earnings by quantity or quality of production; or (iv) a differential based on any other factor other than sex."[33] As the last of these exceptions makes clear, all of these allowable differences are based on some "factor other than sex." Read literally, the Bennett Amendment is therefore wrong on two counts: the Equal Pay Act does not "authorize" any differences in pay and it does not explicitly allow any differences in pay "on the basis of sex."

The Supreme Court addressed the problems posed by the Bennett Amendment in *County of Washington v. Gunther*,[34] interpreting the amendment to allow only differences in compensation within exceptions (i) through (iv) of the Equal Pay Act. This holding is not free from difficulty, since exceptions (i), (ii), and (iii) are nearly the same as exceptions already included in Title VII, indeed in the same subsection where the Bennett Amendment is found.[35] Moreover, exception (iv) appears only to emphasize that the Equal Pay Act does not prohibit differences in pay on a basis other than sex, a limitation that applies equally to the broad prohibition against sex discrimination in Title VII. The Court's

---

32. § 703(h), codified as 42 U.S.C. § 2000e–2(h) (2000).

33. 29 U.S.C. § 206(d)(1) (2000).

34. 452 U.S. 161 (1981).

35. § 703(h), codified as 42 U.S.C. § 2000e–2(h) (2000).

interpretation of the Bennett Amendment appears to make the amendment entirely redundant.

To counter this objection, the Court suggested, but did not decide, that the Bennett Amendment requires proof of disparate treatment—not just disparate impact—in order to prove discrimination in pay under Title VII. By incorporating exception (iv) of the Equal Pay Act into Title VII, the Court suggested, the Bennett Amendment precludes liability for disparate impact based on "any other factor other than sex." Reasoning along the same lines, a circuit court has held that the Bennett Amendment did not incorporate the proviso to the Equal Pay Act requiring equal pay to be achieved only by raising pay. A violation of Title VII can be cured by any means, including reducing the pay of men to the level paid to women.[36]

The significance of *Gunther*, however, does not lie in the scope of the defenses under the Equal Pay Act, but in the scope of liability under Title VII. Despite the Bennett Amendment, the broad prohibition against sex discrimination in Title VII overrides the narrow prohibition in the Equal Pay Act, which is conditioned upon proof of equal work. As interpreted in *Gunther*, Title VII imposes an unconditional obligation on employers not to discriminate in compensation on the basis of sex. To this extent, Title VII departs from the deference to employers and to the market that is characteristic of the Equal Pay Act. It allows judges to reevaluate employers' decisions about the worth of different jobs. Nevertheless, in suggesting that proof of intentional discrimination is still required, the opinion in *Gunther* does not depart very far from a conception of equality as colorblindness. It still requires proof that sex was a factor in the decision to pay women less than men. The opinion does not adopt a remedial conception of equality that would require a closer look at the structural features of employment that lead women systematically to receive lower pay than men.

This conclusion is confirmed by the unusual facts of *Gunther*, which made it especially easy for the plaintiffs to prove discrimination in pay. The plaintiffs were female guards at a county jail who were paid less than male guards at the same facility. Although they performed different tasks than the male guards, and so did not perform "substantially equal work" under the Equal Pay Act, the county's own study revealed that they should have been paid more than they were, and in particular, that there was no justification

36. Norris v. Arizona Governing   1986).
Comm., 796 F.2d 1119, 1123 (9th Cir.

for paying all of the male guards more than any of the female guards. As the Court emphasized, the case did not require an independent judicial comparison of the worth of different jobs.[37] Consequently, *Gunther* only opened the door to claims of comparable worth under Title VII. Some circuits have concluded that it does not open the door very far, relying on the Court's suggestion that the theory of disparate impact might not apply to claims of comparable worth.[38] And, in fact, few such claims have been brought under Title VII, revealing how its prohibition against sex discrimination tends to receive a formal interpretation, forbidding only employment decisions based explicitly or implicitly on sex. This is the subject of the next section of this chapter.

C. The Formal Interpretation of the Prohibition Against Sex Discrimination

The prohibition against sex discrimination in Title VII follows the model of racial discrimination in one crucial respect: it is in large part a formal prohibition, against considering sex in any decision related to employment. It departs from the model of race in other ways, such as admitting exceptions that do not apply to racial discrimination, but these exceptions have been narrowly construed. As we have seen, for instance, the Bennett Amendment has been narrowly interpreted to prohibit all forms of intentional sex discrimination with respect to pay. And outside the scope of the Bennett Amendment, claims of sex discrimination can also be established under the theory of disparate impact. So a formal interpretation does not exhaust the scope of the prohibition against sex discrimination in Title VII. Nor does a formal interpretation capture all aspects of the law of sexual harassment. Yet a formal interpretation goes surprisingly far in explaining the prohibition against sex discrimination in Title VII and in enhancing the employment opportunities available to women.

The Supreme Court adopted a formal interpretation of Title VII in *City of Los Angeles Department of Water & Power v. Manhart*,[39] a case concerned with the use of sex-based actuarial tables to compute pension benefits payable upon retirement. Insurance companies traditionally have used sex-based actuarial tables to estimate the life expectancy of individuals covered by life insurance policies and annuities, and before *Manhart*, employers used these tables in

---

37. 452 U.S. at 181.

38. American Nurses' Ass'n v. Illinois, 783 F.2d 716, 723 (7th Cir. 1986); American Fed'n of State, County & Mun. Employees v. Washington, 770 F.2d 1401, 1405–08 (9th Cir. 1985).

39. 435 U.S. 702 (1978).

providing similar fringe benefits for their employees. Such tables reflect the apparently greater life expectancy of women than men. In the pension plan at issue in *Manhart*, sex-based actuarial tables required women to pay more than men for pension benefits that were payable in equal monthly amounts from the date of retirement until the date of death. Because women live longer on average than men, they had to pay more for monthly benefits than they did for men. At least, that was the justification offered in support of the disputed pension plan.

It was not accepted by the Supreme Court, however, which held that Title VII prohibits employers from using sex-segregated actuarial tables to grant different benefits to male and female employees. The Court reasoned that Title VII prohibits all classifications on the basis of sex unless they fall within one of the exceptions specifically allowed by the statute. Sex-segregated actuarial tables fall outside the Bennett Amendment because they are not based on any of the exceptions (i) to (iv) in the Equal Pay Act. Nor are they permitted by the exception for bona fide occupational qualifications (BFOQ's) on the basis of sex because, as the term implies, it covers only occupational qualifications, not compensation.[40] The Court appeared to allow sex-based classifications in actuarial tables in only two situations related to employment. First, since Title VII only regulates the relationship between employer and employee, an employer remains free to pay cash to its employees, who can then purchase life insurance or annuities from independent insurance companies.[41] If allowed by state law, the latter are free to use sex-segregated actuarial tables. However, as the Supreme Court has subsequently held, any use of such tables in an employer's fringe-benefit plan, even if it is administered by an insurance company, violates Title VII.[42] Second, the Court allowed an employer to take into account the proportion of men and women in its work force in computing unisex actuarial tables.[43] This use of sex-based classification is needed to ensure the solvency of insurance and pension plans, at least in the absence of any practical predictor of life expectancy that is better than sex. For similar reasons, the Court has refused to make its decisions on the use of sex-based actuarial tables retroactive, applying them only to payments based on contributions made after the decisions were rendered.[44]

40. *Id.* at 712–13.

41. *Id.* at 717–18.

42. Arizona Governing Comm. v. Norris, 463 U.S. 1073 (1983) (per cu-

riam); Florida v. Long, 487 U.S. 223, 233 (1988).

43. 435 U.S. at 718 & n.34.

44. *Id.* at 718–23; *Norris*, 463 U.S. at 1074–75 (1983) (per curiam).

The larger significance of *Manhart* concerns its treatment of the factual support for sex-based actuarial tables. The Court assumed that such tables were accurate, but concluded that they were prohibited by Title VII regardless of how accurate they were. What was crucial was the form that the employer's pension plan took, not its factual basis. Taking account of sex, whether or not it improved the accuracy of predictions of life expectancy, was prohibited. The Court's opinion would have been little different if it had concerned a race-based actuarial table, which has as much factual support as a sex-based actuarial table. Staying close to the model of race enabled the Court to give content to the prohibition against sex discrimination without going beyond the meager legislative history that surrounded its addition to Title VII. It has other advantages as well.

The working hypothesis that discrimination on the basis of sex is to be treated just like discrimination on the basis of race, in the absence of compelling reasons to the contrary, assigns equal priority to eliminating both forms of discrimination. It does not relegate women to the second-class status characteristic of sexual stereotypes. It also allows most of the law developed in decisions on racial discrimination to be transferred unchanged to cases of sex discrimination. This generalization of legal doctrine achieves efficiencies that make enforcement of the prohibition against sex discrimination easier to achieve and compliance more likely to be forthcoming. It also avoids controversial questions about the appropriate role of gender in public life, confining it to a few narrow exceptions to the prohibition against sex discrimination. A formal interpretation of the prohibition does not even permit the question to be raised whether "a woman's place is in the home." As the following sections discuss in more detail, all such questions are confined to the interpretation of highly specialized provisions of Title VII.

D. Classifications on the Basis of Pregnancy

The first test of whether Title VII's prohibition against sex discrimination would be given a broad or a narrow interpretation concerned the coverage of pregnancy. The Supreme Court originally examined discrimination on the basis of pregnancy in constitutional cases, revealing yet again the influence of constitutional law on the statutory law of employment discrimination. The Court first held that a public employer could not impose mandatory pregnancy leaves of fixed duration because they rested on an unconstitutional, irrebuttable presumption; they presumed that women in the later stages of pregnancy were physically incapable of working as teachers.[45] But in *Geduldig v. Aiello*,[46] the Court held that classifications on the basis of pregnancy simply were not classifications on the basis of sex. It reasoned that the exclusion of pregnancy from a state disability program was not an exclusion based on sex because it did not distinguish women from men, but only pregnant persons from nonpregnant persons.[47] In two subsequent cases, the Court applied this reasoning to Title VII, holding that employers could exclude benefits for pregnancy from disability and sick-leave plans.[48]

In response to these decisions, Congress enacted the Pregnancy Discrimination Act,[49] which overruled the Court's pregnancy decisions under Title VII. It did so by rejecting both the reasoning and the holdings of these decisions. It rejected the reasoning by defining "because of sex" or "on the basis of sex" to include "because of or on the basis of pregnancy, childbirth, or related medical conditions." And it rejected the holdings by generally requiring that pregnant women be "treated the same for all employment-related purposes" as others "similar in their ability or inability to work" and by specifically applying this requirement to "receipt of benefits under fringe benefit programs."[50]

The net effect of these changes was to ratify and expand a formal interpretation of the prohibition against sex discrimination. By defining sex to include pregnancy under Title VII, the act prohibited any consideration of pregnancy by an employer, unless specifically allowed by another provision of Title VII. The Pregnancy Discrimination Act itself contained one such exception, for benefits related to abortions,[51] a provision added to avoid the constitutional controversy over this subject. The provision for BFOQ's on the basis of sex constitutes another such exception, to be discussed in the next section of this chapter. If no such exception applies, however, the formal interpretation prevents an employer from taking account of pregnancy in any manner that works to the disadvantage of either sex.

45. Cleveland Bd. of Educ. v. La-Fleur, 414 U.S. 632 (1974).

46. 417 U.S. 484 (1974).

47. *Id.* at 496 n.20.

48. General Elec. Co. v. Gilbert, 429 U.S. 125 (1976); Nashville Gas Co. v. Satty, 434 U.S. 136, 143–46 (1977). In the latter case, however, the Court held that denial of accrued seniority because of pregnancy was prohibited by Title VII because it had a disparate impact on women. *Id.* at 141–43.

49. § 701(k), codified as 42 U.S.C. § 2000e(k) (2000).

50. *Id.*

51. "This subsection shall not require an employer to pay for health insurance benefits for abortion...." *Id.* This provision is then subject to its own exceptions for women who would be endangered if the fetus were carried to term, for medical complications arising from an abortion, and allowing employers to provide abortion benefits in collective bargaining agreements.

The full implications of the formal interpretation became apparent in *Newport News Shipbuilding & Dry Dock Co. v. EEOC*,[52] a case concerned, paradoxically, with a claim for pregnancy benefits by male employees seeking such benefits for their wives. Under the employer's medical insurance plan, the husbands of female employees received full coverage of all medical conditions, but the wives of male employees received only limited coverage of pregnancy and childbirth. The Supreme Court held that this limitation upon pregnancy benefits constituted a classification on the basis of sex in violation of Title VII. Just as in *Manhart*, the Court did not inquire into the value of the benefits provided to male and female employees (in this case, in terms of coverage of spouses) but only into the form that those benefits took. The limitation on pregnancy benefits alone amounted to a classification on the basis of sex that was not otherwise allowed by Title VII. By contrast, if the employer had not provided any coverage for spouses, either of male or female employees, its medical insurance plan would have fully complied with Title VII; the plan would have been completely neutral on the basis of sex.[53] This point distinguishes the Pregnancy Discrimination Act from broader legislation that requires employers to grant leave to their employees for pregnancy and other family matters.[54] Under Title VII, employers remain free to grant no benefits at all, so long as they do so equally to both male and female employees.

The constitutional questions raised by the exclusion of pregnancy benefits were not resolved by the Pregnancy Discrimination Act, although it did undercut their significance. In particular, the holding of *Geduldig v. Aiello* that discrimination on the basis of pregnancy is not discrimination on the basis of sex may have some remaining precedential effect in constitutional law. Even so, it does not apply to employers covered by Title VII, which include all private firms with fifteen or more employees, all subdivisions of state and local government, and most parts of the federal government.[55] Another constitutional question, at the opposite extreme, is whether the states can require employers to grant greater benefits for pregnancy than for other disabilities. In *California Federal Savings & Loan Ass'n v. Guerra*,[56] this question was resolved in favor of a state law requiring employers to grant unpaid leave for pregnancy, which allowed pregnant employees to take leave and

52. 462 U.S. 669 (1983).

53. *Id.* at 684 n.25.

54. *E.g.*, Family and Medical Leave Act, codified as 29 U.S.C. §§ 2601 to 2619 (2000) (requiring employers with 50 or more employees to provide up to 12 weeks of unpaid leave per year).

55. §§ 701(b), (f), (h), 717(a), codified as 42 U.S.C. §§ 2000e(b), (f), (h)–16(a) (2000).

56. 479 U.S. 272 (1987).

then return to their jobs without prejudice. The Supreme Court held that this law was not preempted by the Pregnancy Discrimination Act because it served the same basic purpose of increasing the employment opportunities of women.[57] Under these narrow circumstances, a state may allow classifications on the basis of pregnancy, although even this question was left open in *California Federal* because the state law in question did not prevent the employer from extending to all employees the same benefits required for pregnant employees.[58] As a matter of federal law, classifications on the basis of pregnancy are allowed only if they fall within the BFOQ exception applicable to all classifications on the basis of sex.

E. Bona Fide Occupational Qualifications on the Basis of Sex

Title VII specifically permits classifications on the basis of "religion, sex, or national origin in those certain instances where religion, sex, or national origin is a bona fide occupational qualification reasonably necessary to the normal operation of that particular business or enterprise."[59] This provision (the BFOQ) does not allow any classifications on the basis of race. A similar provision in the Age Discrimination in Employment Act allows classifications on the basis of age,[60] but it is the BFOQ for sex in Title VII that has proved to be most controversial. It sharply raises the question how far the law of sex discrimination departs from the model of racial discrimination. In what circumstances can an employer take account of sex, but not race, in making personnel decisions? The short answer is, "not many," because the BFOQ itself turns out to be very narrow.

The Supreme Court has decided two cases on the BFOQ for sex and in both it has emphasized the narrowness of the exception. In the first, *Dothard v. Rawlinson*,[61] the Court applied the exception and held that women could be excluded from positions as prison guards in the violent conditions of the Alabama prison system at that time. In the positions at issue, involving close contact with male inmates, the Court reasoned that female prison guards would be in danger of sexual assault. This danger was increased by the chaotic conditions in the Alabama prisons, which had been held to violate the Eighth Amendment in an unrelated case.[62] Moreover,

---

57. *Id.* at 284–90.

58. *Id.* at 290–92.

59. § 703(e)(1), codified as 42 U.S.C. § 2000e–2(e)(1) (2000).

60. § 4(f)(1), codified as 29 U.S.C. § 623(f)(1) (2000).

61. 433 U.S. 321 (1977).

62. Pugh v. Locke, 406 F.Supp. 318 (M.D. Ala. 1976), *modified on other*

the danger was not just to the women themselves, who could have evaluated it and decided to become prison guards anyway. It also threatened the general security of the prisons by undermining control over the prison population.[63]

In *Dothard*, the Court quoted, but did not explicitly endorse, two tests for applying the BFOQ, both formulated by the Fifth Circuit: whether " 'the *essence* of the business operation would be undermined by not hiring members of one sex exclusively' "[64] or whether the employer " 'had reasonable cause to believe, that is, a factual basis for believing, that all or substantially all women would be unable to perform safely and efficiently the duties of the job involved.' "[65] The Court endorsed only the position that "the bfoq exception was in fact meant to be an extremely narrow exception to the general prohibition of discrimination on the basis of sex" and that "it is impermissible under Title VII to refuse to hire an individual woman or man on the basis of stereotyped characterizations of the sexes."[66] And, indeed, in subsequent cases involving prison and jail guards, the lower courts have distinguished *Dothard* when the defendant failed to submit proof of the need for guards of a single sex.[67]

In the second case, *United Automobile Workers v. Johnson Controls, Inc.*,[68] the Supreme Court held that the BFOQ did not justify the exclusion of fertile women from jobs resulting in exposure to lead in the process of making batteries. The Court applied the same standards as *Dothard*, making clear that the employer had the burden of proof, both of production and persuasion, in making out a BFOQ. Nevertheless, the Court found no BFOQ because the justification offered by the employer for the exclusion of fertile women concerned the safety only of the fetus that they might be carrying.[69] In contrast to *Dothard*, there was no risk to employees or customers.[70] This reasoning appears to be strained

grounds, 559 F.2d 283 (5th Cir. 1977), *rev'd in part on other grounds*, 438 U.S. 781 (1978).

63. 433 U.S. at 336.

64. *Id.* at 333 (quoting Diaz v. Pan Am. World Airways, 442 F.2d 385, 388 (5th Cir.), *cert. denied*, 404 U.S. 950 (1971)).

65. *Id.* (quoting Weeks v. Southern Bell Tel. & Tel. Co., 408 F.2d 228, 235 (5th Cir. 1969)).

66. *Id.* at 333–34.

67. *E.g.*, United States v. Gregory, 818 F.2d 1114, 1117–18 (4th Cir.), *cert. denied*, 484 U.S. 847 (1987). *But cf.* Tor-

res v. Wisconsin Dep't of Health & Soc. Servs., 859 F.2d 1523 (7th Cir. 1988) (en banc), *cert. denied*, 489 U.S. 1017, 1082 (1989) (objective evidence not needed).

68. 499 U.S. 187 (1991).

69. *Id.* at 203–04.

70. *Id.* at 202. On the same ground, the Court also distinguished cases interpreting the BFOQ under the Age Discrimination in Employment Act, 29 U.S.C. § 623(f)(1) (2000). *Id.* at 202–203.

because it makes the result in *Johnson Controls* depend on the obvious, but seemingly irrelevant, fact that fetuses do not participate in the process of making batteries. The safety of the fetus, however, raises distinctive issues under the Pregnancy Discrimination Act.[71] Relying on both this act and an analogy to the constitutional decisions on abortion, the Court left decisions about the safety of children entirely to their parents: "Decisions about the welfare of future children must be left to the parents who conceive, bear, support, and raise them rather than to the employers who hire those parents."[72] These special features of the case may limit its significance, but the opinion itself seizes on these details only to narrow, not to expand, the scope of the BFOQ.

Indeed, apart from the fact that the BFOQ is "extremely narrow," its exact scope has remained quite uncertain. The standards quoted in *Dothard* and applied in *Johnson Controls* leave open difficult questions about the legitimate role of sex-based differences in defining the "essence of the business operation," or what constitutes "stereotyped characterizations of the sexes." For instance, several decisions have allowed the exclusion of members of one sex from jobs involving the physical privacy of members of the opposite sex, such as a nurse on a maternity ward or in a home for elderly, mostly female, patients.[73] Even so, these decisions, particularly those concerned with guards of one sex watching prisoners of another sex, have required proof that there is no other way to protect physical privacy.[74] These decisions depend upon a judgment, but presumably not a stereotype, that physical privacy is more easily violated by members of the opposite sex than members of the same sex.

Other decisions have gone beyond the literal terms of the BFOQ and allowed classifications on the basis of sex as conditions of employment, not as qualifications for employment. The best known of these concern claims that an employer's rules allowing women, but not men, to have long hair violate Title VII.[75] Courts have allowed such rules despite the fact that hair length does not, apart from the attitudes of customers and co-employees, affect the ability to perform most jobs. These decisions, however, have prohibited employers from requiring women to wear sexually revealing

71. § 701(k), codified as 42 U.S.C. § 2000e(k) (2000).

72. 499 U.S. at 206.

73. *E.g.*, Fesel v. Masonic Home of Delaware, Inc., 447 F.Supp. 1346 (D. Del. 1978), *aff'd per curiam*, 591 F.2d 1334 (3d Cir. 1979); Healey v. South-wood Psychiatric Hosp., 78 F.3d 128 (3d Cir. 1996).

74. *E.g.*, Forts v. Ward, 621 F.2d 1210, 1215–17 (2d Cir. 1980).

75. Willingham v. Macon Tel. Publ'g Co., 507 F.2d 1084 (5th Cir. 1975).

costumes when men are subjected to no such requirement.[76] The principal problem in applying the BFOQ, and in extending it to conditions of employment, is in identifying the narrow range of cases in which judgments about sex-based roles are legitimate.

One cautionary note about the BFOQ is necessary. The language of the exception—allowing classifications "reasonably necessary to the normal operation of that particular business or enterprise"—invites confusion with the defendant's burden of showing job relationship and business necessity under the theory of disparate impact. Although the defendant bears the burden of proof on both issues,[77] the similarity ends there. The BFOQ provides a justification for classifications explicitly based on sex, national origin, or religion, and for that reason, is narrowly interpreted. By contrast, the defendant's burden of justification under the theory of disparate impact applies to neutral employment practices, and as we have seen, is of uncertain and ambiguous scope.[78]

F. Sexual Harassment

Claims of sexual harassment pose a challenge for the formal interpretation that otherwise dominates the law of sex discrimination. On the one hand, few such claims involve official action by the employer approving or condoning sexual harassment. Instead, the great majority allege that an individual supervisor or co-employee acted on his own in harassing the plaintiff, often contrary to the employer's explicit policies and directions. On the other hand, when supervisors or co-employees do engage in sexual harassment, they do not simply make decisions based on sex. Everyone in the workplace takes account of the sex of everyone else in a variety of ways, most of them innocuous, from casual conversation to personal manners and appearance. Determining when consciousness of sex becomes sexual harassment inevitably depends upon all of the surrounding circumstances. A formal approach to prohibiting sex discrimination—examining only the official decisions of the employer and only whether these decisions take of account of sex—is inadequate to the complexities of sexual harassment.

76. *E.g.,* EEOC v. Sage Realty Corp., 507 F.Supp. 599, 608–11 (S.D.N.Y. 1981).

77. Rosenfeld v. Southern Pacific Co., 444 F.2d 1219 (9th Cir. 1971); *see* United Auto. Workers v. Johnson Controls, Inc., 499 U.S. 187, 206 (1991) ("We have no difficulty concluding that Johnson Controls cannot establish a BFOQ"). The defendant's burden of proof under the theory of disparate impact is determined by §§ 701(m), 703(k)(1)(A)(i), codified as 42 U.S.C. § 2000e(m), –2(k)(1)(A)(i) (2000).

78. *See* Chapter IV.B.4 *supra.*

These complexities initially led the lower federal courts to doubt that any claims for sexual harassment could be made under Title VII. Such doubts were laid to rest in *Meritor Savings Bank v. Vinson*,[79] in which the Supreme Court followed EEOC guidelines in recognizing claims for sexual harassment generally, and in particular, for creating a hostile work environment. The plaintiff in *Meritor* alleged that her supervisor engaged in a pattern of extended and explicit sexual harassment, including several instances of rape. The Court held that these allegations were sufficient to state a claim for relief, even if the plaintiff did not suffer any tangible economic loss from her supervisor's advances. The plaintiff could recover by proving that the sexual advances and comments were unwelcome and were "sufficiently severe or pervasive 'to alter the conditions of [the victim's] employment and create an abusive working environment.' "[80] The Court distinguished claims of this kind, alleging a hostile environment, from those involving tangible economic loss, but allowed recovery for both. An employee need not suffer the loss of pay, benefits, or the job itself in order to have a claim for sexual harassment. All that is needed is a change in working conditions.

The distinction between the two forms of sexual harassment makes a difference only in determining the vicarious liability of the employer. This issue was addressed, but not definitively resolved, in *Meritor*. The Court reversed the ruling of the court of appeals imposing liability automatically upon the employer, looking instead to common law principles of agency to place some limits on the employer's liability for the acts of its employees.[81] This issue is significant because Title VII does not prohibit discrimination by employees, but only by employers as defined by the statute, including "any agent" of such an employer.[82] If the harassing employee is acting as an agent of the employer, then the employer is liable, and according to the literal terms of the statute, so is the employee. Some courts, however, have held that an individual agent of an employer cannot be held personally liable at all under Title VII,[83] relying on provisions of the Civil Rights Act of 1991 that imposed limited liability for damages, depending upon the size of the em-

79. 477 U.S. 57 (1986).

80. *Id.* at 67 (quoting Henson v. Dundee, 682 F.2d 897, 904 (11th Cir. 1982)).

81. *Id.* at 71–72.

82. §§ 701(b), 703(a), codified as 42 U.S.C. §§ 2000e(b),–2(a) (2000).

83. *E.g.*, Miller v. Maxwell's Int'l Inc., 991 F.2d 583, 587–88 (9th Cir. 1993), *cert. denied*, 510 U.S. 1109 (1994); Lowry v. Clark, 843 F.Supp. 228, 229–31 (E.D. Ky. 1994). Other cases have disagreed. *E.g.*, Raiser v. O'Shaughnessy, 830 F.Supp. 1134, 1137 (N.D. Ill. 1993).

ployer.[84] These decisions have reasoned that if small employers face reduced liability, then individual employees should have none at all. In any event, if the harassing employee is not an agent of the employer, then neither the employer nor the employee is liable under Title VII, although it remains possible that either or both may be liable under state law.[85]

In two more recent decisions, the Supreme Court has resolved some, but not all, of the disputes over liability of employers for sexual harassment. In *Burlington Industries, Inc. v. Ellerth*,[86] the plaintiff was allegedly harassed by a supervisor, who threatened her with various adverse decisions, such as the denial of a raise or a promotion, unless she gave in to his advances. None of his threats were carried out, however, resulting in no "tangible employment action." According to the Court, her claim therefore had to be analyzed as one for sexual harassment based on a hostile environment. Under *Meritor*, this required her to prove that the alleged harassment was "severe or pervasive." It also allowed the employer to avoid liability if it met both elements of an affirmative defense: "(a) that the employer exercised reasonable care to prevent and correct promptly any sexually harassing behavior, and (b) that the plaintiff employee unreasonably failed to take advantage of any preventive or corrective opportunities provided by the employer or to avoid harm otherwise."[87] If the employer failed to establish this defense, then it was vicariously liable for the alleged harassment. As the Supreme Court formulated the defense, the employer must make out both of its elements. Establishing its own reasonable care under the first element is not enough. The employer must also establish the plaintiff's failure to use reasonable care under the second element.

In a companion case, *Faragher v. City of Boca Raton*,[88] the Court clarified the first element of the defense, holding that it had not been satisfied by an employer who had a policy against sexual harassment but had failed to implement it effectively. The employer, a city parks and recreation department, had not disseminated the policy widely enough so that it could reach the relatively remote location, a lifeguard station, where the plaintiffs worked. The employer also had failed to assure employees that they could bypass their immediate supervisors in complaining about harassment by the supervisors themselves, as alleged in this case. Because of the size of the employer and its widely dispersed operations, it was

84. 42 U.S.C. § 1981a (2000).

85. Barbara Lindemann & David D. Kadue, Sexual Harassment in Employment Law ch. 15 (1992 & Supp. 1999).

86. 524 U.S. 742 (1998).

87. *Id.* at 765.

88. 524 U.S. 775 (1998).

required to take more elaborate steps to publicize and implement its policy than a small employer with a single workplace. Although the plaintiffs made only minimal efforts to complain about the harassing conduct, this was an issue only under the second element of the defense. Because the employer had not established the first element, it could not take advantage of the defense at all and accordingly was held liable for the supervisors' harassment.

Where the defense recognized in *Burlington Industries* and *Faragher* is not available, the employer might be exposed either to greater or lesser liability. Its liability is greater in cases in which the plaintiff proves that the harassment was accompanied by a "tangible employment action." A finding to this effect results in strict liability of the employer without any affirmative defense. Because a finding of tangible employment action has such significant consequences, the Court defined the term with some care in *Burlington Industries*. As an initial matter, it means something different from "quid pro quo" sexual harassment, a term used in prior cases to describe demands for sexual favors accompanied by threats or promises of employment-related benefits. As the facts of *Burlington Industries* make clear, an unfulfilled threat does not constitute a tangible employment action. Typically, it involves "hiring, firing, failing to promote, reassignment with significantly different responsibilities, or a decision causing a significant change in benefits."[89]

Because "failing to promote" appears on this list, a significant change in benefits apparently must be judged from the baseline of the benefits that would have been received in the absence of the alleged harassment. Somewhat paradoxically, inaction can be sufficient to create a "tangible employment action." Conversely, a seemingly tangible decision in the form of a constructive discharge might not constitute a "tangible employment action." Since this kind of discharge is constructive, not actual, it does not represent a formal decision by the employer to discharge the employee, but the employee's decision to leave the employer because working conditions are intolerable. It follows, at least according to the Supreme Court, that a constructive discharge must be characterized according to the conditions that led the employee to quit.[90] It constitutes a "tangible employment action" only if the employee's decision resulted from some other tangible employment action, such as a demotion or a pay cut.

89. *Burlington Industries*, 524 U.S. at 761.

90. Pennsylvania State Police v. Suders, 542 U.S. 129 (2004).

Wholly apart from a tangible employment action, other forms of harassment by supervisors can also result in liability of the employer that is not subject to an affirmative defense. If the harassing supervisor is sufficiently high in the employer's management, then his actions are directly attributed to the company as its alter ego.[91] Thus, harassment by the company's president constitutes harassment by the company itself. So, too, harassment explicitly permitted or condoned by the employer results in direct liability, although such cases rarely arise in practice.[92]

At the opposite extreme, the employer is liable for harassment by co-employees only if it is negligent in allowing the harassment to take place. Both *Burlington Industries* and *Faragher* are concerned solely with harassment by supervisors and other managers of the employer. Employees with the same status as the plaintiff are mentioned only in passing, but in terms that restrict the employer's liability to negligence in monitoring their conduct.[93] Because co-employees exercise no authority over the plaintiff, the employer cannot be subjected to vicarious liability on the ground that such employees acted as agents within the scope of their employment. The employer's liability is limited to negligence in allowing a hostile working environment to persist. The entire burden of proof on the issue of reasonable care is therefore on the plaintiff, in contrast to the affirmative defense recognized in *Burlington Industries* and *Faragher*.

In addition to formulating standards for imposing liability upon employers, the Supreme Court has also sought to clarify the standards for determining what constitutes sexual harassment in the first place. A supervisor's request for sexual favors from a subordinate that results in "tangible employment actions" necessarily changes the plaintiff's conditions of employment. Claims of "hostile environment" are more controversial because of the difficulty of distinguishing acceptable and unacceptable conduct in the work place. Individuals at work cannot ignore the sex of the employees they work with, yet they cannot be allowed to impose onerous requests and conditions upon them for that reason either.

The Court has tried to minimize these problems by emphasizing the requirement from *Meritor* that the harassment must be "severe or pervasive." Only the most egregious conduct can support a claim of sexual harassment based on a hostile environment. As the Court subsequently held in *Harris v. Forklift Systems, Inc.*,[94]

---

91. *Id.* at 758.
92. *Id.*
93. *Faragher*, 524 U.S. at 799.

94. Harris v. Forklift Systems, Inc., 510 U.S. 17 (1993).

however, the plaintiff need not introduce evidence of psychological injury in order to establish a hostile environment. As Justice O'Connor said, speaking for the Court, "Title VII comes into play before the harassing conduct leads to a nervous breakdown."[95] She also strongly suggested that the standards for sexual harassment should be determined according to the viewpoint of a "reasonable person," instead of a "reasonable woman" or a "reasonable man."[96]

The latter possibility was taken up in *Oncale v. Sundowner Offshore Services, Inc.*,[97] in which the Supreme Court recognized a claim by a male plaintiff alleging sexual harassment by other male employees. Although this form of harassment is obviously atypical, Title VII does not distinguish between male and female employees, either as victims of sexual harassment or as perpetrators. The formal interpretation of the prohibition against sex discrimination does not allow any such distinction.[98] Exactly when conduct between employees of the same sex becomes sexual harassment presents a more difficult practical question. The Court again stated that it was to be resolved by determining whether the "reasonable person" would find the harassing conduct to be so severe or pervasive as to alter the conditions of employment, emphasizing that such an inquiry depends upon all of the surrounding circumstances.[99]

Some commentators have been critical of this open-ended standard, framing their objections usually in terms of a chilling effect on free speech in the workplace in violation of the First Amendment.[100] These objections seem to gain force from the fact that harassing speech need not be legally obscene in order to give rise to liability under Title VII. Thus, in one widely discussed case, the court found a hostile environment based in part on pervasive displays of soft-core pornography in the workplace.[101] Focusing on speech alone, however, misstates the problems raised by hostile environment claims, to the detriment both of plaintiffs and defendants. Plaintiffs seek to vindicate their right to work in conditions that are free of discrimination. Harassment may, or may not, involve speech of a sexual nature; it involves any course of conduct that makes the workplace more difficult for members of one sex

---

95. *Id.* at 22.

96. The Court used the phrase "reasonable person" twice in stating the standard for liability, and Justice Ginsburg did so again in her concurring opinion. *Id.* at 21, 22; *id.* at 25 (Ginsburg, J., concurring).

97. 523 U.S. 75 (1998).

98. *Id.* at 78–80.

99. *Id.* at 81.

100. *E.g.*, Eugene Volokh, What Speech Does "Hostile Work Environment" Harassment Law Restrict?, 85 Geo. L.J. 627 (1997).

101. Robinson v. Jacksonville Shipyards, Inc., 760 F.Supp. 1486 (M.D. Fla. 1991).

than for members of the other. Speech is likely to figure in resolving this issue primarily as evidence of discriminatory intent, not as the very discrimination at issue. Claims of sexual harassment do not involve supervisors or co-employees who have exercised their right to speak out on issues of public significance, like the proper relations between the sexes. The speech and related conduct of alleged harassers is far too personal—too focused on the plaintiff and too revealing of themselves—to contribute to public debate.

Objections to the law of sexual harassment are more properly framed in exactly the opposite terms: as an invasion of privacy, that it is none of the government's business how alleged harassers conduct themselves towards members of the opposite sex (or, in cases like *Oncale*, members of the same sex). Yet the constitutional protection of privacy is necessarily attenuated in places of employment. Government employers have broad rights to search the offices of their employees and most businesses are subject to comprehensive regulations and correspondingly broad government investigations.[102] Upon entering the public sphere, employees lose much of the privacy that they would otherwise have at home. The point of the laws against sex discrimination is that women have a right to be in the workplace on the same terms as men. This is not to say that the scope of the prohibition against sexual harassment is not a cause for concern, but only that it is rarely a constitutional concern.

This concern, to the extent that it is legitimate, is fundamentally about the limits of the formal interpretation of the prohibition against sex discrimination in Title VII. People take account of sex and gender roles in a great variety of ways in dealing with one another. It is idle to suppose that they will suddenly abandon these deeply ingrained attitudes and reactions when they go to work. Which forms of conduct are deeply offensive depends on changing cultural standards. Comments on an individual's appearance can vary, often by imperceptible degrees, from casual compliments to obsessive interest in physical features. And conduct apart from speech can vary at least as much. Only the most extreme cases, however, go beyond offensiveness and become "severe or pervasive" harassment. Although this is a question for the jury under existing

---

102. O'Connor v. Ortega, 480 U.S. 709 (1987) (public employers can conduct warrantless searches of offices and desks of their employees); Marshall v. Barlow's, Inc., 436 U.S. 307, 320–21 (1978) (warrant required for search of private business but need only be based reasonable legislative or administrative standards for investigation).

law,[103] it is one of common experience—or more precisely, what goes beyond the outer limits of common experience—that the jury is eminently capable of deciding. Although resolution of these claims by the jury creates some degree of uncertainty, it makes more sense than either of the extremes: either abandoning claims of sexual harassment entirely or using them as a vehicle to impose codes of conduct on employers and their employees. With claims of sexual harassment, the law has encountered the limits of a formal approach to the prohibition against sex discrimination.

These limits became apparent with respect to a distinct but related issue, also raised by *Oncale v. Sundowner Offshore Services, Inc.* It is whether Title VII prohibits discrimination on the basis of sexual orientation. On a formal approach, the sex of someone with whom an employee has sexual relations should not be open to consideration by an employer. Just as an employer cannot allocate different health insurance benefits to employees based on the sex of their spouse, as the Court held in *Newport News Shipbuilding & Dry Dock Co. v. EEOC,*[104] an employer should also be barred from discrimination based on the sex of an employee's sexual partner. No court, however, has taken this step and *Oncale* has been limited to harassment based on the sex of the employee alone.[105]

Bills have been introduced in Congress to amend Title VII to prohibit discrimination on the basis of sexual orientation but have not been passed by either house.[106] In constitutional law, the Supreme Court has recognized a right to engage in gay sex, but not a general right to avoid discrimination on this ground. In *Lawrence v. Texas,*[107] the Court held that the states had no legitimate interest in criminalizing homosexual conduct between consenting adults, overruling its prior decision to the contrary.[108] The Court relied on the Due Process Clause, stopping well short of a holding under the Equal Protection Clause that all classifications on the basis of sexual orientation were suspect and subject to strict scrutiny. As applied to employment, this holding does not reach private employers at all, because they do not engage in state action within the scope of the Fourteenth Amendment. It does extend to government employers, but it may leave them free to discriminate on the basis of sexual orientation, so long as the government stops short of

103. 42 U.S.C. § 1981a(a)(1), (c) (2000).

104. 462 U.S. 669 (1983).

105. *E.g.*, Simonton v. Runyon, 232 F.3d 33, 35 (2d Cir. 2000); Higgins v. New Balance Athletic Shoe, Inc., 194 F.3d 252, 259 (1st Cir. 1999).

106. *E.g.*, Employment Non–Discrimination Act of 2003, S. 1705, 108th Cong. (2003).

107. 539 U.S. 558 (2003).

108. Bowers v. Hardwick, 478 U.S. 186 (1986).

making homosexual conduct criminal. *Lawrence* does support the broader trend, evident in legislation in some states, to extend prohibitions against employment discrimination in this direction,[109] but it does so without equating discrimination on the basis of sexual orientation with discrimination on the basis of sex. On this issue, at least, substance triumphs over form.

109.   *See* Chapter 13.A *infra*.

Chapter VII

OTHER FORMS OF DISCRIMINATION AND DEFENSES UNDER TITLE VII

Title VII extends the model of racial discrimination beyond sex to national origin and religion. These forms of discrimination raise distinctive issues and present further variations on the different approaches—historical, economic, and remedial—that can be brought to bear on employment discrimination law. With respect to discrimination on the basis of national origin, the similarities to racial discrimination are dominant, but with respect to discrimination on the basis of religion, it is the differences that are striking. Like any complex regulatory scheme, Title VII also contains ancillary prohibitions that assist in enforcement of the statute. This chapter discusses those concerned with protection against retaliation and with discrimination in advertising. A few defenses and limits on coverage, which cut across all of the prohibitions in Title VII, also deserve a brief discussion. They raise issues of practical significance and illustrate the compromises embedded in any piece of legislation. Like the other issues treated in this chapter, they serve as a reminder that the logic of the law—and particularly the logic of legislation—must remain subject to the lessons of experience.

A. Discrimination on the Basis of National Origin

The prohibition in Title VII against discrimination on the basis of national origin raises three issues, the first more theoretical than the other two. The first concerns the BFOQ exception for national origin. There is no corresponding exception for race, yet classifications on the basis of race closely resemble those on the basis of national origin. What accounts for the different approach to these two, very similar forms of discrimination? The second issue concerns the uncertain relationship between national origin and citizenship. The law is now clear that Title VII does not prohibit discrimination based on citizenship, or more precisely, lack of citizenship, which often disqualifies an individual from working under the immigration laws. Nevertheless, status as an alien is inevitably intertwined with national origin because virtually all aliens have a foreign national origin. The third issue concerns the impact of "English only" rules in the workplace. Speaking a foreign language again correlates strongly with foreign national origin, so that a seemingly neutral requirement that all employees speak English imposes a significant disadvantage on certain ethnic minorities, such as Hispanics.

The common thread that unites all these issues is the absence of any sharp distinction between race and national origin. A plausible distinction, relying on a genetic definition of race and a cultural definition of national origin, has no basis in fact. Genetic variation within the conventionally accepted races is greater than genetic variation among them. Moreover, as the concept is usually invoked, race has as many cultural as physical components, as revealed, for instance, by the traditional classification of individuals of mixed race as belonging entirely to one race or another. Relying on the concept of national origin creates still more uncertainty because an individual's ancestors may come from several different nations and each nation may be defined in terms of ancestry or geography. Drawing fine distinctions between the contested concepts of race and national origin resembles—and perhaps even requires—an embarrassing analysis of what constitutes "purity of blood."[1]

In the abstract, it is easy to find cases in which the distinction between race and national origin can be drawn. A person of Japanese ancestry, for instance, might suffer discrimination based on racial status as an Asian or discrimination based on national origin as Japanese. Claims of discrimination on either of these grounds would have to be supported by different evidence that varies, for instance, with the treatment of Asians from other nations. All that these examples establish, however, is that particular individuals have multiple affiliations and that discrimination on the basis of any of them might be illegal. It is obviously possible to draw these distinctions, but not at all obvious that they should be drawn, causing discrimination on one ground to be treated differently from discrimination on the other.

The BFOQ for national origin squarely raises this issue, even more so than the BFOQ for sex. It is available only when an otherwise prohibited characteristic is "a bona fide occupational qualification reasonably necessary to the normal operation of that particular business or enterprise."[2] The BFOQ creates a narrow exception to the prohibitions against discrimination on the basis of

---

1. *See* Fullilove v. Klutznick, 448 U.S. 448, 533–35 & n.5 (1980) (Stevens, J., dissenting) (comparing distinctions drawn in an affirmative action program to racial laws in Nazi Germany).

2. § 703(e)(1), codified as 42 U.S.C. § 2000e–2(e)(1) (1988); 110 Cong. Rec. 2550, 7271 (1964).

sex, national origin, and religion, but not to the prohibition against discrimination on the basis of race. The omission of a BFOQ for race reflects a deliberate congressional decision to prohibit all racial classifications in employment. It also creates the anomaly that some classifications on the basis of national origin are permissible, while similar classifications on the basis of race are not. At least in constitutional law, the two forms of discrimination have been considered to be so similar that the prohibitions against each have been regarded as equivalent.[3]

As a matter of legal doctrine, the anomaly created by the BFOQ for national origin has been almost entirely eliminated by decisions giving it an exceedingly narrow interpretation. This feature of the BFOQ has been noted earlier in its application to sex discrimination[4] and it is even more pronounced with respect to national origin. The Supreme Court has never upheld a BFOQ for national origin. It has only suggested in dictum that the BFOQ might justify a requirement that executives of a subsidiary of a Japanese corporation be of Japanese origin.[5] Few lower courts have followed up on this suggestion.[6] It is not difficult to see why.

None of the different perspectives on employment discrimination law justifies a departure from the model of race for classifications on the basis of national origin. The history of discrimination against national origin groups, such as Chinese and Hispanics, is fully as worthy of condemnation as discrimination against groups conventionally defined by race. And in the case of some of these national origin groups, like the Chinese, discrimination on the basis of national origin is difficult to distinguish from discrimination on the basis of race. The economic theory of discrimination draws no distinction between racial and national origin groups, relying instead on tastes for discrimination and stereotyping, which apply equally to discrimination on both grounds. The remedial perspec-

---

3. *See* Grutter v. Bollinger, 539 U.S. 306, 316, 331–33 (2003); Korematsu v. United States, 323 U.S. 214 (1944); Hirabayashi v. United States, 320 U.S. 81 (1943).

4. *See* Chapter VI.E *supra.*

5. Sumitomo Shoji America, Inc. v. Avagliano, 457 U.S. 176, 189 n.19 (1982). This decision also raises the further question of the relationship between Title VII and "treaties of freedom and navigation" that allow foreign corporations in the United States to give preferential treatment to citizens of their own country. *See id.* at 178–80; MacNamara v. Korean Air Lines, 863

F.2d 1135, 1138–41 (3d Cir. 1988), *cert. denied*, 493 U.S. 944 (1989) (treaty provision that employers may select managers based on citizenship does not conflict with Title VII, but would conflict with and preempt Title VII if it resulted in a disparate impact on the basis of race or national origin).

6. Tram N. Nguyen, Note, When National Origin May Constitute a Bona Fide Occupational Qualification: The Friendship, Commerce, and Navigation Treaty as an Affirmative Defense to a Title VII Claim, 37 Colum. J. Transnat'l L. 215, 245–47 (1998).

tive, as well, does not presuppose that only racial discrimination requires special compensatory measures to counteract the effects of past discrimination. Each of these perspectives might yield different approaches to different instances of discrimination, but not according to such broad and uncertain categories as race and national origin.

Another form of discrimination, however, must be distinguished from discrimination on the basis of national origin. It is discrimination on the basis of citizenship, or stated negatively, discrimination based on alienage: against individuals who are not citizens. In *Espinoza v. Farah Manufacturing Co.*,[7] the Supreme Court held that discrimination against aliens did not constitute discrimination on the basis of national origin under Title VII. The employer, Farah Manufacturing Co., had located its plant near the Mexican border, but it refused to hire aliens of Mexican citizenship. Nevertheless, of those employed at the plant, 96 percent were American citizens of Mexican national origin. On these facts, the Court held that the exclusion of aliens from employment did not violate Title VII. Disparate treatment on the basis of alienage is not prohibited by Title VII, and at least in this case, it resulted in no disparate impact upon persons of Mexican national origin because they constituted the overwhelming majority of those employed at the plant.[8] In other cases, however, disparate treatment on the basis of alienage may result in disparate impact on the basis of national origin, causing a practical problem in applying the theory of disparate impact, and in particular, in defining the labor market so as to exclude aliens that the employer cannot legally hire.

This is a problem that cannot be easily resolved by judicial decisions. Indeed, as Justice Douglas pointed out in his dissent in *Espinoza*, "national origin" has a systematic connection to alienage because it refers, in its most common usage, to the country which an individual or an individual's ancestors came from.[9] Aliens, by definition, come from another country. Yet the Constitution recognizes the power of Congress "To establish an uniform Rule of Naturalization,"[10] which necessarily includes the power to regulate immigration.

Congress addressed the systematic connection between national origin and alienage in a comprehensive revision of the immigration and naturalization laws, the Immigration Reform and Control Act of 1986.[11] This act contained two complicated prohibitions

---

7. 414 U.S. 86 (1973).

8. *Id.* at 93.

9. *Id.* at 96 (Douglas, J., dissenting).

10. U.S. Const. art I, § 8.

11. Immigration Reform and Control Act of 1986, Pub. L. No. 99–603, 100 Stat. 3359 (1986), as amended, codified

against employment discrimination. The first was designed mainly to protect aliens who were lawfully in this country and had the right to work here despite their status as aliens. It extends, however, to any "protected individual," which includes citizens and several technically defined categories of aliens, and it prohibits any form of discrimination on the basis of "citizenship status." The second prohibition is against discrimination on the basis of national origin, but only by employers who are not covered by Title VII because they have fewer than fifteen employees.[12] Both prohibitions apply only to employers who have at least four employees.[13]

Another distinctive issue about national origin concerns the languages associated with particular ethnic groups. The most controversial cases concern "English only" rules in the workplace. The EEOC has taken the position that a requirement that employees speak English at all times, even on breaks, will be presumed to be discriminatory and that a requirement that employees speak English only at specified times, typically while actually working, must be justified by business necessity.[14] The circuit courts that have addressed this issue have disagreed with the EEOC, at least as to rules of the latter kind. They have applied the theory of disparate impact to such rules, but found insufficient evidence of adverse impact from restrictions on speaking a foreign language, usually Spanish, during working time.[15] The disagreement, as in many issues of employment discrimination law, concerns the burden of proof. The EEOC places the burden of proof on the defendant to justify a practice with a disparate impact on an ethnic minority while the courts impose it on the plaintiff to prove some substantial disadvantage suffered from a prohibition on speaking another language.

Beneath this technical issue, however, lie more basic questions about the nature of discrimination on the basis of national origin. Does it encompass cultural practices associated with national origin, so that harm can be presumed simply from an employer's restriction on those practices? Or is it limited to acting toward an individual based on his or her ancestry, with consequences that can be independently identified as harmful? These questions raise again the desirability of moving beyond a purely colorblind conception of

in 8 U.S.C. and scattered sections of 7, 18, 20, 29, and 42 U.S.C. (2000).

12. *Id.* § 274B(a)(2)(B), codified as 8 U.S.C. § 1324b(a)(2)(B) (2000).

13. *Id.* §§ 274B(a)(2)(A), 316(a), codified as 8 U.S.C. §§ 1324b(a)(2)(A), 1427(a) (2000).

14. 29 C.F.R. § 1606.7 (2006).

15. Garcia v. Spun Steak Co., 998 F.2d 1480, 1485–90 (9th Cir. 1993), *cert. denied*, 512 U.S. 1228 (1994); Garcia v. Gloor, 618 F.2d 264, 270 (5th Cir. 1980), *cert. denied*, 449 U.S. 1113 (1981).

equality and considering a remedial conception of equality—in this case, applied to distinctive cultural practices of particular ethnic groups. As with a remedial conception of sexual equality, the remedy would not be limited to compensating for past discrimination but would extend to conditions and practices related to national origin. On an economic perspective, of course, the employer's duty to adjust to these related characteristics would necessarily be limited. An employer would be given discretion to respond to demand from customers and co-workers for "English only" rules. Yet the competing perspectives on the law of employment discrimination suggest that such rules require a more thorough analysis than they have yet received.

B. Religious Discrimination

Religious discrimination takes a further step beyond racial discrimination in making cultural practices the focus of legal claims. Some religions are closely related to race or national origin, as is the case, for instance, with Judaism. Others have adherents from a variety of different groups, such as Catholicism. All religions, however, require more than simple ancestry as a condition of membership and the prohibition against religious discrimination must therefore identify the range of beliefs and practices that fall within the definition of religion. And, indeed, the degree to which the law protects religious practices, in addition to religious belief, has proved to be a controversial issue under Title VII, as well as the Constitution.

In protecting religions practices, the law imposes an affirmative duty upon employers to take religion into account, in contrast to the negative duty simply to treat employees equally without regard to religion. This represents a step away from a "religion blind" perspective and towards a remedial perspective in which the remedy, as with sex and national origin, is not limited to compensating for past discrimination. It also requires employers to adjust their business operations to the religious practices of their employees.

The scope of this duty, however, is contested and employers can argue from an economic perspective that they should not be forced to bear all of the cost of accommodating religion with employment. The individual employee, or those who share the same religious beliefs, should be required to bear most of the costs of their own religious practices. With respect to religion, this argument takes on added force because accommodating one religion's practices may amount to favoring it over religions with more

144

common practices. Unwarranted accommodation by employers may constitute discrimination on the basis of religion, and if the accommodation is required by law, it may result in an establishment of religion in violation of the First Amendment.

As this last point illustrates, constitutional law exercises a more direct influence over the definition of religious discrimination than over discrimination on other grounds. Most of this influence results from the dual nature of the protection of religion under the First Amendment, both against any law "prohibiting the free exercise" of religion, as well as any law "respecting an establishment of religion." Between these two clauses in the First Amendment, there is only a narrow range left for the permissible operation of the legal prohibitions against religious discrimination.

The contradictory implications of the religion clauses are nowhere better revealed than in the history of the Religious Freedom Restoration Act of 1993 (RFRA).[16] This act was intended to expand upon the constitutional protection of religious practices recognized by the Supreme Court, which required only strict neutrality toward religion.[17] RFRA prohibited the states and the federal government from imposing any substantial burden upon the exercise of religion, even by neutral rules of general application, unless it was accomplished by the least restrictive means available to serve a compelling government interest.[18] When the constitutionality of RFRA was subsequently considered by the Supreme Court, however, the statute was held unconstitutional insofar as it applied to the states.[19] According to the Court, RFRA exceeded the power of Congress to enforce constitutional rights under the Fourteenth Amendment and, instead, sought to define those rights contrary to the Court's own prior decisions. Although the details of this reasoning are complex and controversial, the ultimate result is clear: legislative protection of religious freedom can only operate within a narrow area defined by several different constitutional restrictions.

Title VII has stayed within this narrow area, partly because its provisions concerned with religion are framed flexibly enough to permit a narrow interpretation where one is necessary to avoid a substantial constitutional question. The BFOQ, which applies to religion, as it does to sex and national origin, has the greatest flexibility. It allows decisions based on an employee's religion only if it is a "bona fide occupational qualification reasonably necessary

---

16. 107 Stat. 1488, codified as 42 U.S.C. §§ 2000bb to 2000bb–4 (2000).

17. Employment Div., Dep't of Human Resources v. Smith, 494 U.S. 872, 878–82 (1990).

18. 42 U.S.C. § 2000bb–1 (2000).

19. City of Boerne v. Flores, 521 U.S. 507, 529–36 (1997).

to the normal operation of that particular business or enterprise."[20] Few commercial businesses can carry the burden of proof under this provision.[21] Moreover, the religious organizations most likely to invoke the BFOQ can take advantage of two other provisions that create broader exceptions to the prohibition against religious discrimination. Section 702 creates an exception for employment by religious organizations and schools "of individuals of a particular religion to perform work connected with the carrying on" of their activities[22] and section 703(e)(2) creates a similar, and seemingly redundant, exception for religious schools.[23] As the quoted phrase indicates, these exceptions explicitly allow only consideration of an individual's religion, but some decisions have allowed discrimination on other grounds as well. Thus, in order to avoid constitutional questions, churches have been allowed to discriminate on any ground in hiring ministers.[24] Other positions in religious organizations and schools, however, are excepted only from the prohibition against discrimination on the basis of religion.[25] These decisions have also upheld these exceptions against constitutional arguments, either that they are too narrow under the Free Exercise Clause, because they do not except religious institutions entirely from Title VII, or too broad under the Establishment Clause, because they entangle the government with religious institutions.[26]

These constitutional arguments have had a greater impact on another provision in Title VII, one that expands the prohibition against religious discrimination. Section 701(j) defines "religion" to include "all aspects of religious observance and practice, as well as belief, unless an employer demonstrates that he is unable to reasonably accommodate to an employee's or prospective employee's religious observance or practice without undue hardship on the conduct of the employer's business."[27] This broad definition of

---

20. § 703(e)(1), codified as 42 U.S.C. § 2000e–2(e)(1) (2000).

21. *See* United Auto. Workers v. Johnson Controls, Inc., 499 U.S. 187, 203–04 (1991).

22. § 702, codified as 42 U.S.C. § 2000e–1 (2000).

23. § 703(e)(2), codified as 42 U.S.C. § 2000e–2(e)(2) (2000). Section 702 originally was restricted to employees working in religious activities, but section 703(e)(2) was not. In 1972, however, section 702 was expanded to cover all the activities of religious organizations and schools. H.R. Rep. No. 92–899, at 16 (1972). This change made the exception in section 703(e)(2) for educational institutions largely redundant.

24. EEOC v. Southwestern Baptist Theological Seminary, 651 F.2d 277, 281–84 (5th Cir. 1981), *cert. denied*, 453 U.S. 912 (1981).

25. EEOC v. Mississippi College, 626 F.2d 477, 484–86 (5th Cir. 1980), *cert. denied*, 453 U.S. 912 (1981); Rayburn v. General Conference of Seventh–Day Adventists, 772 F.2d 1164, 1166–67 (4th Cir. 1985).

26. *Mississippi College*, 626 F.2d at 486–89.

27. § 701(j), codified as 42 U.S.C. § 2000e(j) (2000).

"religion" imposes a duty of reasonable accommodation upon employers that requires them to adjust their personnel decisions and policies to the religious practices of their employees.

The Supreme Court considered the extent of this duty in *Trans World Airlines, Inc. v. Hardison*,[28] holding that section 701(j) does not require employers to accommodate an employee's religious practices at "more than a *de minimis* cost."[29] The accommodation sought by the plaintiff in that case—a change in scheduling to allow him to observe the Sabbath as defined by his religion—was held to create an undue hardship. It would have required the employer either to leave the plaintiff's position empty, to pay overtime to another employee, or to transfer another employee with greater seniority rights into the position.[30] The first two of these alternatives would have imposed significant costs on the employer and the third would have subordinated the seniority rights of another employee who did not share the plaintiff's religious beliefs, resulting in unequal treatment on the basis of religion.[31] In narrowly interpreting the duty to accommodate, the Court implied, although it did not hold, that a narrow duty to accommodate was consistent with the Free Exercise Clause and that a broader duty to accommodate might be inconsistent with the Establishment Clause. The Court's narrow interpretation of section 701(j) appears to be designed to avoid these constitutional questions.

Subsequent decisions confirm this conclusion. In *Estate of Thornton v. Caldor, Inc.*,[32] the Court held unconstitutional a state statute that gave employees an absolute right to refuse to work on the Sabbath of their choice. The Court held that this statute violated the Establishment Clause because it conferred a benefit only on employees who observed the Sabbath and because it allowed for no exceptions, as, for instance, when the employer had attempted to make other reasonable accommodations. In a concurring opinion, Justice O'Connor suggested that these facts distinguished the reasonable accommodation provision in section 701(j) from the state statute before the Court.[33] In accord with this suggestion, the Court has held that the duty to accommodate under Title VII does not require the employer to accept an employee's proposed accommodation if its own accommodation is otherwise

28. 432 U.S. 63 (1977).
29. *Id.* at 84.
30. *Id.* at 84–85.
31. *Id.* at 84.
32. 472 U.S. 703 (1985).

33. *Id.* at 711–12 (O'Connor, J., concurring). *Accord*, Protos v. Volkswagen of America, Inc., 797 F.2d 129, 135–37 (3d Cir.), *cert. denied*, 479 U.S. 972 (1986).

adequate.[34]

These decisions illustrate the limits of a remedial approach to discrimination on the basis of religion. At least as the Supreme Court currently interprets the religion clauses of the First Amendment, the legislature can only require evenhanded treatment of employees regardless of religious belief, or nonbelief. This restriction necessarily supports a "religion blind" interpretation of Title VII and undermines any attempt to confer significant advantages upon adherents of any one religion. As a constitutional matter, these arguments apply only to religious discrimination. A provision for reasonable accommodation of disabilities in the Americans with Disabilities Act, framed in almost the same terms as the duty of reasonable accommodation of religious practices under Title VII, does not raise any such constitutional questions.

Yet wholly apart from constitutional questions, a remedial conception of equality raises questions, most apparent from an economic perspective, about how broadly to define the affirmative obligations upon employers to accommodate their employees' religious practices. They have no control over their employees' religious affiliations and therefore cannot control most of the cost of accommodating different religious practices. Title VII recognizes these limits on the affirmative obligations of employers by requiring only "reasonable" accommodation and only "without undue hardship." The point, however, is a more general one. Employers cannot be required to eliminate all of the consequences of religious belief (or other personal characteristics defined as grounds of discrimination). Requiring them to do so might lead to inequality in other respects: towards the employers themselves, who may not be able to shift the cost elsewhere, and towards other employees who do not benefit from special remedial measures. The latter inequality, of course, is what has motivated most of the opposition to affirmative action. The duty to accommodate religious practices illustrates, in another form, how the remedial perspective on employment discrimination law is limited by arguments derived from alternative perspectives.

C. Retaliation

Like many comprehensive statutes, Title VII contains substantive provisions that safeguard the operation of its procedures for enforcement. In Title VII, these are prohibitions against retaliation: personnel decisions and other actions by employers that discourage

---

34. Ansonia Bd. of Educ. v. Philbrook, 479 U.S. 60 (1986).

or punish attempts to enforce rights under the statute. Section 704(a) protects employees and applicants for employment from retaliation for having asserted their rights in two separate ways: for having "opposed any practice made an unlawful employment practice by this title" or for having "made a charge, testified, assisted, or participated in any manner in an investigation, proceeding, or hearing under this title."[35] The first of these clauses, protecting opposition by self-help, has generally been more narrowly interpreted than the second, protecting participation in enforcement proceedings.

Opposition under the first clause raises questions about whether it uses the right forms of protest. Some forms, such as violence or destruction of property, are clearly unprotected. The difficult questions concern the traditional methods of unions and labor organizers, such as strikes, picketing, and boycotts. In a case arising under the National Labor Relations Act (NLRA), the Supreme Court held that picketing in protest of allegedly discriminatory practices was not protected from employer retaliation when it was not authorized by the union that represented the employees involved.[36] Although the Court did not decide the question whether the employees' conduct was protected under section 704(a),[37] its holding would have been inconsequential if the employees were protected from retaliation under Title VII for conduct that was unprotected under the NLRA. In any event, other federal courts have held that protection for opposition through economic pressure is less extensive under section 704 than under the corresponding provision of the NLRA.[38] This result is generally correct, since Title VII sets up a scheme of administrative and judicial remedies for employment discrimination, whereas the NLRA sets up a scheme of collective bargaining that contemplates the use of economic pressure by both labor and management.

The only respect in which the opposition clause has been broadly construed concerns the permissible aims, not the permissible means, of protest. In order to gain protection, the protest need not be against an employment practice known to be unlawful. The person engaged in opposition need only have a reasonable belief that the practice is prohibited by Title VII.[39] These rules justifiably take account of the difficulty—and perhaps for nonlawyers, the

---

35. § 704(a), codified as 42 U.S.C. § 2000e–3(a) (2000).

36. Emporium Capwell Co. v. Western Addition Community Org., 420 U.S. 50 (1975).

37. *Id.* at 70–73.

38. NLRA § 7, codified as 29 U.S.C. § 157 (2000). *See, e.g.,* Hochstadt v. Worcester Found. for Experimental Biology, 545 F.2d 222 (1st Cir. 1976).

39. *E.g.,* Berg v. La Crosse Cooler Co., 612 F.2d 1041 (7th Cir. 1980).

impossibility—of determining whether a disputed employment practice actually violates Title VII.

In contrast to the opposition clause, the participation clause has been construed to protect virtually all means of participation in enforcement proceedings. The clause protects participation in state proceedings related to enforcement of Title VII,[40] and it protects all other forms of participation, even those that might be defamatory under state law.[41] In the latter case, the employer's remedy is not by way of self-help, through retaliation, but through a lawsuit in state court.[42] Any adverse action taken by an employer after an employee has commenced enforcement proceedings, or participated in them in any way, can support a claim of retaliation. For this reason, the participation clause plays an important role in private litigation under Title VII. It often furnishes an added claim for relief, in addition to the claim of discrimination that gave rise to enforcement proceedings in the first place.

The general structure of proof for claims of retaliation follows *McDonnell Douglas Corp. v. Green*[43] in shifting the burden of production from the plaintiff to the defendant. The plaintiff has the burden of producing evidence that he engaged in protected activity, that he suffered an adverse decision from the employer, and that there was a causal connection between his protected activity and the employer's decision. The adverse decision need not involve harms related to employment or at the workplace, but need only be "materially adverse to a reasonable employee or job applicant" and "harmful to the point that they could well dissuade a reasonable worker from making or supporting a charge of discrimination."[44] Once the plaintiff establishes the causal connection between such an adverse decision and protected activity, the defendant has the burden of producing a legitimate, nondiscriminatory reason for its decision. And the plaintiff has the burden of producing evidence that the offered reason is a pretext for retaliation.[45] As with individual claims of disparate treatment, the burden of persuasion remains entirely on the plaintiff.[46]

40. Hicks v. ABT Assocs., Inc., 572 F.2d 960, 968–69 (3d Cir. 1978) (dictum).

41. Pettway v. American Cast Iron Pipe Co., 411 F.2d 998, 1003–08 (5th Cir. 1969).

42. *Id.* at 1007 n.22.

43. 411 U.S. 792 (1973).

44. Burlington Northern & Santa Fe Ry. Co. v. White, 126 S.Ct. 2405, 2409 (2006).

45. Jalil v. Avdel Corp., 873 F.2d 701, 706 (3d Cir. 1989), *cert. denied*, 493 U.S. 1023 (1990); Taitt v. Chemical Bank, 849 F.2d 775, 777 (2d Cir. 1988); Miller v. Fairchild Industries, Inc., 797 F.2d 727, 731 (9th Cir. 1986), *cert. denied*, 494 U.S. 1056 (1990).

46. *Jalil*, 873 F.2d at 706.

A claim of retaliation, if it is supported by sufficient evidence to be submitted to the jury, raises the value of the plaintiff's potential recovery in two ways. First, a plaintiff who has been the victim of retaliation has a greater chance of winning the sympathy of the jury on the underlying claim of discrimination. And second, proof of retaliation also goes a long way toward justifying an award of punitive damages, which are available only upon proof that the defendant acted "with malice or with reckless indifference to the federally protected rights of an aggrieved individual."[47] As with claims of discrimination, the crucial issue in retaliation claims is whether the plaintiff has presented sufficient evidence to survive a motion for summary judgment or a motion for judgment as a matter of law, in order to have the claim submitted to the jury.

D. Discrimination in Advertising

Section 704(b) generally prohibits discrimination in advertising for employment.[48] Because it regulates the press, section 704(b) raises questions under the First Amendment, but these are easily resolved. If the underlying activity can be prohibited—consider selling narcotics—then advertisements to do the activity can be prohibited as well. Accordingly, the Supreme Court has readily upheld statutory prohibitions against discrimination in "help wanted" advertising.[49]

Section 704(b), however, does raise a difficult issue of standing. The individuals harmed by advertising in violation of section 704(b) are only those who have been deterred from applying for the job advertised. Those who applied for the job, even if they were rejected, were not harmed by the advertisement, even if they suffered discrimination in hiring. By definition, the latter individuals applied for the job despite the advertisement. Nevertheless only those least likely to sue—deterred nonapplicants—appear to have standing to assert claims under section 704(b). Enforcement of this provision therefore has mainly been by its impact on other claims of discrimination, but it has not been the less effective for that. Few forms of evidence are as compelling as discriminatory advertising to support an underlying claim of discrimination.

E. Seniority Systems

An important exception to the prohibition against discrimination in Title VII is the seniority clause of section 703(h). It provides

47. 42 U.S.C. § 1981a(b)(1) (2000).

48. § 704(b), codified as 42 U.S.C. § 2000e–3(b) (2000).

49. *E.g.*, Pittsburgh Press Co. v. Pittsburgh Comm'n on Human Relations, 413 U.S. 376 (1973).

that differences in terms and conditions of employment pursuant to bona fide seniority systems do not violate the statute, "provided that such differences are not the result of an intention to discriminate because of race, color, religion, sex, or national origin." The effect of this provision, at least in the years immediately following enactment of Title VII, was to protect white employees with accumulated seniority. They were allowed to retain the higher-level jobs that they held—possibly as a result of past discrimination in hiring and promotions—and to receive priority for further promotions and protection from layoffs under the seniority system. These employees were allowed to keep the benefits of high seniority even if it had been gained through decisions that Title VII now made illegal. Protecting the job security of incumbent employees spread the cost of eliminating past discrimination so that it did not fall disproportionately upon them by causing them to lose their jobs. Yet it inevitably had the consequence of impeding the progress of minority employees and women into jobs from which they had previously been excluded.

The ultimate fairness of this compromise might be questioned, but not its necessity. Protecting the seniority rights of white employees plainly resulted in a disparate impact upon minority employees and women who, through past discrimination, had never had an opportunity to accumulate seniority. In the abstract, it is difficult to justify striking any particular balance between the interests of incumbent white employees, who might not have engaged in discrimination themselves, with the claims of victims of past discrimination, who deserve full compensation. Obtaining democratic support for the laws against discrimination, however, required some such balance to be struck. And, indeed, unions sought the seniority clause of section 703(h) in order to protect the expectations of their members based on existing seniority systems.[50] This lesson extends beyond the compromises necessary in the legislative process. Laws against employment discrimination cannot be effectively implemented and enforced without the cooperation of the great majority of employers and fellow workers who are subject to their provisions. Assuring their support is essential to making lasting changes in the workplace. Compromises like the seniority clause of section 703(h) are more than a concession to the exigen-

---

50. *See* Hugh Davis Graham, The Civil Rights Era: Origins and Develop- ment of National Policy 1960–72 139–40 (1990).

cies of democratic politics. They are a recognition of the only way to achieve lasting change in a democratic society.

Seemingly contrary to this reasoning, the lower federal courts initially gave the seniority clause a narrow interpretation, holding that it did not protect departmental seniority systems that worked to the particular advantage of white employees in higher-level jobs.[51] But in *International Brotherhood of Teamsters v. United States*,[52] the Supreme Court held that all seniority systems were protected, whether departmental or plant-wide. In order to establish that a seniority system violates Title VII, a plaintiff must prove that it is not "bona fide" or is "the result of an intention to discriminate." This is equivalent to proof of disparate treatment, so that the seniority clause in section 703(h) does not create an exception to claims on this ground. It does, however, bar claims of disparate impact, preventing attacks upon seniority systems based solely on their discriminatory effects. In subsequent cases, the Court has reaffirmed this holding, applying it to all seniority systems created after the effective date of Title VII,[53] and to one that favored a group of "permanent employees," all of whom were white, because they had worked at least forty-five weeks in a single calendar year.[54]

The Court has left unclear, however, how disparate treatment in a seniority system is to be proved. In a procedural ruling, the Court held that the district court's findings on this issue must be accepted on appeal unless clearly erroneous,[55] but apart from the suggestion in *Teamsters* that a seniority system was illegal if it had its "genesis in racial discrimination,"[56] the Court has not elaborated on the ways in which disparate treatment can be proved. The disparate impact of a seniority system may be difficult to distinguish from disparate treatment. Seniority systems carry forward the effects of past discrimination by awarding seniority to white employees who benefitted from past discrimination against blacks. *Teamsters* implies that such disparate impact alone does not establish disparate treatment. Additional evidence of discrimination in related employment practices may be sufficient, such as employer's decision to replace a plant-wide seniority system with a departmen-

51. Local 189, United Papermakers v. United States, 416 F.2d 980 (5th Cir. 1969), *cert. denied*, 397 U.S. 919 (1970); Quarles v. Philip Morris, Inc., 279 F.Supp. 505 (E.D. Va. 1968).

52. 431 U.S. 324 (1977).

53. American Tobacco Co. v. Patterson, 456 U.S. 63 (1982).

54. California Brewers Ass'n v. Bryant, 444 U.S. 598 (1980).

55. Pullman–Standard v. Swint, 456 U.S. 273 (1982).

56. *International Bhd. of Teamsters*, 431 U.S. at 356.

tal seniority system as soon as blacks were allowed to work in lower-level jobs.[57]

The Court has formulated clear rules on two issues related to seniority systems: statutes of limitations and remedies. In *United Air Lines, Inc. v. Evans*,[58] the Court held that a bona fide seniority system did not preserve a claim of discriminatory discharge that was otherwise barred by the statute of limitations. The alleged discrimination arose independently of the seniority system, involving a "no marriage" rule that applied only to female flight attendants. The seniority system was implicated only in perpetuating the effects of this initial discriminatory act. As explained more fully in the next chapter,[59] the holding in *Evans* applies at least to the timeliness of claims based on a single discriminatory act. As to claims of discrimination in the seniority system itself, these are now governed by a separate provision in Title VII which starts the limitation period running from three different events, whichever occurs latest: when the seniority system is adopted, when the plaintiff is subject to the seniority system, or when the plaintiff is injured by the application of the seniority system.[60] This provision was added by the Civil Rights Act of 1991 to liberalize the limitation period for these claims and to overrule a more restrictive decision of the Supreme Court.[61]

On the issue of remedies, in *Franks v. Bowman Transportation Co.*,[62] the Court held that section 703(h) does not limit awards of remedial seniority to victims of discrimination. They may receive awards of seniority to determine fringe benefits payable by the employer and to determine rights in competition with other employees, such as protection from layoffs. The district court's discretion to make such awards is to be exercised according to the same standard applicable to awards of back pay. Remedial seniority is to be denied "only for reasons which, if applied generally, would not frustrate the central statutory purposes of eradicating discrimina-

---

57. Myers v. Gilman Paper Co., 527 F.Supp. 647 (S.D. Ga. 1981). Several decisions vacated and remanded by the Supreme Court eventually resulted in findings that a seniority system was not bona fide. Terrell v. United States Pipe & Foundry Co., 644 F.2d 1112 (5th Cir. 1981), *vacated and remanded sub nom.* International Ass'n of Machinists v. Terrell, 456 U.S. 955 (1982), *on remand* 696 F.2d 1132 (5th Cir. 1983), *on remand*, 39 Fair Empl. Prac. Cas. (BNA) 571 (N.D. Ala. 1985); United States v. Georgia Power Co., 634 F.2d 929 (5th Cir. 1981), *vacated and remanded sub nom.* Local

Union Number 84, Int'l Bhd. of Elec. Workers, 456 U.S. 952 (1982), *on remand*, 695 F.2d 890 (5th Cir. 1983).

58. 431 U.S. 553 (1977).

59. *See* Chapter VIII. A.4 *infra*.

60. § 706(e)(2), codified as 42 U.S.C. § 2000e–5(e)(2) (2000).

61. The overruled decision is Lorance v. AT & T Tech., Inc., 490 U.S. 900 (1989).

62. 424 U.S. 747 (1976).

tion throughout the economy and making persons whole for injuries suffered through past discrimination." Section 703(h) does not limit the broad power of the federal courts to remedy proven violations of Title VII. It only limits the circumstances in which such violations can be found based on the operation of a seniority system.

F. Coverage

The coverage of Title VII raises numerous issues of varying significance. The main provisions on coverage apply Title VII to all employers with fifteen or more employees in an industry affecting commerce; all labor organizations in an industry affecting commerce; and all employment agencies that regularly provide employment to statutorily defined employers.[63] The statutory definition of "employer" includes state and local government, but excludes the United States and related entities, Indian tribes, and certain private membership clubs.[64] The exception for the United States and related entities is largely, but not entirely, offset by the special provisions for coverage of employees of the United States.[65]

These provisions reflect diverse concerns, such as protecting the freedom of association of smaller employers, or at least leaving them to be regulated only by state law; recognizing the greater ability of larger employers to comply with a complex statutory scheme; and providing a special remedy for federal employees that is consistent with the remedies available under the civil service system. The limit on the size of employers, together with provisions in the Civil Rights Act of 1991 limiting liability for damages based on the size of the employer, has led most of the circuits to hold that individual agents of an employer are not covered by the statute at all.[66] This issue has been most frequently litigated in sexual harassment cases, in which the plaintiff has sued both the employer and a supervisor who has allegedly engaged in harassment.[67]

---

63. § 701(b)–(e), codified as 42 U.S.C. § 2000e(a)–(e) (2000).

64. § 701(a)–(b), codified as 42 U.S.C. § 2000e(a)–(b) (2000).

65. § 717(a), codified as 42 U.S.C. § 2000e–16(a) (2000). The Civil Rights Act of 1991 also added special provisions for claims by employees of the Senate (but not the House of Representatives, who are subject to provisions in the House Rules). §§ 301–25, codified as 2 U.S.C. §§ 1201 to 1224 (2000).

66. *E.g.*, Tomka v. Seiler Corp., 66 F.3d 1295 (2d Cir. 1995); Miller v. Maxwell's Int'l Inc., 991 F.2d 583 (9th Cir. 1993), *cert. denied*, 510 U.S. 1109 (1994).

67. *E.g.*, Paroline v. Unisys Corp., 879 F.2d 100 (4th Cir. 1989), *vacated in part on other grounds*, 900 F.2d 27 (4th Cir. 1990); Grant v. Lone Star Co., 21 F.3d 649 (5th Cir. 1994).

Apart from routine litigation over the question whether an employer has fifteen or more employees,[68] most of the questions about coverage have addressed two additional issues of general significance: whether Title VII extends to all aspects of employment and whether it extends to employees who work outside the United States. The first question has been resolved in favor of coverage, reaching such conditions and benefits from employment as eligibility for partnership in a law firm[69] and pension benefits.[70] The question of coverage of employees working overseas was first resolved by the Supreme Court against coverage,[71] but this decision was overruled by the Civil Rights Act of 1991, which explicitly extends coverage to United States citizens employed overseas by United States employers and corporations controlled by United States employers.[72] This extension of coverage is subject to a defense that compliance with Title VII would violate the law of the country of employment.[73]

68. *E.g.*, Clackamas Gastroenterology Associates v. Wells, 538 U.S. 440 (2003); Walters v. Metropolitan Educ. Enters., Inc., 519 U.S. 202 (1997).

69. Hishon v. King & Spalding, 467 U.S. 69, 74–76 (1984).

70. Arizona Governing Comm. v. Norris, 463 U.S. 1073 (1983) (per curiam); City of Los Angeles Dep't of Water & Power v. Manhart, 435 U.S. 702, 708–11 (1978).

71. EEOC v. Arabian Am. Oil Co., 499 U.S. 244 (1991).

72. §§ 701(f), 702(c), codified as 42 U.S.C. §§ 2000e(f),–1(c) (2000).

73. § 702(b), codified as 42 U.S.C. § 2000e–1(b) (2000).

Chapter VIII

PROCEDURES UNDER TITLE VII

Title VII establishes an enforcement scheme that is divided into three stages: state or local administrative proceedings; investigation and conciliation by the Equal Employment Opportunity Commission (EEOC); and litigation by private individuals, or by the EEOC or the Attorney General. This three-stage scheme is inherently more complicated than any simple mechanism for purely administrative or judicial enforcement. Questions repeatedly have been raised about the relationship among the different stages of enforcement, the time limits that apply at each stage, and the effect that these have on the remedies ultimately available to the plaintiff. As a result, the legal doctrine governing these issues has become ever more complex, making litigation of employment discrimination cases highly technical and specialized. The doctrinal complexity, moreover, does not point in a single direction, but serves a variety of different purposes, some favorable to plaintiffs, others to defendants.

Any scheme of procedures and remedies must promote, at least to some degree, the fair and efficient enforcement of the obligations defined by substantive law. In Title VII, these are obligations not to discriminate. Title VII thus gives individuals who believe they are victims of discrimination a fair opportunity to raise their claims in an administrative or judicial forum, and correspondingly, it gives employers an opportunity to defend against these claims. By requiring resort to administrative proceedings, Title VII also attempts to reduce the cost of resolving claims of discrimination, and at the remedy stage, it provides a full range of legal and equitable relief to compensate for past discrimination and to deter future discrimination. Superimposed on these standard procedural values, however, are additional policies concerned with protecting federalism, fostering settlement, limiting administrative enforcement, and assisting plaintiffs in obtaining legal counsel. All of these additional values can be implemented, on an optimistic view, without detracting from the fair and efficient enforcement of the statute. But on a pessimistic view, these additional values inevitably require some compromise with the standard procedural values of fairness and efficiency. Even if these values coincide in support of some procedures and remedies, they diverge and conflict with respect to others.

157

The first stage of Title VII enforcement, through state and local administrative remedies, illustrates how values of federalism complicate the resolution of Title VII claims. These remedies must be exhausted, but only if a state or locality has enacted a statute or ordinance against employment discrimination.[1] An EEOC regulation contains an authoritative list of states and localities with appropriate agencies.[2] The EEOC must give "substantial weight" to the findings of state and local agencies,[3] but the courts are not bound by any administrative findings, whether by state or local agencies or by the EEOC.[4] Federal courts, however, are bound by the decisions of state courts reviewing the decisions of state or local administrative agencies.[5] Thus, a plaintiff who wants to preserve her right to bring a Title VII claim in federal court must, first, exhaust state or local administrative proceedings, but second, avoid state judicial proceedings that would preclude a further claim or litigation on issues in federal court.

The second stage of enforcement, through administrative proceedings in the EEOC, reveals both the policy in favor of settlement and the restrictions on administrative authority under Title VII. The EEOC exercises no adjudicatory authority, except in cases filed by federal employees or by certain high-level state employees, for which special procedures apply.[6] The only powers of the EEOC are to investigate charges, to determine whether there is reasonable cause to support them, to attempt to reach a settlement through conciliation, and to decide whether to sue or, if the charge is filed against a state or local government agency, to refer it to the Attorney General for a decision whether or not to sue.[7] If conciliation does not result in a settlement that is satisfactory to the charging party and if the EEOC or the Attorney General decides

---

1. § 706(c), (d), codified as 42 U.S.C. § 2000e–5(c), (d) (2000); 29 C.F.R. § 1601.70 (2006).

2. 29 C.F.R. § 1601.74 (2006).

3. § 706(b), codified as 42 U.S.C. § 2000e–5(b) (2000).

4. Astoria Fed. Sav. & Loan Ass'n v. Solimino, 501 U.S. 104, 110–14 (1991); University of Tennessee v. Elliott, 478 U.S. 788, 795–96 (1986); McDonnell Douglas Corp. v. Green, 411 U.S. 792, 798–99 (1973). However, the federal courts may be bound by the unreviewed decisions of state agencies as they affect claims under other federal statutes. *University of Tennessee*, 478 U.S. at 796–99.

5. Kremer v. Chemical Constr. Corp., 456 U.S. 461 (1982).

6. § 717, codified as 42 U.S.C. § 2000e–16 (2000); Civil Rights Act of 1991, Pub. L. No. 102–166, § 321, 105 Stat. 1071, 1097. Employees of the House of Representatives and the Senate are subject to separate procedures for each house. Civil Rights Act of 1991, Pub. L. No. 102–166, § 117, 301–19, 105 Stat. 1071, 1080, 1088–96. Presidential employees also are subject to special procedures. Pub. L. No. 102–166 § 320, 105 Stat. 1071, 1096–97.

7. § 706(f), codified as 42 U.S.C. § 2000e–5(f) (2000); EEOC v. Illinois State Tollway Auth., 800 F.2d 656 (7th Cir. 1986).

not to sue, the EEOC issues a right-to-sue letter to the charging party.[8] Apart from the requirement of exhaustion of state and local administrative remedies and timely filing with the EEOC, the details of prior administrative proceedings are not generally significant in Title VII litigation.

At the third stage, after receipt of a right-to-sue letter, the charging party can sue in either federal or state court.[9] At that point, the statute encourages plaintiffs to sue by providing for an award of attorney's fees to prevailing parties,[10] a provision that has been interpreted to favor plaintiffs by requiring an award of attorney's fees to them in most cases in which they prevail. By contrast, prevailing defendants are seldom entitled to an award of attorney's fees.[11] As so interpreted, this provision subsidizes the plaintiff's litigation costs, creating a contingent fee that does not come out of the plaintiff's own monetary recovery but out of an independent award against the defendant. Plaintiffs and their attorneys are therefore more likely to sue, particularly on claims that would not support a large award of back pay or damages but that nevertheless have a significant prospect of success.

Considered separately, each of the policies implemented at each stage of a Title VII case appears to have some plausible support. Encouraging resort to state and local remedies generates greater support for the ultimate goal of eliminating employment discrimination. Fostering settlement avoids the further costs of litigation. Limiting the power of the EEOC as a federal agency assures that cases will ultimately be resolved by the impartial authority of the courts. And encouraging plaintiffs to sue through an award of attorney's fees provides individuals with an opportunity to obtain full legal representation, even if they would not otherwise have the means to do so. Yet considered together, these policies yield a complex system of enforcement that threatens to sidetrack employment discrimination cases into a multitude of collateral procedural issues.

Nowhere is the complexity of these procedures more apparent than in the statute of limitations that governs claims under Title VII. This chapter begins with a detailed discussion of this issue, followed by an analysis of the distinctive procedures for public actions. A section on private actions then considers the role that private actions, and particularly class actions, play in enforcement

---

8. § 706(f), codified as 42 U.S.C. § 2000e–5(f) (2000).

9. Yellow Freight Sys., Inc. v. Donnelly, 494 U.S. 820 (1990).

10. § 706(k), codified as 42 U.S.C. § 2000e–5(k) (2000).

11. Christiansburg Garment Co. v. EEOC, 434 U.S. 412, 416–17, 421 (1978).

of the statute. Actions by federal employees are treated in a separate section that discusses the unique procedures for their claims. A concluding section then examines the preclusive effect of judgments under Title VII and the extent to which they are affected by judgments in other proceedings. The topic of remedies, which is closely related to these issues of procedure, is taken up in the following chapter.

A. Statute of Limitations

The time limits for filing claims of discrimination have been the most frequently litigated issue under the enforcement provisions of Title VII. Defendants have raised this issue because, if they are successful on it, they obtain a complete defense to a claim of discrimination. As the Supreme Court said in one of its leading decisions on this subject, a discriminatory act which is not the subject of a timely charge "is merely an unfortunate event in history which has no present legal consequences."[12] Moreover, even if the defense is not entirely successful, it can still limit the defendant's liability by restricting the period for which back pay and damages can be awarded. Just as defendants have strong reasons to raise the defense, plaintiffs have equally strong reasons to oppose it. If they do not establish that they have complied with the applicable time limits, they lose their right to relief regardless of the underlying merits of their claims.

Defendants can raise the issue of failure to comply with the statute of limitations at each stage of a Title VII case. They typically do so after a claim has been filed in court, but the defense can concern failure to comply with the time limits for administrative proceedings also. It is therefore useful to consider the statute of limitations as it applies at each successive stage of a Title VII case.

1. State or Local Administrative Proceedings

The statute of limitations for filing with a state or local administrative agency affects only the ability of a plaintiff to pursue a claim under state or local law. It has no effect on a plaintiff's claim under Title VII. Although a plaintiff must exhaust state and local administrative remedies in a timely fashion in order to pursue a claim under state or local law, a plaintiff need not do so in order to pursue a claim under Title VII. The Supreme Court reached this

12. United Air Lines, Inc. v. Evans,
431 U.S. 553, 558 (1977).

conclusion in *Oscar Mayer & Co. v. Evans*,[13] a case under the Age Discrimination in Employment Act, but one concerning a provision on exhausting state and local administrative remedies identical to that in Title VII. This provision requires only "the filing of a written and signed statement of the facts upon which the proceeding is based" in order to commence state or local proceedings. Relying extensively on the legislative history of Title VII, the Court reasoned that this provision listed all of the requirements for a filing sufficient to exhaust state or local remedies. Since filing within the state or local limitation was not listed, it was not necessary.[14]

This reasoning might be doubted, since the provision in question seems to concern pleading requirements rather than time limits for filing, but whatever its merits, it has one undoubted attraction. It simplifies the application of the statute of limitations, which would otherwise become impractically complex through the interaction of the different time limits for filing with state or local agencies and for filing with the EEOC. As the next subsection reveals, the time limits for filing with the EEOC alone are already complex enough.

2. EEOC Proceedings

The time limits for filing with the EEOC depend upon the existence of a state or local agency to enforce a statute or ordinance against employment discrimination. In a state or locality without such an agency, of which very few are left, a charge must be filed with the EEOC within 180 days of the alleged discrimination.[15] In a state or locality with such an agency, a charge must be filed with the EEOC within 300 days of the alleged discrimination or within 30 days of notice of termination of state or local proceedings, whichever period expires first.[16] Moreover, if a charge is filed with the EEOC without first exhausting appropriate state or local administrative remedies, the EEOC must defer action on the charge for 60 days or until the termination of state or local proceedings, whichever occurs first.[17]

In an effort to simplify this network of overlapping time limits, the EEOC has taken steps to make the process of filing a charge easier for individual plaintiffs, who at this stage of a Title VII case may well be acting without the assistance of counsel. These steps,

---

13. 441 U.S. 750 (1979).

14. *Id.* at 759.

15. § 706(e), codified as 42 U.S.C. § 2000e–5(e)(1) (2000).

16. *Id.*

17. § 706(c), (d), codified as 42 U.S.C. § 2000e–5(c), (d) (2000).

taken under the EEOC's authority to issue procedural regulations and to enter into "worksharing agreements" with state and local agencies,[18] have been approved by the Supreme Court in a series of decisions. The resulting procedures accommodate the otherwise conflicting policies of preserving federalism and of providing an efficient means of resolving claims of discrimination. Plaintiffs must still exhaust available state and local remedies, but the EEOC assists them in meeting the technical requirements for filing a timely charge. Although these procedures are not perfectly clear or simple, they are a great improvement over the literal terms of the statute.

In Love v. Pullman Co.,[19] the Supreme Court approved the first of the EEOC's innovations in handling charges that should have been filed with a state or local agency initially but instead had been filed with the EEOC. The statute, read literally, prohibits filing with the EEOC until available state and local remedies have been exhausted.[20] By regulation, however, the EEOC undertook to refer such erroneously filed charges to the appropriate state or local agency, and then, after expiration of the deferral period for exclusive state or local consideration, to reactivate such charges within its own proceedings.[21] The Supreme Court upheld this regulation as a desirable simplification of the exhaustion requirement under Title VII that facilitated compliance by individual plaintiffs.[22]

In *Mohasco Corp. v. Silver*,[23] the Court examined the effect of this practice of automatic referral on the statute of limitations for filing with the EEOC. Essentially, the Court combined the 300–day limitation for filing with the EEOC with the 60–day deferral period for state or local proceedings. The result was the "240–day maybe" rule. The 240–day branch of the rule derives from the 300–day branch of the statute of limitations, less the 60–day deferral period. The Court reasoned that a charge initially filed with the EEOC without exhausting state or local administrative proceedings is effectively filed with the EEOC, 60 days after transfer to the state or local agency, when the charge is reactivated by the EEOC.[24] Consequently, the original limitation of 300 days for effective filing with the EEOC must be shortened by 60 days to 240 days for initial filing. Sixty days of the 300–day limitation are taken up by the deferral period in which the EEOC cannot act on the charge. The

---

18. §§ 709(b), 713(a), codified as 42 U.S.C. § 2000e–8(b), –12(a) (2000).

19. 404 U.S. 522 (1972).

20. § 706(c), (d), codified as 42 U.S.C. § 2000e–5(c), (d) (2000).

21. 29 C.F.R. § 1601.13 (2006).

22. 404 U.S. at 526–27.

23. 447 U.S. 807 (1980).

24. *Id.* at 815–817; 29 C.F.R. § 1601.13 (2006).

"maybe" branch of the rule derives from the part of the deferral rule that ends the deferral period upon termination of state or local proceedings. Even if a charge is initially filed with the EEOC more than 240 days after the alleged discrimination, it may still be effectively filed with the EEOC within 300 days of the alleged discrimination if state or local administrative proceedings terminate in fewer than 60 days. Termination of these proceedings ends the deferral period and, under EEOC regulations, automatically reactivates the charge with the EEOC before the expiration of the 300–day limitation.[25]

The principal defect of the "240–day maybe" rule of *Mohasco Corp. v. Silver* is that a 240–day limitation period appears nowhere in the statute. This makes the "240–day maybe" rule difficult to find and understand, especially for individual plaintiffs who are supposed to be able to file charges with the EEOC without the assistance of counsel.[26] The principal argument for the "240–day maybe" rule is that it is the only rule that results in equal treatment of those who file charges initially with the EEOC and those who file charges with the EEOC only after exhausting state or local administrative remedies. Both have 300 days from the date of the alleged discrimination and 240 days after the deferral period to file a timely charge with the EEOC.[27]

The EEOC has alleviated much of the uncertainty created by the "240–day maybe" rule by entering into worksharing agreements with state and local agencies. Such agreements typically provide for waiver of jurisdiction of the state or local agency if it is necessary to ensure that a charge is timely filed with the EEOC. These provisions become critical if the plaintiff has filed with the EEOC or the state agency within the "maybe" period identified in *Mohasco*: more than 240 days, but not more than 300 days, after the alleged discrimination. In *EEOC v. Commercial Office Products Co.*,[28] the Supreme Court held that waiver of state or local jurisdiction over charges filed in this period, followed by automatic referral of these charges to the EEOC, satisfies the 300–day limitation period. Although the worksharing agreements effectively reduce the length of the 60–day deferral period to whatever is left of the 300–day limitation period, they follow the principle, endorsed in *Love v. Pullman*, that the EEOC can assist nonlawyers in complying with the complex procedures created by Title VII. Moreover, workshar-

25. § 706(c), (d), codified as 42 U.S.C. § 2000e–5(c), (d) (2000); 29 C.F.R. § 1601.13(a)(3)(ii) (2006).

26. Love v. Pullman Co., 404 U.S. 522, 527 (1972).

27. *Mohasco*, 447 U.S. at 825.

28. 486 U.S. 107 (1988).

ing agreements do not encroach upon the power of state and local agencies to process charges during the 60–day deferral period since they have, by definition, consented to such agreements.

The EEOC has also made it easier to comply with the time limits for filing a charge by liberally allowing amendment of charges to cure defects in the charge as originally filed or to add related allegations of discrimination. Any such amendment relates back to the original date of filing, according to a regulation of the EEOC subsequently upheld by the Supreme Court.[29]

3. Judicial Proceedings

For private actions, the time limit for filing in court is 90 days from receipt of a right-to-sue letter.[30] This time limit must be satisfied in addition to the time limit for filing with the EEOC. It has, however, provoked less litigation, both because it is simpler and because it is defined by two easily established dates: when the plaintiff receives a right-to-sue letter and when the plaintiff files a claim in court. Nevertheless, a few cases have considered what happens when a plaintiff, acting without an attorney, files the right-to-sue letter as a complaint. These decisions have held that this filing does not usually satisfy the 90–day limitation period, or even toll its running until a proper complaint can be filed.[31] If the right-to-sue letter is accompanied by the charge filed with the EEOC, however, it may constitute "a short and plain statement of the claim showing that the pleader is entitled to relief" sufficient to constitute a properly filed complaint under the Federal Rules of Civil Procedure.[32]

For public actions brought by the EEOC or the Attorney General, Title VII specifies no time limit at all. Only the equitable defense of laches imposes a time limit upon public actions.[33]

4. General Principles

In addition to considering the effect of each of the specific time limits under Title VII, the Supreme Court has rendered several decisions of more general significance in interpreting the statute of limitations. These decisions, like the EEOC regulations on exhaustion of state and local administrative remedies, have an overall simplifying effect, although unlike the EEOC regulations, they do

29. Edelman v. Lynchburg College, 535 U.S. 106 (2002).

30. § 706(f)(1), codified as 42 U.S.C. § 2000e–5(f)(1) (2000).

31. Baldwin County Welcome Center v. Brown, 466 U.S. 147 (1984).

32. Fed. R. Civ. P. 8(a)(2). *See* Judkins v. Beech Aircraft Corp., 745 F.2d 1330 (11th Cir. 1984).

33. Occidental Life Ins. Co. v. EEOC, 432 U.S. 355 (1977).

not always work to the advantage of plaintiffs. Thus, the Court has held that the time limits under Title VII are not tolled during resort to grievance and arbitration procedures under a collective bargaining agreement,[34] and conversely, that the time limits under other employment discrimination statutes are not tolled during resort to administrative proceedings under Title VII.[35] Together, these decisions stand for the general principle that the special procedures, and in particular, the time limits, for pursuing different remedies for employment discrimination must be satisfied independently. Several different claims might arise out of one act of discrimination, but insofar as they are based on different sources of law, the special procedures for each of them must be separately satisfied.

The Supreme Court has also held that the time limits under Title VII, like statutes of limitations generally, are not jurisdictional, so that they are subject to waiver, estoppel, and equitable tolling,[36] and that they are tolled during the pendency of a class action.[37] In a case involving the discharge of a university professor, the Court held that the limitation period began to run when the university decided to deny him tenure, not when his employment ended a year later.[38] This holding has uncertain implications for practices that are less formal than those for denying tenure, and it has been applied by the lower federal courts only when the plaintiff receives formal notice of official action taken by the employer.[39] Nevertheless, in these cases, it makes the date of the employment decision, rather than the date the decision takes effect, decisive in determining when the statute of limitations begins to run.

The Court's most important decisions interpreting the limitations under Title VII concern the theory of continuing violations, which was invoked frequently in the early years after the enactment of Title VII. This theory allows plaintiffs to seek relief for a continuing series of discriminatory acts, many of which precede any filed charge by several years and so, considered in isolation, can no

34. Electrical Workers v. Robbins & Myers, Inc., 429 U.S. 229 (1976).

35. Johnson v. Railway Express Agency, 421 U.S. 454 (1975) (claim under 42 U.S.C. § 1981).

36. Zipes v. Trans World Airlines, 455 U.S. 385 (1982).

37. Crown, Cork & Seal Co. v. Parker, 462 U.S. 345 (1983).

38. Delaware State College v. Ricks, 449 U.S. 250 (1980).

39. Smith v. United Parcel Serv. of Am., Inc., 65 F.3d 266, 268 (2d Cir. 1995) (ADA claim); Hoesterey v. Cathedral City, 945 F.2d 317, 320 (9th Cir. 1991), *cert. denied*, 504 U.S. 910 (1992) (civil rights claim); Colgan v. Fisher Scientific Co., 935 F.2d 1407, 1420 (3d Cir.), *cert. denied*, 502 U.S. 941 (1991) (ADEA claim). Although these cases arise under statutes other than Title VII, the Supreme Court has made clear that *Ricks* applies in the same fashion to all civil rights claims. Chardon v. Fernandez, 454 U.S. 6 (1981) (per curiam).

longer be the subject of a timely claim of discrimination. The theory of continuing violations, in effect, stretches the statute of limitations backward and allows recovery for past instances of discrimination when it would not otherwise be available. Such an extended remedy follows directly from the remedial perspective, with its emphasis on identifying and compensating for the continuing consequences of past discrimination. Yet it also raises concerns from an economic perspective about the ability of employers to bear the costs of litigation over events that might be long past. The very purpose of the statute of limitations is to protect defendants from exposure to liability over periods of time longer than the limitation period itself. If a claim is not brought within the period specified by the statute of limitations, then the defendant is entitled to ignore the claim and to make business and other arrangements free of the risk of liability.

The Supreme Court addressed this tension underlying the theory of continuing violations in *United Air Lines, Inc. v. Evans.*[40] This case concerned a charge filed with the EEOC in 1973 that alleged a discriminatory discharge in 1968. The plaintiff was subsequently rehired in 1972, but she was denied any seniority that had earlier accrued to her. She argued that the continuing effect of this denial of accrued seniority supported a timely charge of discrimination that ultimately could be traced back to her discharge in 1968. The Supreme Court rejected this argument, relying partly on the protection of seniority systems in section 703(h), discussed in the previous chapter.[41] The Court reasoned that a seniority system that did not itself violate Title VII also did not revive claims of discrimination that were otherwise barred by the statute of limitations. The Court also, however, relied on more general reasoning about the purpose and effect of statutes of limitations:

> A discriminatory act which is not made the basis for a timely charge is the legal equivalent of a discriminatory act which occurred before the statute was passed. It may constitute relevant background evidence in a proceeding in which the status of a current practice is at issue, but separately considered, it is merely an unfortunate event in history which has no present legal consequences.[42]

Taken literally, this reasoning would completely abolish the theory of continuing violations.

Subsequent decisions, however, have not taken this reasoning so far and have distinguished between claims of discrimination

---

40.   431 U.S. 553 (1977).

41.   *See* Chapter VII.E *supra.*

42.   *Evans,* 431 U.S. at 558.

concerned with discrete events and those involving a continuing course of conduct. In *National Railroad Passenger Corp. v. Morgan*,[43] the Supreme Court considered both types of claims. The plaintiff alleged that he suffered from a variety of racially discriminatory acts and retaliation over the course of his employment by the defendant. Because these were discrete acts, they could be the subject of a timely claim only if each act occurred within 300 days before a charge was filed with the EEOC. However, the plaintiff also alleged that he suffered from a racially hostile environment at work, involving a series of acts that constituted a single unlawful practice. The Court held that this claim was timely if a single act in the series fell within the 300–day limitation period: "Provided that an act contributing to the claim occurs within the filing period, the entire time period of the hostile environment may be considered by a court for the purposes of determining liability."[44] Relief could accordingly extend to acts outside the limitation period, so long as it conformed to other restrictions on remedies under Title VII.

Among these restrictions is the two-year limit on awards of back pay under section 706(g), allowing awards of back pay for a period within two years prior to the filing of a charge with the EEOC.[45] In the absence of the theory of continuing violations, this provision would be entirely redundant, since the longest limitation period for filing charges with the EEOC is only 300 days and awards of back pay ordinarily cannot extend back any earlier before filing with the EEOC. Under *National Railroad Passenger Corp.*, a continuing hostile environment that began less than two years before filing a charge with the EEOC, but included acts that occurred within the limitation period, would support an award of back pay for the entire course of conduct. As the Court also made clear, however, the plaintiff's recovery might be limited by the equitable doctrine of laches, if the plaintiff delayed too long after filing a charge with the EEOC in obtaining a right-to-sue letter and in filing suit.[46] Likewise, the continuing violation theory would be entirely unavailable to a plaintiff who alleged only a discrete act of harassment, such as firing or some other tangible employment action. This act would have to occur within the limitation period in order to be actionable.

A related question is whether claims of discrimination in pay involve discrete or continuing violations of Title VII. In *National Passenger Railroad Corp.*, the Court stated that they are discrete,

---

43. 536 U.S. 101 (2002).

44. *Id.* at 117 (footnote omitted).

45. § 706(g)(1), codified as 42 U.S.C. § 2000e–5(g)(1) (2000).

46. 526 U.S. at 121–22.

allowing recovery only for claims based on paychecks within the appropriate limitation period.[47] Earlier decisions had upheld such claims based on evidence of discrimination that occurred much earlier, but without addressing the further question whether the decision to engage in discrimination, in addition to the paycheck itself, must occur within the limitation period.[48] That issue is currently before the Court.[49]

Another example of a continuing violation, one explicitly endorsed by the Civil Rights Act of 1991, concerns claims of discrimination in seniority systems. For these claims, the limitation period starts to run from any of three different events, effectively making the last of them the only one that counts: when the seniority system is adopted, when the plaintiff is subject to the seniority system, or when the plaintiff is injured by the application of the seniority system.[50] This provision was intended to overrule a more restrictive decision of the Supreme Court that started the limitation running when the seniority system was adopted or changed.[51] It endorses the theory of continuing violations, but only for the rare claim that attacks the validity or operation of a seniority system.

B. Public Actions

Title VII authorizes the EEOC to sue private employers and the Attorney General to sue state and local government employers.[52] In addition, it authorizes commissioners of the EEOC to initiate administrative proceedings by filing charges with the EEOC.[53] In purely quantitative terms, public actions have not been a significant factor in enforcing Title VII. Most litigation under Title VII, like other civil rights laws, has been brought by private individuals. Yet when the EEOC or the Attorney General has sued, it has often been in landmark cases that establish new theories of liability, or that involve the practices of an entire industry, or that result in settlements on behalf of a large number of employees. The special procedures for these actions distinguish them from ordinary private litigation under Title VII.

Public actions can be filed only after investigation and conciliation efforts have failed, and in any event, no sooner than 30 days

47. *Id.* at 111–12.

48. E.g., Bazemore v. Friday, 478 U.S. 385, 394–97 (1986).

49. Ledbetter v. Goodyear Tire & Rubber Inc., 126 S.Ct. 2965 (2006) (granting certiorari).

50. § 706(e)(2), codified as 42 U.S.C. § 2000e–5(e)(2) (2000).

51. The overruled decision is Lorance v. AT & T Technologies, Inc., 490 U.S. 900 (1989).

52. § 706(f), codified as 42 U.S.C. § 2000e–5(f) (2000).

53. § 706(b), codified as 42 U.S.C. § 2000e–5(b) (2000).

after a charge has been pending in the EEOC, after the 60–day deferral period for exclusive action by a state or local agency.[54] In general, more exacting compliance with administrative procedures is required in public actions than in private actions because the EEOC is held responsible for its own mistakes.[55] On the other hand, a very broadly worded charge filed by an EEOC commissioner was held sufficient to meet the requirements of specificity and notice prescribed by Title VII and EEOC regulations.[56] If a public action is filed, the charging party has a right to intervene, and conversely, if a private action is filed, the EEOC or the Attorney General may seek permissive intervention after certifying that the case is of general public importance.[57]

Public actions may be brought under either section 706 or section 707.[58] Section 706 actions usually allege discrimination against a small number of individuals, whereas section 707 actions allege a "pattern or practice" of discrimination against a class of employees. Nothing turns on the difference between the two sections, however. The Supreme Court has held that the EEOC or the Attorney General can bring section 706 actions on behalf of a class of employees without certification of a class action under the Federal Rules of Civil Procedure.[59] Moreover, the allocation of authority to sue is the same in section 707 actions as in section 706 actions: the EEOC can sue private employers and the Attorney General can sue state and local government employers. The language of the statute, however, is confused on this point, and it was only clarified by an executive reorganization plan.[60]

C.　Private Actions

Private actions can be brought by any individual who filed a charge with the EEOC, or on whose behalf a charge was filed.[61] This last clause indicates the prominent role that class actions have played in the enforcement of Title VII. Under the principle that "racial discrimination is by definition class discrimination," class

---

54. § 706(f)(1), codified as 42 U.S.C. § 2000e–5(f)(1) (2000).

55. *See* EEOC v. Raymond Metal Prods. Co., 530 F.2d 590 (4th Cir. 1976).

56. EEOC v. Shell Oil Co., 466 U.S. 54 (1984). It met the requirements of section 706(b), codified as 42 U.S.C. § 2000e–5(b) (2000), and 29 C.F.R. § 1601.12(a)(3) (2006).

57. § 706(f)(1), codified as 42 U.S.C. § 2000e–5(f)(1) (2000).

58. §§ 706, 707, codified as 42 U.S.C. §§ 2000e–5, 6 (2000).

59. Fed. R. Civ. P. 23; General Tel. Co. v. EEOC, 446 U.S. 318 (1980).

60. § 707(e), codified as 42 U.S.C. § 2000e–6(e) (2000); Reorg. Plan No. 1 of 1978, § 5, 3 C.F.R. 322 (1978), reprinted in 5 U.S.C. app. at 1574 (2000).

61. § 706(f)(1), codified as 42 U.S.C. § 2000e–5(f)(1) (2000).

actions were frequently certified in the period immediately following enactment of Title VII. This trend was abruptly halted by a
series of decisions by the Supreme Court in the late 1970s. In
subsequent years, private litigation has remained a significant
means of enforcing Title VII, but mainly through individual actions,
which have largely determined the kinds of claims, the nature of
relief, and the types of plaintiffs that are most common in employment discrimination cases. The conditions and restrictions on private actions have accordingly exercised a pervasive influence over
the development of the law under Title VII.

These begin with the requirement of exhaustion of administrative remedies and the time limits for filing administrative charges
with the EEOC. Assuming that a charge has been timely filed with
the EEOC and properly deferred to a state or local agency, then the
EEOC will investigate the charge, determine whether it is supported by reasonable cause, and if it is, engage in attempts at
settlement. Most charges lead to the issuance of a right-to-sue
letter, which authorizes the charging party to file an action within
90 days. In the rare instances in which the EEOC itself or the
Attorney General decides to sue on the charge, the private individual is limited to a right to intervene.[62] Otherwise, the private
individual may sue on any charge that has not been settled,
whether or not the EEOC has found reasonable cause to support it.
Indeed, a private individual can request a right-to-sue letter at any
time after a charge has been pending before the EEOC for 180
days.[63] Charging parties, and those on whose behalf a charge is
filed, can also receive from the EEOC the results of its investigation, despite a general prohibition in Title VII against the public
disclosure of the results of an investigation in advance of litigation
on the charge. The Supreme Court has held that these individuals
do not constitute members of the general public within the scope of
the prohibition on disclosure.[64]

Class actions played a distinctive role in expanding the scope of
private litigation of Title VII, particularly in the first decade of
enforcement of the statute. The statutory procedures for exhaustion of administrative remedies are broadly consistent with class
action practice. The statute itself provides that a named plaintiff
can exhaust administrative remedies on behalf of the class and
judicial decisions have interpreted the exhaustion requirement to
be satisfied by any claim that was the subject of a charge or that

62. *Id.*

63. *Id.*

64. § 706(b), codified as 42 U.S.C.
§ 2000e–5(b) (2000); EEOC v. Associated Dry Goods Corp., 449 U.S. 590
(1981).

could reasonably have been expected to grow out of the EEOC's investigation of a charge.[65] A line of cases, originating in the Fifth Circuit, initially adopted a principle of liberal certification of Title VII class actions.[66] These cases applied the requirements of Federal Rule of Civil Procedure 23 loosely in Title VII cases and certified "across-the-board" classes that included all employees who suffered from discrimination throughout an employer's operations.

Liberal certification of class actions furthered the remedial goals of Title VII by expanding the beneficiaries of private litigation from individual plaintiffs to entire classes of employees and applicants for employment. Any resulting remedy could then work to the benefit of the designated class, resulting in broad awards of compensatory relief and injunctions that restructured whole plants and companies. All of these benefits were available, however, only if the plaintiff class prevailed. If it lost, or if its claims were settled on inadequate terms, all of the class members were barred from seeking relief individually.

It was for this reason that the Supreme Court eventually halted the trend toward liberal certification, in two cases in which certification of broad classes had been approved by the Fifth Circuit. In *East Texas Motor Freight System, Inc. v. Rodriguez*,[67] the Court held that a class had been erroneously certified on appeal, relying on a variety of different reasons: the named plaintiffs had not sought certification before trial; the case had not been tried as a class action; the relief requested by the employees had been rejected in a union vote by most of the class members; and the named plaintiffs had lost on their individual claims at trial. In *General Telephone Co. v. Falcon*,[68] the Court again held that a class action had been erroneously certified, this time by the district court, because the class consisted of applicants for employment, but the named plaintiff was an employee who alleged discrimination on his own behalf only in promotions. In *Rodriguez* the Court stated: "We are not unaware that suits alleging racial or ethnic discrimination are often by their very nature class suits, involving class-wide wrongs. Common questions of law or fact are typically present. But careful attention to the requirements of Fed. Rule Civ. Proc. 23 remains nonetheless indispensable."[69] In *Falcon*, the Court added that the "across-the-board" rule led to neglect of the requirements of Rule 23, but it left open the possibility that employment prac-

---

65. Sanchez v. Standard Brands, Inc., 431 F.2d 455 (5th Cir. 1970).

66. *E.g.*, Johnson v. Georgia Highway Express, Inc., 417 F.2d 1122 (5th Cir. 1969).

67. 431 U.S. 395 (1977).

68. 457 U.S. 147 (1982).

69. 431 U.S. at 405.

tices applicable to employees and applicants might justify certification of an equally broad class.[70] A similar possibility led to its later decision in *Bazemore v. Friday*[71] affirming the denial of class certification in some respects, but not others, based on differences in the conditions of employment of class members working at different locations.

The Supreme Court continued to limit the scope of Title VII class actions in *Cooper v. Federal Reserve Bank*,[72] but in a manner more immediately favorable to individual plaintiffs. The Court held that the judgment in a class action dismissing claims of a pattern or practice of discrimination in promotions did not preclude subsequent individual claims by class members. Although the individual plaintiffs testified at trial in the class action, the district court denied their motions to intervene and did not adjudicate their individual claims. Consequently, they were bound by the judgment in the class action, but only with respect to pattern-or-practice claims covering the same period as the class action. This decision only made explicit what was already implicit in the Court's earlier decisions: that the desirability and extent of class certification depends on the nature of the claims asserted on behalf of the class and that doubts should be resolved in favor of protecting the rights of absent class members.

A similar conflict between individual litigation and alternative remedies is reflected in the decisions on mandatory arbitration of employment discrimination claims. In *Gilmer v. Interstate/Johnson Lane Corp.*,[73] the Supreme Court held that claims under the Age Discrimination in Employment Act, which are normally adjudicated according to procedures very similar to those under Title VII, could be made subject to binding arbitration. The Court distinguished an earlier Title VII case holding that employees were not bound by arbitration under a collective bargaining agreement[74] on the ground that an individual agreement constitutes a waiver of the employee's right to sue.[75] By contrast, under a collective bargaining agreement, the union controls both negotiation of the agreement and the process of arbitration, so that the arbitrator's decision is only entitled to "such weight as the court deems appropriate."[76] More recently, the Supreme Court has emphasized that a collective

70. 457 U.S. at 157–160 & n.15.

71. 478 U.S. 385 (1986).

72. 467 U.S. 867 (1984).

73. 500 U.S. 20 (1991).

74. Alexander v. Gardner–Denver Co., 415 U.S. 36 (1974).

75. *Gilmer*, 500 U.S. at 35.

76. *Alexander*, 415 U.S. at 60.

bargaining agreement can waive the individual's right to sue only if it does so in "clear and unmistakable" terms.[77]

Other decisions have confirmed both the policy favoring arbitration and its limits in the law of contract. In *Circuit City Stores, Inc. v. Adams,*[78] the Court broadly interpreted the Federal Arbitration Act to promote arbitration of claims arising out of individual employment contracts. The act itself contains an exception for "contracts of employment of seamen, railroad employees, or any other class of workers engaged in foreign or interstate commerce,"[79] but the Court construed this exception to apply only to workers engaged in foreign or interstate transportation, rather than the much larger class of workers engaged in industries "affecting commerce." Despite such decisions vindicating the policy in favor of arbitration, that policy still is limited to parties who have agreed to this form of dispute resolution. The Court made this limitation clear in *EEOC v. Waffle House, Inc.,*[80] a case brought by the EEOC on behalf of an employee who had entered into an arbitration agreement. The EEOC sued under the Americans with Disabilities Act, invoking procedures that identical to those under Title VII. The Court held that the EEOC's authority to sue was conferred independently of any claim by the employee and so fell outside the scope of his agreement to arbitrate.[81]

D. Actions by Federal Employees

As noted in the previous chapter,[82] federal employees fall outside the ordinary provisions of Title VII and are covered instead by the special provisions in section 717. These provisions make the federal government subject to the same prohibitions against discrimination as other employers, but through procedures that attempt to merge enforcement of Title VII with administration of the federal civil service laws.[83] Under these procedures, the EEOC takes on the role—unique for it under Title VII—of an adjudicative agency, succeeding to some of the powers of the former Civil Service Commission.

In order to bring claims under Title VII, federal employees, like other employees, must first exhaust administrative remedies and must do so within strict and complicated time limits. The remedies,

---

77. Wright v. Universal Maritime Serv. Corp., 525 U.S. 70, 79–80 (1998).

78. 532 U.S. 105 (2001).

79. 9 U.S.C. § 1 (2000).

80. 534 U.S. 279 (2002).

81. *Id.* at 297–98.

82. *See* Chapter VII.F. *supra.*

83. § 717, codified as 42 U.S.C. § 2000e–16 (2000).

however, are entirely within the federal government and begin with those within the employing agency itself. A federal employee must make a complaint to an EEO counselor in the agency within 45 days of the alleged discrimination and file a written complaint with the agency within 15 days of the final interview with the EEO counselor.[84] If the federal employee then takes the case to the EEOC, a charge must be filed with the EEOC within 30 days of receipt of the final decision of the employing agency.[85] If not, an action can be filed in federal court within 90 days of notice of the agency's final decision or, if the agency has not reached a final decision, at any time after 180 days of filing with the agency.[86] If a charge is filed with the EEOC, then the EEOC acts in an adjudicative capacity.[87] If the federal employee is dissatisfied with the results of the EEOC proceedings, then an action may be filed in federal court under the same time limits as an action filed directly from agency proceedings: within 90 days of notice of a final decision of the EEOC or, if the EEOC has not reached a final decision, at any time after 180 days of filing with the EEOC.[88]

Some circuits had held that these time limits are jurisdictional because waivers of sovereign immunity are to be strictly construed, but the Supreme Court has concluded that they are not; they are subject to equitable tolling just like claims against private employers.[89] Actions by federal employees result in de novo judicial review, just like other Title VII actions.[90] On the other hand, actions to enforce, or to review, administrative decisions favorable to federal employees result, at most, in only limited judicial review.[91]

For employees within its coverage, section 717 provides the exclusive remedy for employment discrimination,[92] but its scope extends to all the equitable remedies that are available to private employees, including prejudgment interest.[93] Additional specialized procedures apply to claims of discrimination that are joined with

---

84. 29 C.F.R. §§ 1614.105(a), .106(b) (2006).

85. *Id.* § 1614.402(a) & 65 Fed. Reg. 37659 (1999).

86. § 717(c), codified as 42 U.S.C. § 2000e–16(c) (2000); 29 C.F.R. § 1614.407 (2006).

87. Reorg. Plan No. 1 of 1978, § 3, 3 C.F.R. 321 (1978), reprinted in 5 U.S.C. app. at 1574 (2000).

88. § 717(c), codified as 42 U.S.C. § 2000e–16(c) (2000); 29 C.F.R. § 1614.407 (2006).

89. Irwin v. Department of Veterans Affairs, 498 U.S. 89, 93–96 (1990).

90. Chandler v. Roudebush, 425 U.S. 840 (1976).

91. Moore v. Devine, 780 F.2d 1559 (11th Cir. 1986), *on rehearing*, 767 F.2d 1541 (11th Cir. 1985).

92. Brown v. General Servs. Admin., 425 U.S. 820, 828–29, 832–35 (1976); *see* FDIC v. Meyer, 510 U.S. 471, 483–86 (1994) (no implied right of action under the Fifth Amendment against federal agencies).

93. § 717(d), codified as 42 U.S.C. § 2000e–16(d) (2000).

claims under the civil service laws, which would ordinarily be brought before the Merit Systems Protection Board.[94] By its terms, however, section 717 does not apply to all federal employees, excluding various positions in the military or outside the civil service.[95] The Supreme Court has held that excluded federal employees have an implied right of action for disparate treatment in violation of the Fifth Amendment.[96] Employees of the Senate and presidential appointees, however, now have statutory remedies created by the Civil Rights Act of 1991.[97]

E. Preclusion

The usual rules of preclusion generally apply to actions under Title VII, subject only to complications involving the exhaustion of administrative remedies, and more controversially, litigation over affirmative action plans. Thus, federal courts are bound by the decisions of state courts under the ordinary rules of full faith and credit, even if those decisions simply review decisions of state or local administrative agencies.[98] So, too, a conciliation agreement that awards a job to a charging party under Title VII does not bar another individual, who is displaced from the same job, from suing for violation of a collective bargaining agreement that awards the job to him.[99]

Exhaustion of administrative remedies complicates these general rules only slightly. As noted earlier, a court that considers a Title VII claim is not bound by the decision of an administrative agency, whether by a state or local agency or by the EEOC itself.[100] This result is necessary so that the statutory requirement of exhaustion of administrative remedies does not become the effective equivalent of administrative adjudication. According binding effect to the decision of an administrative agency would make its decision final by precluding any inconsistent decision by a court.

---

94. 5 U.S.C. § 7702 (2000); 5 C.F.R. §§ 1201.151–.175 (2006) & 65 Fed. Reg. 25624 (2000); 29 C.F.R. §§ 1614.302– .310 (2006) & 65 Fed. Reg. 37659 (1999). Claims of discrimination involving collective bargaining result in still further complexity because they could otherwise be brought before an arbitrator or before the Federal Labor Relations Authority. 5 U.S.C. §§ 7118, 7121–23 (2000).

95. § 717(a), codified as 42 U.S.C. § 2000e–16(a) (2000). For an illustration of a court refusing to apply Title VII to the uniformed military, see Roper v. De-

partment of the Army, 832 F.2d 247 (2d Cir. 1987).

96. Davis v. Passman, 442 U.S. 228 (1979).

97. Civil Rights Act of 1991, Pub. L. No. 102–166, § 117, 301–20, 105 Stat. 1071, 1080, 1088–97.

98. Kremer v. Chemical Constr. Corp., 456 U.S. 461 (1982).

99. W.R. Grace & Co. v. Local Union 759, 461 U.S. 757, 771 (1983).

100. *See* note 4 *supra.*

Litigation over affirmative action is subject to more complex and uncertain treatment. The Supreme Court initially applied the usual rules of preclusion to consent decrees that established programs of affirmative action attacked by white employees or the union that represented them. In two cases, the Court held that consent decrees were binding only on the parties who signed the decrees and on others in privity with them.[101] In the more controversial of the cases, the Court held that persons who were not a party to the underlying action were under no duty to intervene to object to the consent decree in order to preserve their rights.[102]

The Civil Rights Act of 1991 sought to change this result, but the Supreme Court's decision may have been based on constitutional considerations immune from legislative revision. The act itself contains elaborate provisions making judgments and consent decrees binding on nonparties with actual notice of the proposed order and an opportunity to object to it, as well as on nonparties whose interests were adequately represented by an existing party.[103] This extended preclusive effect, however, is subject to several limitations,[104] the most important being those imposed by the Due Process Clause. These limit the preclusive effect of any judgment rendered in a proceeding to which an individual was neither a party nor adequately represented by a party.[105] Whether an opportunity to become a party through intervention upon notice of an action satisfies the requirements of due process remains an open question.

---

101. Martin v. Wilks, 490 U.S. 755, 761–63 (1989); Local No. 93 v. Cleveland, 478 U.S. 501, 528–29 (1987).

102. *Martin*, 490 U.S. at 761–63.

103. § 703(n)(1)(B), codified as 42 U.S.C. § 2000e–2(n)(1)(B) (2000).

104. § 703(n)(2), codified as 42 U.S.C. § 2000e–2(n)(2) (2000).

105. Hansberry v. Lee, 311 U.S. 32 (1940).

Chapter IX

REMEDIES

Once a violation of Title VII has been established, the plaintiff's case moves from allegations and evidence of discrimination to the need to devise appropriate remedies for the violations of the law that have already been found. The issue is no longer whether the defendant is liable, but how much, and in particular, to what extent the defendant is subject to various remedies for past discrimination. The burden of proof undergoes a corresponding shift, from being primarily on the plaintiff to falling primarily on the defendant. Subject to only a few exceptions, the plaintiff is now presumed to be entitled to a broad array of remedies and the defendant subject to equally broad liability.

For reasons having to do more with history than logic, Title VII initially authorized only judicially ordered equitable relief. Such relief could take the monetary form of back pay, but not damages, which can be awarded in federal court only if accompanied by the right to jury trial. Both damages and the right to jury trial were made available under Title VII only by the Civil Rights Act of 1991.[1] That act extended to Title VII the remedy of damages available under the Reconstruction civil rights acts, and particularly section 1981, first enacted in the Civil Rights Act of 1866.[2] This right to damages carries with it the right to jury trial, which can be invoked by either party. Unlike damages under section 1981, however, damages under Title VII are subject to caps, depending on the size of the employer. In another, more complete analogy to the Reconstruction civil rights acts, attorney's fees have always been available to prevailing plaintiffs under Title VII.[3] This remedy has obviously increased both the total liability of defendants and the net recovery of plaintiffs under Title VII, but more importantly, it has also affected the incentives of attorneys to represent plaintiffs under Title VII and to pursue claims on their behalf.

This chapter will take up each of these types of relief in turn: equitable remedies, legal remedies, and attorney's fees. Each reflects the trend toward granting ever more complete relief under Title VII. This abstract principle is easily stated and admits of only a few qualifications, although its application to any concrete case in

---

1. 42 U.S.C. § 1981a (2000).

2. 42 U.S.C. § 1981 (2000).

3. § 706(k), codified as 42 U.S.C. § 2000e–5(k) (2000).

177

computing an award of back pay or damages or in formulating an injunction can become quite complicated. Moreover, because Title VII provides the model for other laws against employment discrimination, the remedies available under Title VII, and the issues that they raise, largely determine the scope and nature of relief under other statutes prohibiting employment discrimination.

A. Equitable Remedies

Equitable remedies can take a variety of forms, from injunctions prohibiting future discrimination or restructuring employment practices, to individual awards of back pay and seniority. The early predominance of equitable relief in the enforcement of Title VII resulted from the presumed disadvantages of jury trial, which is constitutionally required for claims supporting an award of damages. As originally enacted, Title VII authorized only "equitable relief," taking the traditional equitable form of the injunction as the model for most remedies, but including monetary relief in the form of back pay among the available remedies.[4] Following the practice in equity, the nature and amount of the remedies awarded were left to the discretion of the district court. Allocating these issues to the court necessarily took them away from the jury, along with any role in adjudicating the underlying claims of discrimination. This removed the possibility of jury nullification, thought to be a significant threat in the South in the years immediately after the enactment of Title VII. Although damages are now available to remedy violations of Title VII—and with them, the right to jury trial—questions about the nature and amount of equitable relief continue to dominate the remedial phase of Title VII cases.

In all its forms, equitable relief is presumptively available to any proven victim of discrimination. A finding that the defendant has violated Title VII justifies the issuance of an injunction against the discriminatory practice almost as a matter of course,[5] at least absent changed circumstances that would make an injunction inappropriate.[6] A finding of violation also justifies the award of compensatory relief to individual victims of discrimination. As the Supreme Court has said of an award of back pay, it "should be denied only for reasons which, if applied generally, would not frustrate the central statutory purposes of eradicating discrimination throughout

---

4. This provision is now found in § 706(g)(1), codified as 42 U.S.C. § 2000e–5(g)(1) (2000).

5. International Bhd. of Teamsters v. United States, 431 U.S. 324, 361 (1977).

6. Albemarle Paper Co. v. Moody, 422 U.S. 405, 436 (1975).

the economy and making persons whole for injuries suffered through past discrimination."[7]

This principle, which is fundamental to the remedial phase of Title VII cases, contrasts markedly with the discretion traditionally accorded to trial judges in formulating equitable relief. It is explicable, however, by the complications that inevitably attend any attempt to devise full compensatory and deterrent relief in a manner consistent with fairness toward the defendant. One reason, for instance, that might justify the limitation on such relief is unjustified delay in asserting a claim for back pay.[8] This reason, by its very nature, would not generally frustrate the compensatory and deterrent purposes of Title VII, since most plaintiffs seek back pay as a matter of course, but it does protect defendants from the assertion of claims for back pay that would not otherwise be timely. This limitation can be developed by analogy to the equitable doctrine of laches, which bars claims asserted after an unjustifiable delay that has worked to the prejudice of the defendant.

Other complications in formulating remedies under Title VII arise from requirements and limits found in the statute itself. As an initial matter, a plaintiff must establish that she is a victim of discrimination. Although this conclusion follows automatically from a finding of liability in an individual action, in a class action or a pattern-or-practice action, each member of the plaintiff class must make this preliminary showing, as discussed more fully later in this chapter.[9] After the plaintiff's status as a victim of discrimination is established, the defendant has the opportunity to prove that the plaintiff would have been rejected for an entirely legitimate reason wholly apart from any previously established discriminatory motive.[10] This burden in the remedy phase of the case rests entirely on the defendant, and is distinct from the burden of proof on the issue of pretext in the liability phase of the case, which rests on the plaintiff. If the defendant carries the burden of proving that the plaintiff would have received the same treatment in the absence of discrimination, then the court may award only declaratory relief, prospective injunctive relief, and attorney's fees and costs.[11] If the

---

7. *Id.* at 421.

8. *Id.* at 423–24. *See* City of Los Angeles Dep't of Water & Power v. Manhart, 435 U.S. 702, 718–23 (1978) (decision that employers could not use sex-segregated actuarial tables does not justify award of retroactive monetary relief); Arizona Governing Comm. v. Norris, 463 U.S. 1073, 1075 (1983) (per curiam) (same).

9. *See* Section C *infra.*

10. § 706(g)(2)(B), codified as 42 U.S.C. § 2000e–5(g)(2)(B) (2000). For further discussion see Chapter III.D *supra.*

11. § 706(g)(2)(B)(i), codified as 42 U.S.C. § 2000e–5(g)(2)(B)(i) (2000). This subsection addresses only claims of intentional discrimination under § 703(m), codified as 42 U.S.C. § 2000e–

defendant fails to carry this burden, then the plaintiff is almost always entitled to an award of back pay according to the general principle in favor of full compensatory and deterrent relief, quoted earlier.

The amount of such relief, however, requires detailed computations. Putting the plaintiff in the position that she would have been in if she had not been a victim of discrimination turns out to be more complex than at first appears. The first complication concerns the offset for "[i]nterim earnings or amounts earnable with reasonable diligence" which the statute itself requires.[12] What the plaintiff earned in other jobs while the litigation was pending, or more speculatively, what she might have earned with reasonable diligence, operates as a restriction on the amount that she can otherwise recover. Along the same lines, the defendant can also take steps to mitigate the plaintiff's losses by making an unconditional offer of reinstatement (or initial hiring or promotion). In particular, the defendant can stop the accrual of back pay liability by making an unconditional offer to return the plaintiff to the position from which she was discriminatorily excluded. This offer stops the accrual of back pay liability, whether or not it is accepted by the plaintiff, and whether or not it is accompanied by the offer of retroactive benefits, such as seniority for the time that she was not employed.[13]

A further complication in determining awards of back pay concerns their tax status as wages. Like most awards of monetary relief in employment discrimination cases, these awards are now taxable as income to the employee. Only awards for "personal physical injuries or physical sickness" are automatically excluded from income.[14] There are further questions, however, about whether the defendant must withhold payroll taxes on the awards[15] and whether the plaintiff is entitled to compensation for the adverse tax consequences of receiving back pay for several years in a single lump sum taxed in a single year.[16]

2(m) (2000). Claims of disparate impact apparently fall under the preceding subsection, § 706(g)(2)(A), codified as 42 U.S.C. § 2000e–5(g)(2)(A) (2000).

12. § 706(g)(1), codified as 42 U.S.C. § 2000e–5(g)(1) (2000).

13. Ford Motor Co. v. EEOC, 458 U.S. 219, 228–39 (1982).

14. 26 U.S.C. § 104(a)(2) (2000). Recoveries for "emotional distress" are not excludable as compensation for physical injury or physical sickness.

15. *Compare* Rasimas v. Michigan Dep't of Mental Health, 714 F.2d 614, 627 (6th Cir. 1983), *cert. denied*, 466 U.S. 950 (1984) (no withholding of income tax), *with* Melani v. Board of Higher Educ., 652 F.Supp. 43, 47–48 (S.D.N.Y. 1986) (requiring withholding).

16. *Compare* Blim v. Western Elec. Co., 731 F.2d 1473, 1480 (10th Cir.), *cert. denied*, 469 U.S. 874 (1984) (no extra compensation for tax liability for lump sum award of back pay), *with* Arneson v. Callahan, 128 F.3d 1243, 1247 (8th Cir. 1997), *cert. denied*, 524

All of these complications are multiplied when the award of relief concerns fringe benefits, and in particular, seniority. The Supreme Court has stated that the same general principle in favor of full compensatory relief applies to awards of fringe benefits and remedial seniority, just as it does to awards of back pay.[17] This extension of the principle is obvious enough with respect to fringe benefits for which employees do not directly compete, such as medical insurance and vacation time. These fringe benefits are just forms of compensation in kind, fully analogous to compensation in cash, and should be subject to the same general remedial principle. Even so, the complexity of most fringe benefit plans requires the court to exercise considerable discretion in determining exactly what benefits the plaintiff would have received in the absence of discrimination.

Awards of competitive seniority, however, introduce complications of an entirely different order. The plaintiff's gain is necessarily another employee's loss, whether or not the other employee is also a victim of discrimination or of the same race or gender as the plaintiff. The Supreme Court has stated that the same general principle of full compensation still applies, but in a limited and qualified way. In particular, it justifies only awards of "rightful place" seniority, resulting in placement of the plaintiff in the job which she was discriminatorily denied, with full remedial seniority, only after a vacancy develops in that job.[18] Contrary to the implication of the term, an award of "rightful place" seniority does not immediately put the victim of discrimination in her rightful place, because it does not allow incumbent employees to be bumped out of their jobs to create a vacancy. Some courts have awarded "front pay" to victims of discrimination to compensate for the period between entry of the judgment and occurrence of a vacancy that allows them to achieve their rightful place.[19] Front pay differs from back pay only in providing compensation for the effects of discrimination that occur after, instead of before, entry of the judgment, but it is not awarded as routinely as back pay because of the difficulty of ascertaining the future effects of past discrimination.[20] All of these determinations, and especially the need to balance the interests of plaintiffs against the vested seniority rights of incumbent employees, require the exercise of discretion by the district

U.S. 926 (1998) (awarding such compensation).

17. Franks v. Bowman Transp. Co., 424 U.S. 747, 770–71 (1976).

18. *Id.* at 776–78.

19. *E.g.*, White v. Carolina Paperboard Corp., 564 F.2d 1073, 1091 (4th Cir. 1977); Patterson v. American Tobacco Co., 535 F.2d 257, 269 (4th Cir.), *cert. denied*, 429 U.S. 920 (1976).

20. *E.g.*, Dillon v. Coles, 746 F.2d 998, 1005–06 (3d Cir. 1984).

courts,[21] leaving them with considerable power over the formulation of the relief actually awarded.

Because the relief accorded to proven victims of discrimination is so extensive, the occasions for court-ordered affirmative action, which by definition confers benefits on individuals who have not established that they are victims of discrimination, must necessarily be limited. The statute itself contains a clause that might be taken to bar such relief to nonvictims entirely, but as discussed in an earlier chapter,[22] it does not bar the award of affirmative action. Affirmative action is nevertheless awarded only as a last resort, to remedy egregious discrimination. In contrast to other equitable remedies, it is not routinely available, but rather is hardly ever awarded.[23]

B. Damages and the Civil Rights Act of 1991

The Civil Rights Act of 1991 greatly expanded the remedies available under Title VII by authorizing the award of damages for intentional discrimination.[24] With the award of damages, the act also granted the right to jury trial.[25] Together these changes moved the litigation of Title VII claims even closer to the model of personal injury litigation: more is at stake and more is determined by the jury. Plaintiffs and their attorneys now have greater incentives to pursue claims under Title VII, particularly by augmenting judicially awarded attorney's fees with contingent fees. As discussed later in this chapter,[26] the award of attorney's fees to prevailing plaintiffs already increases the attractiveness of these claims. The addition of a contingent fee, drawn from an award of damages, provides an alternative source of compensation for plaintiffs' attorneys, one that is particularly significant in cases settled well in advance of trial. And, of course, the prospect of recovering damages gives plaintiffs themselves a further reason to undertake the expense and stress of litigation.

The provision that added damages to the remedies available under Title VII was enacted as a separate section of the United States Code, section 1981a. This purely formal separation of rights and remedies resulted from the expanded scope of section 1981a,

---

21. International Bhd. of Teamsters v. United States, 431 U.S. 324, 376 (1977).

22. *See* Chapter V.A *supra*.

23. Local 28, Sheet Metal Workers' Int'l Ass'n v. EEOC, 478 U.S. 421, 448–50 (opinion of Brennan, J.); *id.* at 483 (Powell, J., concurring and concurring in the judgment).

24. 42 U.S.C. § 1981a(a)(1) (2000).

25. *Id.* § 1981a(c).

26. *See* Section D *infra*.

which also provides for the award of damages for violations of the Rehabilitation Act of 1973 and the Americans with Disabilities Act of 1990.[27] Partly, too, Congress wanted to emphasize the parallel between actions for damages under Title VII and actions for damages under section 1981, which is, however, limited to discrimination on the basis of race and national origin.[28] Section 1981a establishes a damage remedy for discrimination on the basis of sex, religion, and disability similar to that already available for discrimination on the basis of race and national origin under section 1981.

Despite the parallel with damages under section 1981, section 1981a itself is limited in several respects. First, damages can be recovered under section 1981a only if they cannot be recovered under section 1981. Plaintiffs who have a claim under section 1981 must rely on it for any recovery of damages.[29] Second, damages are available only for claims of disparate treatment, not for claims of disparate impact.[30] This limitation aligns section 1981a with section 1981, which imposes liability only for disparate treatment, but at the cost of departing from Title VII which, of course, allows recovery on claims of disparate impact. Third, recovery of punitive damages is available only against private employers and only upon proof that the defendant acted "with malice or with reckless indifference to the federally protected rights of an aggrieved individual."[31] Fourth, monetary relief that can be recovered under Title VII, mainly in the form of back pay, cannot be recovered under section 1981a.[32] And fifth, the amount of damages for future pecuniary losses, nonpecuniary losses, and punitive damages are capped at different amounts depending on the size of the employer, from $50,000 for employers with 15 to 100 employees, to $300,000 for employers with more than 500 employees.[33]

Further limits on punitive damages were imposed by the Supreme Court in *Kolstad v. American Dental Association*,[34] a case concerned with the employer's vicarious liability for the decision of its employees. The Court rejected a test that would require a finding that the employer engaged in independently "egregious" conduct to be held liable for punitive damages and, instead, adopted a test similar to the one for vicarious liability for sexual harassment. An employer, the Court held, was liable for the malicious or recklessly indifferent decisions of its managerial agents only if those decisions were "contrary to the employer's good-faith efforts

---

27. *Id.* § 1981a(a)(2), (3).

28. *See* Ch. X.B *infra*.

29. 42 U.S.C. § 1981a(a)(1) (2000).

30. *Id.*

31. *Id.* § 1981a(b)(1).

32. *Id.* § 1981a(b)(2).

33. *Id.* § 1981a(b)(3).

34. 527 U.S. 526 (1999).

to comply with Title VII."[35] Thus an employer can protect itself from punitive damages by establishing internal controls against obviously discriminatory practices.

These limits on damages, while significant, do not impose equally strict limits on the right to jury trial. Awards of back pay and injunctive relief still are made by the judge because these are forms of equitable relief awarded by the court, but under the Seventh Amendment, the jury's decision on the issue of liability on a claim for damages is binding on the judge. Or, more precisely, to the extent that claims for legal relief and claims for equitable relief involve common issues, the jury's decision of those issues takes priority over the judge's because of the right to jury trial under the Seventh Amendment.[36] So, for instance, when the plaintiff alleges intentional discrimination, seeks damages and back pay, and requests a jury trial, the issue of liability is submitted to the jury along with the issue of damages. The judge decides the claim for back pay, but in doing so, must accept the jury's verdict on the issue of intentional discrimination. Only on claims of disparate impact does the judge determine the issue of liability because these claims do not support an award of damages.

Wholly apart from the issue of damages, the Civil Rights Act of 1991 modified the remedies available under Title VII in various other ways. The only common theme in these provisions is that they overruled, either partially or wholly, several prior decisions of the Supreme Court. As discussed earlier,[37] the act introduced the partial defense that the plaintiff would have been rejected for an entirely legitimate reason even if the employer had not engaged in discrimination.[38] This provision allows the award of declaratory relief, prospective injunctive relief, and attorney's fees and costs, even if the defense is made out, thereby partially overruling a decision that had recognized a full defense on the same grounds.[39] What appears mainly to have been at stake was the award of attorney's fees to prevailing plaintiffs.[40] On a related subject, the act also authorizes the award of fees for experts as costs,[41] overrul-

---

35. *Id.* at 545 (citation and internal quotation marks omitted).

36. Lytle v. Household Mfg., Inc., 494 U.S. 545, 550–54 (1990); Dairy Queen, Inc. v. Wood, 369 U.S. 469, 473 (1962); Beacon Theatres, Inc. v. Westover, 359 U.S. 500, 510–11 (1959).

37. *See* Section A and Chapter III.D *supra.*

38. § 706(g)(2)(B), codified as 42 U.S.C. § 2000e–5(g)(2)(B) (2000).

39. Price Waterhouse v. Hopkins, 490 U.S. 228, 245–46 (1989).

40. This provision is in some tension with the general principles governing the award of attorney's fees, because it authorizes the award of attorney's fees based solely on a finding that the statute has been violated. *See* Section D *infra.*

41. § 706(k), codified as 42 U.S.C. § 2000e–5(k) (2000).

ing a decision that had restricted fees for expert witnesses to the same fees for other witnesses.[42] Another provision authorizes the award of prejudgment interest against the United States,[43] which is also generally available against other defendants.[44] In yet another overruling provision, the act restricts collateral attack upon judgments and consent decrees by persons who were not parties to the underlying action.[45] This provision was designed mainly to protect court-ordered and court-approved affirmative action plans from claims of reverse discrimination, but it cannot, of course, deny anyone an opportunity to be heard under the Due Process Clause.[46]

C.   Remedies in Class Actions and Pattern–or–Practice Actions

Class-wide relief can be sought either in class actions brought by private plaintiffs or pattern-or-practice actions brought by the government. The shift from individual to class claims does not change the standards governing relief under Title VII, but it does change the way in which those standards are applied. It also invites consideration of how a broad remedial conception of equality can be brought to bear through large-scale litigation. Awards of compensatory relief to plaintiffs in individual actions, no matter how comprehensive, do not directly change the employment practices of institutional employers. Relief in class actions and pattern-or-practice actions can directly accomplish this result. And, indeed, for victims of discrimination with claims too small to support an individual action, class claims are the only practical means to award any relief to them at all. Such relief often can only be approximate because of the difficulties of determining how an entire class of employees would have fared in the absence of discrimination, and in fact, it usually results from a partial or complete settlement of the claims asserted on behalf of a class. These necessary departures from the ideal of perfect compensation reveal both the limitations of individ-

---

42. The overruled decision is *Crawford Fitting Co. v. J.T. Gibbons, Inc.*, 482 U.S. 437 (1987). Expert witness fees remain excluded, however, from awards of attorney's fees under civil rights statutes other than Title VII and 42 U.S.C. §§ 1981, 1981a. *See* 42 U.S.C. § 1988 (2000); West Virginia Hosps., Inc. v. Casey, 499 U.S. 83 (1991).

43. § 717(d), codified as 42 U.S.C. § 2000e–16(d) (2000). The decision in *Library of Congress v. Shaw*, 478 U.S. 310 (1986), was overruled only to the

extent that it disallowed the award of interest, not to the extent that it allowed an award of back pay.

44. Loeffler v. Frank, 486 U.S. 549, 554–57 (1988).

45. § 703(n), codified as 42 U.S.C. § 2000e–2(n) (2000). The overruled decision is *Martin v. Wilks*, 490 U.S. 755 (1989).

46. The provision itself recognizes this point. § 703(n)(2)(D), codified as 42 U.S.C. § 2000e–2(n)(2)(D) (2000).

ual litigation as a remedy for discrimination and the desirability of alternative forms of relief, including affirmative action.

The departure from individual litigation begins with the way in which class litigation is structured. Such litigation is usually bifurcated into a "liability" stage that determines whether the defendant has violated Title VII and a "recovery" stage that determines the eligibility of individual class members for compensatory relief. These stages approximate the distinction between class-wide issues and individual remedies, but they do not follow it exactly. After a class-wide finding of violation, the court usually decides the issue of class-wide relief, typically an injunction that prospectively prohibits the discriminatory practice.[47] Usually it is only after deciding that issue that the court turns to the more difficult issue of individual relief for class members.

Some opinions complicate the transition from the liability to the remedy stage still further by introducing the confusing terminology of "prima facie" case to describe the effect of finding a violation of Title VII.[48] This is a mistake, first because the terminology of "prima facie" case can carry so many different meanings, but second, and more fundamentally, because there is nothing "prima facie" about a finding of violation: the defendant has been found to have violated the law. Accordingly, just as in individual actions, most of the burden of proof should shift from the plaintiff to the defendant.

This principle of shifting most of the burden of proof to the defendant, in fact, was first developed in judicial decisions concerned with class litigation, anticipating the partial defense, codified by the Civil Rights Act of 1991, allowing the defendant to avoid liability for compensatory relief by proving that the plaintiff would have been rejected for an entirely legitimate reason despite the discrimination found at the earlier stage of the case.[49] The act allocates the burden of proof on this defense entirely to the defendant. So, too, in class actions and pattern-or-practice actions, a class member need only prove that she applied for the job in question. The burden then shifts to the employer to prove that she was not a victim of discrimination, for instance, because she lacked the necessary qualifications for the job or there was no opening when she applied.[50] In order to obtain reinstatement, class members

---

47. International Bhd. of Teamsters v. United States, 431 U.S. 324, 361 (1977).

48. *E.g.*, United States v. United States Steel Corp., 520 F.2d 1043, 1053–54 (5th Cir. 1975), *cert. denied*, 429 U.S. 817 (1976).

49. § 706(g)(2)(B), codified as 42 U.S.C. § 2000e–5(g)(2)(B) (2000).

50. *Teamsters*, 431 U.S. at 361–62.

must also be qualified at the time that reinstatement is offered, an issue upon which the employer apparently bears the burden of proof.[51]

An employee who did not apply for the job at issue has the "not always easy burden of proving that he would have applied for the job" in the absence of discrimination.[52] This requires a showing that the plaintiff was deterred from applying for the job and that he possessed the qualifications that would have been revealed in an application.[53] If a nonapplicant makes this showing, he is treated just like an applicant; the employer bears the burden of proving that he was not a victim of discrimination.[54] The Supreme Court has granted compensatory relief to class members who have applied for a job, whether or not they were already employed by the employer, and to class members who were employees but who did not apply for a job.[55] Class members who are neither applicants nor employees, however, present a more difficult case for compensation because they are difficult to distinguish from members of the public at large.[56]

All of these intricate doctrinal rules presuppose a precise determination of who is entitled to relief, and as the previous section discussed, in what amount. Such precision is more likely to be achieved in theory than in practice. Indeed, even in theory, it is difficult to ascertain which of several class members would have been hired or promoted for a single open position. Even if they were all discriminatorily excluded from consideration for the position, only one would have received it in the absence of discrimination. As the Fifth Circuit has characterized this inquiry, it is "the quagmire of hypothetical judgments,"[57] one that only becomes deeper as the number of positions and discriminatory decisions multiply and the hypothetical judgments become ever more speculative. As with the attempt to precisely tailor individualized relief to the situation of a particular plaintiff, the greater the precision that is sought, the greater also the uncertainty of any relief that is ultimately formulated. The tendency of class litigation to be settled before trial, or in any event, before a full-fledged adjudication on the issue of liability, alleviates this problem only by recognizing that it cannot be solved.

---

51. *See* Franks v. Bowman Transp. Co., 424 U.S. 747, 772–73 nn. 31–32 (1976).

52. *Teamsters*, 431 U.S. at 367–68.

53. *Id.* at 367–71.

54. *Id.* at 369 & n.53.

55. *Id.* at 367–71; *Franks*, 424 U.S. at 771–72.

56. *See Teamsters*, 431 U.S. at 368 n.52.

57. Pettway v. American Cast Iron Pipe Co., 494 F.2d 211, 260 (5th Cir. 1974).

The costs of fully individualized adjudication would consume the benefits of precisely tailored relief.

These departures from the ideal of perfectly individualized relief support a remedial conception of equality that goes beyond compensation of identified victims of discrimination. Any such relief is necessarily approximate, both in determining who has been wronged and in determining what they would have received in the absence of discrimination. Perfect compensation is an unattainable ideal, which should not be pursued to the exclusion of more broadly defined remedies. Prospective remedies, of course, also are necessary, in the form of injunctions against future discrimination or orders restructuring discriminatory business practices. But these purely forward-looking remedies do not address the continuing consequences of past discrimination. As noted earlier, affirmative action can rarely be ordered by a court under Title VII. For all these reasons, the remedial perspective looks beyond remedies in the narrow sense of court orders entered after a finding of liability. It seeks, instead, to change the rules of liability themselves in order to encourage employers to take steps on their own to compensate for the effects of past discrimination. The theory of disparate impact and voluntary affirmative action are two means of doing so. A close look at conventional judicial remedies reveals the need for a remedial perspective that endorses other ways of alleviating the effects of past discrimination.

D. Attorney's Fees

Section 706(k) authorizes the award of attorney's fees to "the prevailing party" in Title VII cases.[58] Despite its reference to "the prevailing party," this provision has been applied in diametrically opposed ways to prevailing plaintiffs and prevailing defendants. Prevailing plaintiffs almost always recover an award of attorney's fees; prevailing defendants almost never do. The Supreme Court reached this result in *Christiansburg Garment Co. v. EEOC*,[59] holding that prevailing plaintiffs are entitled to an award of attorney's fees " 'unless special circumstances would render such an award unjust,' "[60] but that prevailing defendants are entitled to an award of fees only if " 'the action brought is found to be unreasonable, frivolous, meritless or vexatious.' "[61] The Court reasoned that

58. § 706(k), codified as 42 U.S.C. § 2000e–5(k) (2000).

59. 434 U.S. 412 (1978).

60. *Id.* at 416–17 (quoting Newman v. Piggie Park Enters., 390 U.S. 400, 402 (1968)).

61. *Id.* at 421 (quoting Carrion v. Yeshiva Univ., 535 F.2d 722, 727 (2d Cir. 1976)).

fee awards to prevailing plaintiffs further the statutory purpose of eliminating discrimination, but that fee awards to prevailing defendants succeed only in discouraging meritless litigation.[62]

This rationale seemingly follows directly from the remedial conception of equality. A presumption in favor of awarding attorney's fees to prevailing plaintiffs both gives them full compensation for past discrimination and provides them, through their attorneys, with a strong incentive to pursue claims under Title VII. On closer examination, however, it has a more limited impact, mainly favoring claims on which plaintiffs are likely to prevail and for which they are likely to recover a significant award of back pay and damages. These are claims predominantly by current or former employees, who are acquainted with the defendant's personnel practices and who, if successful, are likely to recover enough in back pay and damages to make litigation worthwhile. Only these claims provide an attorney with a sufficient prospect of recovering a substantial award of attorney's fees, at the outset of the litigation when the decision to sue is made.

Yet these cases do not open up new job opportunities for minorities or women to the same extent as cases brought by applicants for employment. Current or former employees have already passed the initial hurdle to acceptance by an employer, and although they may allege discrimination in working conditions, promotions, or termination decisions, they do so as much to preserve existing opportunities as to expand them. Preserving existing opportunities is a worthy goal, but it is more appropriate to the conventional historical perspective on employment discrimination law, rather than the broad remedial perspective. It envisages limited changes through individual litigation, rather than far-reaching reforms through procedural devices such as class actions. This tendency towards incremental change is reinforced by the method for computing attorney's fees.

The leading decision on computing the amount of an award of attorney's fees is *Hensley v. Eckerhart*.[63] It established a two-step process, applicable to all statutes that authorize an award of attorney's fees to the prevailing party.[64] First, the court should compute the "lodestar": the number of hours reasonably expended

---

62. *Id.* at 420.

63. 461 U.S. 424 (1983).

64. This case did not itself involve a claim of employment discrimination, but a claim under the general civil rights statute, 42 U.S.C. § 1983 (2000). The same principles, however, apply to the award of attorney's fees in all civil rights actions, so that precedents under other civil rights statutes also apply to the award of attorney's fees under Title VII. *Id.* at 433 n.7.

multiplied by a reasonable hourly rate. Second, the court should adjust the lodestar figure up or down to take account of other factors, chief among them, the results obtained by the plaintiff. If the plaintiff has been only partially successful, the lodestar figure must be reduced so that it reflects only hours reasonably expended on claims on which the plaintiff prevailed or on related claims that contributed to the successful claims. Conversely, if the plaintiff has been exceptionally successful, the lodestar figure may be enhanced. In determining which hours were reasonably expended, "the most critical factor is the degree of success obtained."[65] Other factors may also be taken into account in adjusting the lodestar figure up or down, but only to the extent that they are not already reflected in the lodestar figure itself.[66] This last qualification is important, since it has been interpreted in subsequent decisions to eliminate virtually all upward adjustments in the lodestar. The lodestar also includes the hours reasonably expended by paralegals and law clerks,[67] and under Title VII, awards of costs can also include fees for experts,[68] essentially treating other professionals like attorneys.

The lodestar method of calculating awards of attorney's fees has been largely confirmed by the Supreme Court's subsequent decisions. In *Blum v. Stenson*,[69] the Court held that a 50% increase in the lodestar figure was not justified by the complexity or novelty of the issues, the skill of counsel, the results obtained, or the risks of litigation. None of these factors was out of the ordinary and all were adequately reflected in the lodestar figure. In *Pennsylvania v. Delaware Valley Citizens' Council*,[70] the Court twice considered, but did not definitively resolve, the question whether the lodestar figure can be adjusted upward to take account of the plaintiff's risk of loss and counsel's risk of not being compensated at all. In *City of Burlington v. Dague*,[71] the Court finally held that no enhancement of the lodestar was permitted on these grounds. To the extent that the risk of loss reflected factors that should be used to enhance the award—such as the difficulty of the case—these were already taken into account in computing the lodestar. To the extent that the risk of loss reflects the merits of the case, it should not be used to enhance awards of attorney's fees or to encourage plaintiffs to bring weak cases.[72]

65. *Id.* at 436.

66. *Id.* at 434 n.9.

67. Missouri v. Jenkins, 491 U.S. 274, 284–89 (1989).

68. § 706(k), codified as 42 U.S.C. § 2000e–5(k) (2000). This provision also applies to claims under 42 U.S.C.

§§ 1981, 1981a. *See* 42 U.S.C. § 1988(c) (2000).

69. 465 U.S. 886 (1984).

70. 478 U.S. 546 (1986), on reargument, 483 U.S. 711 (1987).

71. 505 U.S. 557 (1992).

72. *Id.* at 562–63.

The principal criticism of the lodestar method of calculating fee awards is that it creates the wrong incentives for plaintiffs' attorneys. Because it does not compensate attorneys at all for cases that they lose, it encourages them only to take cases that they are likely to win. In the cases they actually win, they receive the lodestar amount but without any enhancement for the difficulty or riskiness of the case. In cases that they lose, they recover nothing at all from the defendant and, on the assumption that employment discrimination plaintiffs have limited means, they receive only minimal compensation directly from the plaintiffs. They gain no net benefit, and are likely to suffer a net loss, from taking risky cases. They are better off taking only the cases described earlier, in which the plaintiff is well acquainted with the defendant's employment practices and is likely to obtain a substantial recovery of back pay or damages.

The need for a substantial recovery by the plaintiff, although not strictly speaking a prerequisite for an award of attorney's fees under Title VII, nevertheless follows from the emphasis in *Hensley v. Eckerhart* on "the degree of success obtained." Several subsequent decisions have denied an award of attorney's fees altogether when the plaintiff has not obtained any judicially ordered relief or received only nominal relief. In *Hewitt v. Helms*,[73] the plaintiffs obtained an opinion that state prison officials had acted in violation of the Constitution but that they were immune from liability for damages, the only relief that the plaintiffs sought. Despite the fact that the prison officials revised their regulations to conform to the opinion, the plaintiffs were not prevailing parties entitled to an award of attorney's fees.[74] In *Farrar v. Hobby*,[75] the plaintiff obtained nominal damages of one dollar and thus was a prevailing plaintiff, but because he had failed to establish a claim to any other form of relief, he was not entitled to an award of attorney's fees.

Other decisions have supported an award of attorney's fees based on a disproportionately low recovery by the plaintiff, but these decisions are exceptional. *Texas State Teachers Association v. Garland Independent School District*[76] allowed an award of attorney's fees when the plaintiff succeeded on " 'any significant issue in litigation which achieve[d] some of the benefit the parties sought in bringing suit.' "[77] The Court cautioned, however, that a "material

---

73. 482 U.S. 755 (1987).

74. *Id.* at 759–64. *Accord,* Rhodes v. Stewart, 488 U.S. 1 (1988) (no award of attorney's fees where prisoner's claims became moot before district court entered declaratory judgment in their favor).

75. 506 U.S. 103 (1992).

76. 489 U.S. 782 (1989).

77. *Id.* at 791–92 (quoting Nadeau v. Helgemoe, 581 F.2d 275, 278–79 (1st Cir. 1978)).

alteration of the legal relationship of the parties" was necessary and that "purely technical or *de minimis*" success was inadequate.[78] And a divided decision in *City of Riverside v. Rivera*[79] affirmed an award of $245,000 in attorney's fees to plaintiffs who had recovered a total of $33,000 against police officers arising from an illegal search and arrest. For a plurality of four, Justice Brennan held that the district court's findings were sufficient to support the lodestar figure as a reasonable fee award.[80] Justice Powell concurred in the judgment on the ground that the district court's detailed findings of fact justified the fee award, but he expressed "serious doubts as to the fairness of the fees awarded in this case."[81] Only the elaborate documentation of the fee award, supported by the public interest in preventing police misconduct, justified a fee award greatly in excess of the plaintiffs' own recovery.

A special provision added to Title VII by the Civil Rights Act of 1991 might blunt the effect of the decisions recounted in the last two paragraphs, none of which arose under Title VII. This provision explicitly authorizes an award of attorney's fees upon a finding that Title VII has been violated, even if no monetary relief or other compensatory relief is awarded to the plaintiff.[82] Nevertheless, in the absence of an award of injunctive relief that confers a benefit upon the plaintiff or upon others similarly situated, it is difficult to justify a substantial award of attorney's fees under the lodestar. Hours reasonably expended by an attorney under *Hensley v. Eckerhart* must be related to some claim on which the plaintiff prevailed. Minimal relief might justify an award of attorney's fees, but only if it is minimal as well.

The proportionality typically required between the award of attorney's fees and the relief obtained by the plaintiff raises yet another problem with the lodestar method of calculating fee awards. A plaintiff's attorney with the likely prospect of obtaining substantial relief has a strong incentive to prolong the case in order to maximize the number of hours he can reasonably expend upon it. Early settlement works to the disadvantage of attorneys who are compensated only or mainly through the award of attorney's fees. Although the plaintiff retains ultimate control over the decision whether or not to settle, the attorney's advice about the relative benefits of litigation over settlement is often likely to be dispositive. Contingent fee agreements between the attorney and the plaintiff

---

78. *Id.* at 792–93.

79. 477 U.S. 561 (1986).

80. *Id.* at 569–73 (opinion of Brennan, J.).

81. *Id.* at 586 (Powell, J., concurring).

82. § 706(g)(2)(B), codified as 42 U.S.C. § 2000e–5(g)(2)(B) (2000).

can eliminate this disincentive to settle, without jeopardizing the plaintiff's ability to obtain an award of attorney's fees from the defendant,[83] but these arrangements are contractual and not mandatory. The lodestar method does not guarantee that such agreements will be made, or more broadly, that the most significant employment discrimination claims will be brought and vigorously pursued.[84]

83. Blanchard v. Bergeron, 489 U.S. 87, 93 (1989).

84. A further complication involves the tax consequences to the plaintiff of an award of attorney's fees, which go to the plaintiff individually before any payment to the attorney. These awards are included in the plaintiff's gross income, often causing it to rise above the threshold for applying the Alternative Minimum Tax (AMT), a complex set of provisions that imposes a higher tax rate and allows fewer deductions to individuals with high annual income. Among the disallowed deductions are those that would ordinarily apply to the plaintiff's payment of attorney's fees, but in a recent amendment to the Internal Revenue Code, Congress reinstated these deductions with respect to the AMT. 26 U.S.C. § 62(20) (2000). Specifically, the amendment redefines adjusted gross income to exclude any award of costs and fees to offset its inclusion in gross income.

Chapter X

RECONSTRUCTION CIVIL RIGHTS ACTS

Several civil rights acts were passed during Reconstruction, contemporaneously with the ratification of the Thirteenth, Fourteenth, and Fifteenth Amendments. The most general of these is section 1983, enacted as part of the "Ku Klux Klan" Act of 1871.[1] It creates a private right of action for deprivation of federal rights under color of state law. Although it literally applies to the deprivation of any federal right, its most common application is to the deprivation of federal constitutional rights. And in most cases, it is limited to claims against the officials of state and local government, both because most constitutional rights apply only against the government and because section 1983 itself requires action under color of state law.

Section 1981, another civil rights act from the same era, applies to a broader range of employers, although not to a broader range of rights, than section 1983. Section 1981 was first enacted as part of the Civil Rights Act of 1866.[2] In its current version, it grants to all persons the same right "to make and enforce contracts . . . as is enjoyed by white citizens." This provision applies only to contracts, but it applies to all contracts, whether public or private. Section 1981 therefore applies, just like Title VII, to private employers.

Both section 1983 and section 1981 have complicated histories of enactment, reenactment, interpretation, and reinterpretation, which to some extent are intertwined. The legislative acts and judicial decisions that eventually gave content to these statutes make the historical perspective particularly significant in interpreting their provisions. Sections 1981 and 1983 can only be understood against the background of the constitutional rights first recognized during Reconstruction and the subsequent revitalization of those rights after *Brown v. Board of Education*.[3] No source of employment discrimination law is more heavily influenced by the development of constitutional law. And indeed, just like the constitutional prohibition against racial discrimination in the Fourteenth Amendment itself, both of these statutes fell into nearly a century of neglect before they were revived by the Warren Court.

1. 42 U.S.C. § 1983 (2000).   3. 347 U.S. 483 (1954).
2. *Id.* § 1981.

The predominance of the historical perspective in interpretation of these statutes has both expansive and limiting consequences. The expansive consequences are most apparent in section 1983, which is simply a vehicle for enforcing constitutional rights, including rights against discrimination. The limiting consequences have to do with the need to prove intentional discrimination and, under section 1983, the further requirement of proof of state action. Both requirements leave claims of employment discrimination under these statutes significantly narrower in scope than those under Title VII. Only on the issue of remedies, and particularly damages, have these statutes expanded the scope of liability beyond that in Title VII.

This chapter begins with a brief summary of the law under section 1983. An exhaustive treatment would require an entire book, but the role of constitutional law stands out so clearly under section 1983 that it serves to illustrate its influence over all of civil rights law. The following section examines section 1981 and takes up both its similarities and contrasts with constitutional law and its parallel development with interpretation of Title VII. The chapter concludes with a short discussion of another highly technical statute enacted during Reconstruction, section 1985(3), which nevertheless has some bearing on employment discrimination claims.

A.　Section 1983

The modern law of section 1983 begins with *Monroe v. Pape*,[4] which interpreted the statute to provide a remedy for all deprivations of constitutional rights under color of state law, even if state law itself provided a remedy. This holding made section 1983 the vehicle for enforcing all constitutional rights against the state, including those based on the constitutional prohibitions against discrimination. Before the enactment of Title VII and its amendment to cover states and localities as employers, section 1983 already provided a remedy for employment discrimination by state and local officials. Moreover, with the subsequent recognition of a constitutional prohibition against sex discrimination, section 1983 covered all the same grounds of discrimination as Title VII: race, national origin, sex, and religion.[5] Employees of state and local

---

4.　365 U.S. 167 (1961).

5.　The Fourteenth Amendment also prohibits discrimination on the basis of alienage, except in positions bound up with the operation of the states as government entities, such as police or

teachers. Ambach v. Norwick, 441 U.S. 68 (1979); Foley v. Connelie, 435 U.S. 291 (1978). In this respect, it is broader than Title VII, which does not cover discrimination on this ground at all, and it is likewise broader than the Fifth

government therefore have overlapping remedies for employment discrimination under section 1983 and Title VII. The overlap results, however, not from the terms of the statutes themselves but from the prohibition of the same forms of discrimination by both the Constitution and Title VII.

This overlap, of course, is only partial. Title VII's great innovation was to extend the constitutional prohibition against discrimination to private employment. Section 1983 expressly refrains from taking this step by requiring action under color of state law, a statutory requirement that follows the Fourteenth Amendment's limitation to state action. And even when this requirement is satisfied, the content of the prohibitions differs in significant respects. The constitutional prohibition enforced by section 1983 extends only to intentional discrimination, not to practices that have a disparate impact.[6] As under Title VII, evidence of disparate impact may be used to prove intentional discrimination, but an additional inference about the intent of government officials must be drawn in order to reach this conclusion. Disparate impact alone does not constitute a violation of the Constitution.

Likewise, the statutory and constitutional prohibitions against sex discrimination are not identical. Title VII prohibits any employment practice that classifies on the basis of sex, subject only to a narrow exception for bona fide occupational qualifications.[7] Constitutional decisions, by contrast, take a more flexible approach, prohibiting classifications on the basis of sex unless they have an "exceedingly persuasive justification."[8] The nuances of the statutory and constitutional standards against discrimination on other grounds, such as religion, might also yield different results in particular cases. From the historical perspective, these differences reveal only that Title VII developed from constitutional law, not that it is identical to it.

The different procedures under section 1983 and Title VII make this point clearer still. A claim under section 1983 need not be preceded by attempts to exhaust administrative remedies. A plaintiff need only file an action in court within the applicable

---

Amendment, which permits most forms of discrimination on the basis of alienage by the federal government. Hampton v. Mow Sun Wong, 426 U.S. 88 (1976) (discrimination against aliens not permitted because not specifically authorized by Congress or the President); Mathews v. Diaz, 426 U.S. 67 (1976) (discrimination permitted because authorized by Congress).

6. Washington v. Davis, 426 U.S. 229, 238–39 (1976).

7. United Auto. Workers v. Johnson Controls, Inc., 499 U.S. 187, 200–01 (1991).

8. United States v. Virginia, 518 U.S. 515, 531 (1996).

statute of limitations, borrowed for this purpose from state law.[9] A claim under section 1983 can be joined with one under Title VII, but the procedural requirements of each statute must be separately satisfied for each claim.[10] In particular, the elaborate time limits for filing a claim under Title VII are not affected by joining a claim under section 1983, even if it challenges exactly the same employment decision.

The remedies available under the two statutes also are a study in contrasts. Most of the restrictions on remedies under section 1983 developed outside of employment discrimination cases, resulting in legal rules that seem better suited for other kinds of cases, such as those alleging police brutality or denial of due process by administrative action. This consequence follows from the role of section 1983 as a vehicle for enforcing any constitutional right involving state action. The broad scope of these claims gives rise to the need for equally broad defenses, particularly with respect to recovery of damages. Thus, damages can be recovered from a government employer only if it is a subdivision of the state, but one that remains separate from the state itself, such as a city or county. Otherwise, the Eleventh Amendment bars the recovery of money directly from the state treasury.[11] Moreover, even if this requirement is met, the government employer is directly liable only for alleged discrimination resulting from the execution of official policy or custom.[12] Insofar as the claim is against an individual state or local officer, which it often is, then none of the preceding restrictions apply, but others come into play. The officer is liable for damages only if a defense of partial or complete immunity cannot be made out.[13] To complicate the remedial issues still further, injunctive relief and the award of attorney's fees are available

9. All claims under section 1983 are subject to the state statute of limitations for claims for personal injury. Wilson v. Garcia, 471 U.S. 261, 271–75 (1985). If a state has more than one such statute— for instance, one for intentional torts and one for all other torts—the general or residual statute should be applied. Owens v. Okure, 488 U.S. 235 (1989).

10. *See* Johnson v. Railway Express Agency, 421 U.S. 454, 460–62 (1975). By the same token, the reference in section 1983 to enforcing all federal rights under the Constitution "and laws" does not encompass enforcement of rights under statutes, like Title VII, that have their own enforcement mechanism. *See* Middlesex County Sewerage Auth. v.

National Sea Clammers Ass'n, 453 U.S. 1, 19–21 (1981).

11. Quern v. Jordan, 440 U.S. 332, 338 (1979). The Eleventh Amendment applies only to actions in federal court, but section 1983 itself contains a corresponding exception for actions against the states in state court. Will v. Michigan Dep't of State Police, 491 U.S. 58, 66 (1989).

12. City of St. Louis v. Praprotnik, 485 U.S. 112, 128 (1988); Owens v. City of Independence, 445 U.S. 622, 657 (1980).

13. *See, e.g.*, Scheuer v. Rhodes, 416 U.S. 232 (1974).

against the officer without regard to immunity.[14]

None of these Byzantine rules applies under Title VII because Congress has chosen to make state and local governments directly liable for damages and other forms of relief. In doing so, Congress relied upon its power to enforce the Fourteenth Amendment by appropriate legislation and thereby abrogated the protection afforded to the states under the Eleventh Amendment.[15] This is not to say that the remedial scheme under Title VII is simple. As the preceding chapters reveal, it is not, but it is complex for entirely different reasons. The remedies and defenses specific to section 1983 have had no effect on those under Title VII.

Section 1983 has exercised a far more direct influence over claims under section 1981, by way of the decision of the Supreme Court in *Jett v. Dallas Independent School District*,[16] which held that claims under section 1981 against state and local officials must be brought under section 1983. The Court's reasoning was that section 1981 only created a right, while section 1983 created the remedy for enforcing that right.[17] There is some question, explored in the next section of this chapter, whether this decision survives the Civil Rights Act of 1991, but even if it does, its effect is limited by the very nature of claims of intentional discrimination and their interaction with the defenses available under section 1983.

The various defenses under section 1983 (as well as those under the Eleventh Amendment) usually confine liability for monetary relief to claims against individual state or local officials. Substituting these officials as defendants does not deprive the plaintiff of the right to recover damages and other monetary relief, but it makes any such recovery subject to a defense, usually of qualified immunity. Qualified immunity is available to state officials who act under the reasonable belief that their conduct does not violate the Constitution. Yet the only claims of discrimination that can be brought under section 1983 or section 1981 are claims of intentional discrimination. At this late date, over fifty years after *Brown v. Board of Education*, state and local officials can rarely claim, with any credibility, that they engaged in intentional discrimination under a reasonable belief that they did so consistently with the Constitution. The only exceptions to this rule involve

14. *See, e.g.*, Hafer v. Melo, 502 U.S. 21 (1991). The award of attorney's fees is authorized by 42 U.S.C. § 1988, which applies to claims under all of the Reconstruction civil rights acts. As discussed in Chapter IX.D, section 1988 is interpreted in generally the same way as the corresponding provision in Title VII for the award of attorney's fees.

15. Fitzpatrick v. Bitzer, 427 U.S. 445, 456 (1976).

16. 491 U.S. 701 (1989).

17. *Id.* at 731–36.

areas of continuing controversy, such as affirmative action and perhaps some instances of sex discrimination. Otherwise, in employment discrimination cases, section 1983 makes more of a difference in form—in determining who is sued—rather than in substance—in determining what is recovered.

B. Section 1981

The interpretation of section 1981 depends even more on an historical perspective than does section 1983. In its current form, section 1981 prohibits any intentional discrimination on the basis of race in contracting, whether it is public or private or whether it involves making, performing, or enforcing contracts.[18] The scope of this prohibition extends beyond section 1983, because it reaches private discrimination, but it also extends beyond Title VII, because it reaches all kinds of contracts, not just contracts of employment. In a society heavily dependent upon contracts, in all their various forms throughout the economy, section 1981 represents a remarkable extension of the principle against discrimination. How section 1981 acquired this exceedingly broad scope, now codified by amendments to the statute made by the Civil Rights Act of 1991, is a complicated story. In the end, it has less to do with a single considered judgment of Congress than with the interaction of judicial decisions and amending legislation.

Section 1981 provides that all persons "shall have the same right in every State and Territory to make and enforce contracts . . . as is enjoyed by white citizens."[19] It was first enacted as part of the Civil Rights Act of 1866, in the exercise of the newly acquired powers of Congress to enforce the Thirteenth Amendment. A companion statute, section 1982, which prohibits racial discrimination in transactions related to land, was enacted at the same time. Because the Thirteenth Amendment prohibits slavery in all its forms, whether public or private, both section 1981 and section 1982 could plausibly be given the same broad scope. During Reconstruction, however, doubts arose about the constitutionality of the Civil Rights Act of 1866 and parts of it, including those enacting sections 1981 and 1982, were reenacted in the Voting Rights Act of 1870, relying upon additional powers conferred upon Congress by the Fourteenth Amendment. Reenactment raised the question whether sections 1981 and 1982, like the Fourteenth Amendment, were limited to state action. This was the dominant, if largely tacit, understanding of these statutes for over a century. If they reached

18. 42 U.S.C. § 1981 (2000).   **19.** *Id.* § 1981(a).

only discrimination by the states, their scope would not have exceeded that of section 1983.

But just as section 1983 was revived by a judicial decision in the midst of the Civil Rights Era, sections 1981 and 1982 were revived and extended beyond state action in the same manner. In *Jones v. Alfred H. Mayer Co.*,[20] the Supreme Court held that section 1982 prohibited housing discrimination by private individuals, as well as by public officials, relying upon the enactment of the Civil Rights Act of 1866 under the Thirteenth Amendment, with its power to reach entirely private conduct. The reasoning of this decision was then applied without further question to claims under section 1981 alleging discrimination by private employers. This decision, *Johnson v. Railway Express Agency*,[21] interpreted section 1981 to provide a remedy for employment discrimination that is entirely independent of Title VII. Yet the enactment of Title VII only a few years earlier plainly diminished the practical significance of the extension of section 1981 to private discrimination. Insofar as it applied to employment discrimination, section 1981 mainly prohibited conduct that was already prohibited by Title VII.

The same theme underlies subsequent decisions interpreting section 1981: it imposes no greater burden upon employers than does Title VII. The Supreme Court has, for instance, interpreted section 1981 to reach claims of discrimination on the basis of national origin,[22] in addition to claims of racial discrimination, although the lower federal courts are divided on whether it also covers discrimination against aliens.[23] The Supreme Court has also limited section 1981 to claims of disparate treatment, excluding liability for disparate impact.[24] Along similar lines, the lower federal courts have interpreted section 1981 so that it does not impose liability for employment practices allowed by specific exceptions in Title VII.[25]

---

20. 392 U.S. 409, 437–39 (1968).

21. 421 U.S. 454 (1975).

22. Saint Francis College v. Al-Khazraji, 481 U.S. 604 (1987).

23. *Compare* Bhandari v. First National Bank of Commerce, 887 F.2d 609 (5th Cir. 1989), *cert. denied*, 494 U.S. 1061 (1990) (not covered independently of racial discrimination) *with* Duane v. GEICO, 37 F.3d 1036 (4th Cir. 1994) (private discrimination against aliens covered), *cert. voluntarily dismissed*, 515 U.S. 1101 (1995) Early decisions of the Supreme Court, before section 1981 was extended to cover private discrimination, applied it to government discrimination against aliens. Takahashi v. Fish and Game Comm'n, 334 U.S. 410 (1948).

24. General Building Contractors Ass'n v. Pennsylvania, 458 U.S. 375 (1982).

25. *E.g.*, Johnson v. Ryder Truck Lines, 575 F.2d 471 (4th Cir. 1978), *cert. denied*, 440 U.S. 979 (1979) (seniority system permitted by Title VII not prohibited by section 1981).

Nevertheless, in three respects, section 1981 is broader than Title VII. The first and most important of these concerns the award of damages. Section 1981 supports the award of damages as a remedy,[26] and it gives rise to a right to jury trial under the Seventh Amendment.[27] This originally set it apart from Title VII, which was limited to equitable relief, without any right to jury trial. The Civil Rights Act of 1991 corrected this discrepancy, but did not entirely eliminate it, authorizing the award of damages under Title VII under certain conditions. Damages are available under Title VII only for claims of intentional discrimination and only if a remedy is not available under section 1981. Moreover, damages under Title VII are subject to caps that depend on the size of the employer.[28] Second, section 1981 covers all employers (and indeed, all private contracting parties), while Title VII only covers employers with fifteen or more employees.[29] And third, section 1981 has independent procedures for filing suit, which do not require exhaustion of administrative remedies. A claim under section 1981, like one under section 1983, need only be filed in court within the time allowed by the applicable statute of limitations.

This last issue has created some complications because the applicable statute of limitations depends upon the nature of the plaintiff's claim. For claims involving discrimination in hiring, or any new employment contract, the statute of limitations is the one governing personal injury actions in the state in which the district court sits.[30] The state statute of limitations does not apply of its own force, but is "borrowed" only to fill a gap in federal law and is interpreted according to federal principles.[31] This borrowed statute of limitations applies to all claims under section 1981 as it existed before the Civil Rights Act of 1991. As to all other claims, a new federal catch-all statute of limitation applies. This new, four-year limitation period applies to all federal statutes enacted after 1990 that do not have their own limitation period.[32] In *Jones v. R.R.*

---

26. Johnson v. Railway Express Agency, 421 U.S. 454, 460 (1975).

27. *E.g.*, Setser v. Novack Investment Co., 638 F.2d 1137, 1139–40 (8th Cir.), *modified on other grounds*, 657 F.2d 962 (8th Cir.) (en banc), *cert. denied*, 454 U.S. 1064 (1981); Moore v. Sun Oil Co., 636 F.2d 154, 156 (6th Cir. 1980); *cf.* Curtis v. Loether, 415 U.S. 189, 195–96 (1974) (action for damages under Fair Housing Act gives rise to Seventh Amendment right to jury trial in federal court).

28. 42 U.S.C. § 1981a (2000).

29. § 701(b), codified as 42 U.S.C. § 2000e(b) (2000).

30. This is the limitation for filing tort claims for personal injuries, not the generally shorter limitation for filing administrative complaints, Burnett v. Grattan, 468 U.S. 42 (1984), or the generally longer limitation for filing contract actions. Goodman v. Lukens Steel Co., 482 U.S. 656 (1987).

31. *Johnson*, 421 U.S. at 462–66.

32. 28 U.S.C. § 1658.

Donnelley & Sons Co.,[33] the Supreme Court held that section 1981(b) was one such statute because claims for "performance, modification, and termination of contracts" had not been previously recognized under section 1981.

The reason for this change in the statute goes back to debates over its scope and origins. The broader remedies available under section 1981 apparently led the Supreme Court to have second thoughts about extending the statute to all forms of private discrimination. In *Patterson v. McLean Credit Union*,[34] the Court held that the literal terms of section 1981, as it then read, covered only discrimination in making or enforcing contracts, leaving claims of discrimination in conditions of employment to be remedied only under Title VII. This decision prompted Congress to amend section 1981 in two significant respects in the Civil Rights Act of 1991. First, Congress put to rest any debate over the application of section 1981 to private discrimination by explicitly providing that the statute applied equally to "nongovernmental discrimination" and discrimination under color of state law.[35] Second, Congress specifically overruled the holding in *Patterson* and made section 1981 applicable to all aspects of any contractual relationship, including conditions of employment.[36]

The doctrinal intricacy of the law under section 1981, although of immediate significance mainly to the practitioner, also reveals the profound and unforeseeable effects of history on employment discrimination law. How section 1981 came to acquire its present form cannot be explained as a matter of logical development of policy. Instead, it involves the interaction of statutes and judicial decisions issued more than a century apart. It is difficult to imagine that section 1981 initially would have received an interpretation that applied it to private discrimination, or that it could have eventually received such an interpretation without the prior enactment of Title VII, which far more explicitly achieved the same result. Even the recent amendments to section 1981 accomplished by the Civil Rights Act of 1991 would have been impossible if they had not responded to intervening judicial decisions. So, too, the addition of a damage remedy to Title VII responded to the availability of a damage remedy under section 1981.

Yet, just as these developments expanded the scope of section 1981 by building upon prior enactments and judicial decisions, they

33. 541 U.S. 369 (2004).

34. 491 U.S. 164 (1989).

35. 42 U.S.C. § 1981(c) (2000). For the debate over the scope of section 1981, see Gerhard Casper, *Jones v. May-*

er: Clio, Bemused and Confused Muse, 1968 Sup. Ct. Rev. 89.

36. 42 U.S.C. § 1981(b) (2000).

limited it as well. Section 1981 does not expand upon the prohibitions against intentional discrimination on the basis of race and national origin already found in Title VII and the Constitution. As applied to section 1981, the historical perspective looks back to earlier enactments and earlier decisions and the forms of discrimination that they sought to remedy. Because it looks backward, it invariably imposes limits on the innovation that can be accomplished to address newly recognized forms of discrimination.

C. Section 1985(3)

Section 1985(3) prohibits employment discrimination in a narrow range of cases involving conspiracies to deny equal protection, resulting in an injury to any person or property or a deprivation of any federal right or privilege.[37] It provides for the same remedies and is enforced according to the same procedures as section 1983. Also like section 1983 (and section 1981 as well), it suffered a century of neglect before it was revived by a judicial decision in the Civil Rights Era.

That decision, *Griffin v. Breckenridge*,[38] interpreted section 1985(3) to reach purely private conspiracies involving "class-based, invidiously discriminatory animus." This last phrase closely follows the constitutional prohibition against government reliance upon "suspect classifications" and the scope of this statute has accordingly been limited to discrimination against groups defined in those terms. Thus, nonunion workers are not among the groups protected by the statute.[39] As we have just seen, this limitation to constitutionally recognized forms of discrimination is a natural consequence of the historical perspective on civil rights laws.

A further limitation on section 1985(3) also follows from this limitation. The "class-based, invidiously discriminatory animus" may result in the deprivation of rights that overlap with those protected by Title VII, but these rights must be derived from other sources of law, such as the Constitution. Section 1985(3) cannot be used to enforce rights granted solely by Title VII, which must be enforced according to the remedial scheme in Title VII itself. Thus, in *Great American Federal Savings & Loan Ass'n v. Novotny*,[40] the Supreme Court held that section 1985(3) did not provide a remedy for retaliation in violation of Title VII that could be the subject of a claim under that statute. While this holding is quite narrow, as is

37. *Id.* § 1985(3).

38. 403 U.S. 88, 102 (1971).

39. United Bhd. of Carpenters, Local 610 v. Scott, 463 U.S. 825, 835 (1983).

40. 442 U.S. 366 (1979).

the scope of section 1985(3), it illustrates how the Reconstruction civil rights statutes have been narrowed to conform to Title VII as the basic modern legislation on employment discrimination.

Chapter XI

THE AGE DISCRIMINATION
IN EMPLOYMENT ACT

Unlike the statutes discussed in previous chapters, the Age Discrimination in Employment Act (ADEA) raises issues predominantly under the economic perspective on laws against employment discrimination. No history of discrimination against older workers supports an historical perspective, equating the treatment of older workers with that of racial or ethnic minorities or women. Recent legislation, so far from discriminating against older workers, has conferred benefits upon them, through such major programs as Social Security and Medicare, and even with respect to employment, through protection of pension benefits in the Employment Retirement Income Security Act (ERISA).[1] The ADEA itself is an instance of such specially protective legislation, since it applies only to claims by older workers that they suffered discrimination in favor of younger workers, but not to the corresponding claims by younger workers.[2] Unlike discrimination on the basis of race, national origin, sex, or religion, discrimination on the basis of age is not suspect as a matter of constitutional law.[3]

Nor does age discrimination have the kind of cumulative effects as other forms of discrimination, at least none that would warrant a broad interpretation of the ADEA to remedy the effects of past discrimination. Age discrimination does not apply to a discrete and insular minority, but to individuals who may have had a full range of opportunities and advantages earlier in life. It does not limit the employment opportunities available to a fixed class of people and their descendants. It applies only to an ever changing cohort of older workers. A remedial perspective therefore confronts no persistent effects of age discrimination that need to be remedied.

Only an economic perspective can supply a justification for the ADEA. The most plausible basis for doing so again is distinct from the economic justifications offered for prohibiting other forms of discrimination. Tastes for discrimination cannot be used to condemn an attitude that everyone might have toward their older relatives, and if they live long enough, that their younger relatives might have toward them. Statistical discrimination likewise cannot

---

1. 29 U.S.C. § 1001 et seq. (2000).

2. General Dynamics Land Systems, Inc. v. Cline, 540 U.S. 581 (2004).

3. Massachusetts Bd. of Retirement v. Murgia, 427 U.S. 307, 312–14 (1976).

condemn as a stereotype the truism that everyone at some age suffers from declining ability and energy. These explanations for age discrimination, to the extent that they are persuasive, are descriptive only. They cannot supply a justification for the ADEA, which must be supported on entirely different grounds.

These grounds are usually found in the "life-cycle theory of earnings," which seeks to explain variations in earnings by age as a form of postponed compensation. According to this theory, an employee's compensation at first exceeds his productivity because he receives additional compensation in the form of on-the-job training. As the employee's productivity increases, it soon exceeds the level of current compensation that he receives from an employer, even if his compensation has also increased with seniority and promotions. Although the employee's compensation continues to increase, more or less steadily, his productivity does not, and it eventually decreases below his level of current compensation, causing the employer to suffer a net loss. On the life-cycle theory of earnings, if an employer opportunistically discharges an employee late in his career, the discharge effectively deprives the employee of the postponed compensation for the middle period of his career when his productivity exceeded his pay. Laws against age discrimination are one means of preventing employers from taking advantage of their employees in this way.

Such laws, however, are not the only means of protecting older workers and a justification for the ADEA based on the life-cycle theory stops well short of supporting a general prohibition against age discrimination. Contracts for pension benefits, for instance, could provide employees with the needed protection against exploitation late in their careers, particularly if they were supplemented with statutes like ERISA that restrict the ability of employers to deny or reduce benefits already granted. Only some workers, particularly those who are highly paid, need the benefit of a prohibition against age discrimination. Through a variety of means, by contract or by seeking better terms of employment elsewhere, many workers can protect themselves. Yet the ADEA, adopting much of its language verbatim from Title VII, follows the model of civil rights legislation against racial discrimination, adding only limited exceptions.

The tension between the broad scope of the ADEA and the limited justification for its prohibitions generates interpretive problems across all of the major provisions of the statute. Sometimes these are resolved in favor of following the law as it has developed under Title VII. On several important issues, however, they are resolved in favor of giving the ADEA a distinctive and narrow interpretation. This chapter begins by examining these tensions in the substantive prohibitions and exceptions in the statute. It then turns to an examination of the procedural and remedial provisions of the ADEA, which combine aspects of both Title VII and the Equal Pay Act. The chapter concludes with a brief assessment of the overall significance of the ADEA for the aims and limits of employment discrimination law.

A. Prohibitions and Exceptions

The ADEA prohibits discrimination on the basis of age in almost exactly the same terms as Title VII prohibits discrimination on the basis of race. This should come as no surprise, either as a matter of theory or as a matter of legislative history. Title VII is the single most important enactment in employment discrimination law and it has therefore served as the model for all subsequent legislation in this field. The ADEA itself actually originated in a provision in Title VII requiring a study by the Secretary of Labor of the employment opportunities of older workers. This study found considerable discrimination in hiring of older workers, a finding emphasized in the subsequent legislative debates over the ADEA.[4] Although this finding is at odds with the life-cycle theory of earnings, which emphasizes termination of older workers rather than failure to hire them, it was used to support a prohibition against age discrimination modeled on Title VII and covering all aspects of employment.

The ADEA is narrower than Title VII only in covering a genuine "protected class." The ADEA protects only individuals who are at least 40 years old.[5] This limitation represents a departure from Title VII, which protects all individuals from discrimination within its scope. The ADEA protects only older workers, not younger workers, from age discrimination. Moreover, as originally enacted, the ADEA did not even protect all older workers, but only those who were 65 or younger. This ceiling on coverage was gradually raised until it was abandoned entirely.[6]

Unlimited coverage of older workers, just like protection against discrimination in hiring, does not fit easily with the life-

---

4. Secretary of Labor, The Older American Worker: Age Discrimination in Employment: Report to Congress under Section 715 of the Civil Rights Act of 1964, at 5–20 (1965).

5. 29 U.S.C. § 631 (1988).

6. *Id.* § 631(a). In other provisions on coverage, the ADEA applies to all private employers with at least twenty employees, to state and local government, and to most of the federal government, but not to elected officials or certain of their appointees. *Id.* § 630(f). This exception was applied to state judges in Gregory v. Ashcroft, 501 U.S. 452, 464–65 (1991).

cycle theory of earnings. The life-cycle theory presupposes that, at some point, employees have received as compensation whatever surplus they had earlier conferred upon their employers. At this point, an employer does not engage in opportunism by reducing the pay of its older workers, or even discharging them, so long as their total compensation equals their productivity over their entire career. Although the ADEA recognizes this point in its provisions on early retirement plans, it does so only through a complicated exception to its general prohibition against age discrimination.

This prohibition follows Title VII both in its literal terms and in its interpretation, at least as applied to claims of intentional discrimination. Thus, the method of proving individual claims of intentional discrimination under the ADEA is the same as under Title VII, relying upon the structure of burdens of production from *McDonnell Douglas Corp. v. Green.*[7] This similarity holds despite the existence of different provisions in the ADEA that create specific defenses for employment decisions "based on reasonable factors other than age" and for discipline or discharge "for good cause."[8] These defenses were plainly intended to confer some advantage upon employers, but they arguably do the opposite, by shifting the burden of persuasion onto them to establish the existence of a legitimate, nondiscriminatory reason for a disputed employment decision. Under *McDonnell Douglas*, by contrast, only the burden of production would shift.[9] The easiest way to reconcile these diverging statutory provisions is to interpret the defenses under the ADEA to shift the burden of persuasion to the employer only if the plaintiff proves that age was a factor in the disputed decision.[10] This interpretation of the ADEA would bring it into conformity with provisions of Title VII enacted by the Civil Rights Act of 1991.[11]

Class-wide claims can also be proved by statistical evidence under the ADEA, but subject to greater restrictions than under Title VII.[12] The theory of disparate impact applies to claims under

7. 411 U.S. 792 (1973). *See* Chapter III.B *supra.*

8. 29 U.S.C. § 623(f)(1),(3) (2000).

9. Criswell v. Western Airlines, Inc., 709 F.2d 544, 552–53 (9th Cir. 1983), *aff'd on other grounds*, 472 U.S. 400 (1985); 29 C.F.R. § 1625.7 (2006).

10. *See* Marshall v. Westinghouse Electric Corp., 576 F.2d 588, 590–92 (5th Cir. 1978). The Supreme Court has reserved decision on this question. West-

ern Air Lines v. Criswell, 472 U.S. 400, 408 n.10 (1985).

11. The amendments are those that added §§ 703(m), 706(g)(2)(B), codified as 42 U.S.C. § 2000e–2(m),–5(g)(2)(B) (2000), to Title VII. No corresponding amendments were made to the ADEA.

12. Dace v. ACF Industries, Inc., 722 F.2d 374, 378 (8th Cir. 1983); Criswell v. Western Airlines, Inc., 709 F.2d 544, 552 (9th Cir. 1983), *aff'd on other grounds*, 472 U.S. 400 (1985); Geller v. Markham,

the ADEA, but only in diluted form, as the Supreme Court held in *Smith v. City of Jackson.*[13] The Court was closely divided on recognizing the theory at all under the ADEA, but was unanimous that it applied only in a weaker form than under Title VII. Justice Stevens, with three other justices, found the theory to be based directly on the language of the ADEA,[14] while Justice Scalia found that it was supported by regulations promulgated by the EEOC.[15] The remaining justices would not have recognized the theory under the ADEA, but assuming that it was to be recognized, agreed with the majority that it was in the form adopted in *Wards Cove Packing Co. v. Atonio.*[16] As explained earlier in Chapter 4, that case reduced the defendant's burden of justifying a practice with a disparate impact only to a burden of production and allowed the court only to engage in "a reasoned review of the employer's justification for his use of the challenged practice."[17] This aspect of *Wards Cove* was soon superseded by the Civil Rights Act of 1991, which amended Title VII, but not the ADEA, to codify a stronger version of the theory of disparate that is less favorable to defendants and more favorable to plaintiffs. In *Smith*, the Court took the absence of any amendment to the ADEA to support the continued application of the weaker version adopted in *Wards Cove*. The Court also found support for this conclusion in the defense available under of the ADEA for decisions based on a "reasonable factor other than age."[18] This provision, like *Wards Cove*, supported only limited judicial review of the employer's justification for a practice with disparate impact.

The Court's narrowing of the theory of disparate impact under the ADEA reflects an underlying concern that the model of racial discrimination developed under Title VII cannot be readily transferred to age discrimination. In particular, the remedial perspective that justifies the theory of disparate impact conflicts with the economic perspective and the more limited forms of liability that it justifies. Older workers, on the economic perspective, do not need the extended remedies for the continuing effects of past discrimination that racial minorities and women need. By its very nature, discrimination on the basis of age does not have cumulative effects, either on a single individual or between generations. It applies only

---

635 F.2d 1027, 1032–35 (2d Cir. 1980), *cert. denied*, 451 U.S. 945 (1981).

13. 544 U.S. 228 (2005).

14. *Id.* at 232–40 (opinion of Stevens, J.).

15. *Id.* at 243–48 (Scalia, J., concurring in part and concurring in the judgment).

16. 490 U.S. 642 (1989). *See Smith*, 544 U.S. at 240–41.

17. *Wards Cove*, 490 U.S. at 659. *See* Chapter 4.B. *supra*.

18. 29 U.S.C. § 623(f)(1). *See Smith*, 544 U.S. at 239–41.

to the end of an individual's working life, not over an entire career. Under the life-cycle theory of earnings, older workers are still vulnerable to exploitation, but this can be prevented by a prohibition against intentional discrimination alone. It is not necessary also to prohibit neutral practices that have adverse consequences correlated with age. Of course, in any particular case, it may be difficult to distinguish an employer's reliance on legitimate factors correlated with age from age discrimination itself, but no more so than determining the issue of pretext with respect to discrimination on any other ground.

In *Hazen Paper Co. v. Biggins*,[19] the Supreme Court confronted a similar question: whether a finding of intentional discrimination could be based entirely on a factor correlated with age: the imminent vesting of pension rights which allegedly resulted in the plaintiff's discharge. Although a discharge for this reason violates provisions in ERISA protecting pension benefits,[20] it does not, by itself, justify a finding of age discrimination. According to the Supreme Court, the plaintiff was required to submit additional evidence that age was a factor in the employer's decision.

This holding has implications for a similar, but more pervasive issue: whether an employer can justify the termination of older employees because they receive higher pay than younger employees. Most federal courts hold that they cannot, but these decisions rely in part on the theory of disparate impact limited in *Smith v. City of Jackson*.[21] Under the life-cycle theory of earnings, older workers are likely to be exploited for precisely this reason, but only up to a point in their careers. After that point, they have recouped all of the surplus productivity over current salary previously received by their employers. From an economic perspective, everything depends upon when an employer invokes the higher pay of older employees as a reason to discharge them, or equivalently, to force them into retirement. Yet because this point will vary with each employer, not to mention each employee, it is impossible for a legal rule, and even judges applying a flexible legal standard, to distinguish reliably between discharges that exploit older workers and those that do not.

Instead of allowing discharges for this reason, the ADEA allows employers to take account of the declining productivity of older employees through an exception for voluntary retirement plans.

---

19. 507 U.S. 604 (1993).

20. 29 U.S.C. § 1001 *et seq.* (2000), and scattered sections of 5, 18, and 26 U.S.C. (2000).

21. For an account of the arguments on both sides of this issue, see the opinions in Metz v. Transit Mix, Inc., 828 F.2d 1202 (7th Cir. 1987).

The history of this exception is quite convoluted, involving repeated cycles of enactment and judicial interpretation that eventually created a distinction between mandatory and voluntary retirement plans. As originally enacted, the ADEA created an exception to its prohibitions for "any bona fide employee benefit plan such as a retirement, pension, or insurance plan, which is not a subterfuge to evade the purposes of this chapter."[22] The Supreme Court interpreted this exception to permit various forms of mandatory retirement plans, resulting in the addition of a proviso that "no such seniority system or employee benefit plan shall require or permit the involuntary retirement for any [covered individual] because of the age of such individual."[23] This proviso attempted to drastically narrow the scope of the exception, but the exception was again expanded by the Supreme Court, which continued to read it to allow any form of age discrimination within a pension plan, but not outside it. On this interpretation, employers were free to reduce the retirement benefits of employees who continued to work beyond the age desired by their employer. Congress again amended the statute to overrule this interpretation and maintain the narrowness of the exception.[24] The amendment allows classifications on the basis of age only if they are cost-justified according to EEOC regulations or if they are part of "a voluntary early retirement incentive plan consistent with the relevant purpose or purposes of this chapter."[25]

It is this last provision, along with further, highly technical requirements for permissible employee benefit plans,[26] that allow employers to encourage their employees to take early retirement. In its current form, the statute presupposes a distinction between permissible carrots—added benefits for early retirement—and impermissible sticks—penalties for not taking normal retirement. Whether or not this distinction can be maintained as a conceptual matter, it provides employers with the means to sever their relationship with older employees in a manner consistent with the life-cycle theory of earnings. Although the fit between this provision and the theory is only approximate, it allows employers to bring the employment relationship to an end without denying older employees the postponed compensation that they deserve for their years of work at higher levels of productivity.

Another provision, which is closely related in function if not in form, restricts waiver of claims under the ADEA.[27] All waivers must be for additional consideration, apart from benefits that the em-

22. 29 U.S.C. § 623(f)(2)(A) (2000).

23. *Id.*

24. *Id.* § 623(f)(2)(B).

25. *Id.*

26. *Id.* § 623(j)–(*l*).

27. *Id.* § 626(f).

ployee already receives, and must be subject to waiting periods during which the employee can consider the agreement, and in some instances, revoke it after entering into it.[28] Further restrictions apply to waivers "in connection with an exit incentive or other employment termination program offered to a group of employees."[29] This last provision applies to early retirement plans, but waivers also figure in the settlement of ADEA claims, which frequently involve the payment of retirement benefits to increase the plaintiff's total recovery. These, too, are subject to many of the same restrictions as other waivers.[30] All of these restrictions limit the ability of employers to take advantage of older workers by offering retirement on terms that, while seemingly beneficial to them are, on balance, against their interests. The possibility of a bargain to the mutual benefit of employers and employees nevertheless remains open. The ADEA does not completely displace contracts as a mechanism for determining the rights of older workers.

A variety of other provisions in the ADEA also recognize that its prohibition against age discrimination is weaker than the corresponding prohibitions in Title VII. The ADEA excludes from its coverage certain executives over the age of 65;[31] certain public officials and members of their staffs;[32] and employees who fall within administratively created exceptions.[33] Two different occupations—firefighters and law enforcement officers, and tenured professors at colleges and universities—have been subject to changing statutory provisions. The original exceptions for these occupations allowed employers to impose maximum ages of employment, or what is virtually the same thing, ages of mandatory retirement.[34] These exceptions expired at the end of 1993, only to be reinstated later in different form. States and localities can now set a maximum age for employment of firefighters and law enforcement officers, as well as an age for mandatory retirement.[35] Colleges and universities cannot impose mandatory retirement upon tenured professors, but they can increase the incentives for early retire-

28. *See* Oubre v. Entergy Operations, Inc., 522 U.S. 422, 428 (1998) (allowing employees to revoke waiver without tendering back benefits received under it).

29. 29 U.S.C. § 626(f)(1)(H) (2000).

30. *Id.* § 626(f)(2).

31. *Id.* § 631(c).

32. *Id.* § 630(f).

33. *Id.* § 628. These have exempted only programs of public employment for "the long-term unemployed, handicapped, members of minority groups, older workers, or youth." 29 C.F.R. § 1627.16 (2006).

34. Age Discrimination in Employment Act of 1986, Pub. L. No. 99–592, §§ 3, 6, 100 Stat. 3342 (1986).

35. 29 U.S.C. § 623(j) (2000).

ment.[36]

All of these exceptions depend, to some extent, on the special nature of the positions covered. Firefighters and law enforcement officers need a degree of fitness that is hard to maintain with increasing age. Yet these exceptions also depend upon the qualified nature of the prohibition against age discrimination. Generalizations and stereotypes based on age, in contrast to those based on sex, are more acceptable in a wider range of circumstances. Indeed, with respect to fringe benefit plans, the explicit terms of the ADEA allow employers to alter "retiree health benefits" on the basis of age,[37] while Title VII does not allow any such distinction on the basis of sex.[38]

The most general defense in the ADEA, however, closely follows a similar defense to claims of sex discrimination under Title VII: the exception for bona fide occupational qualifications (BFOQ).[39] As a matter of formal legal doctrine, the Supreme Court gave the BFOQ for age the same interpretation as the BFOQ for sex in *Western Air Lines v. Criswell*.[40] "[L]ike its Title VII counterpart, the BFOQ exception 'was in fact meant to be an extremely narrow exception to the general prohibition' of age discrimination contained in the ADEA."[41]

Whether the BFOQ is applied as strictly to age as it is to sex remains an open question. In *Criswell*, the employer argued that mandatory retirement of flight engineers—the third officer in the cockpit of a passenger airplane—at age 60 was justified on grounds of safety. The jury rejected this argument and the Court held that it had been properly instructed, relying on the Fifth Circuit's decision in *Usery v. Tamiami Trial Tours, Inc.*[42] That case had allowed age as a proxy for safety considerations only in two circumstances: where the employer " 'had reasonable cause to believe, that is, a factual basis for believing, that all or substantially all [persons over the age limit] would be unable to perform safely and efficiently the duties of the job involved' "; or where "it is 'impossible or highly impractical' to deal with older employees on an

---

36. *Id.* § 623(m).

37. *Id.* § 623(*l*)(2)(D).

38. City of Los Angeles, Dep't of Water & Power v. Manhart, 435 U.S. 702, 712–13 (1978).

39. 29 U.S.C. § 623(f)(1) (2000). The provision in Title VII is § 703(e)(1), codified as 42 U.S.C. § 2000e–2(e)(1) (2000).

40. 472 U.S. 400 (1985).

41. *Id.* at 412 (quoting Dothard v. Rawlinson, 433 U.S. 321, 334 (1977)); *see* United Auto. Workers v. Johnson Controls, Inc., 499 U.S. 187, 202 (1991).

42. 531 F.2d 224 (5th Cir. 1976).

individualized basis."[43] Although the employer did not succeed in persuading the jury that either of these conditions were met in *Criswell*, it is apparent that at some age (for instance, 75 or 80), they would be met. The risk of sudden illness or death would be so great, and yet so difficult to predict for any particular individual, that an employer could exclude anyone over a given age from positions involving the safety of others.

Distinctions on the basis of sex do not vary by degrees to such an extent. Men and women are two entirely discrete and virtually unchangeable categories. Allowing discrimination against men or women operates to the disadvantage of the entire sex, and so is seldom allowed by Title VII. Older and younger employees can be distinguished by degrees in innumerable ways. As the life-cycle theory of earnings recognizes, at some point older workers differ so much from their younger colleagues that employers should be allowed to take account of their age. No corresponding argument supports discrimination on the basis of sex.

This difference between discrimination on the basis of age and discrimination on the basis of sex emerged more clearly in a companion case to *Criswell*, *Trans World Airlines v. Thurston*.[44] This case also concerned the qualifications for airline flight officers. Under regulations of the Federal Aviation Administration (FAA), captains and first officers were required to leave their positions when they reached the age of 60. No similar regulations applied to flight engineers. TWA had therefore allowed captains and first officers who were 60 years old to transfer to the position of flight engineer, but subject to restrictions that did not apply to those who transferred before age 60. TWA justified the restriction as a BFOQ based on the regulations applicable to captains and first officers. The parties did not dispute the validity of these regulations,[45] but the Court held that the absence of a BFOQ for the position of flight engineer was decisive. The BFOQ depends only on the nature of the job to which transfer is sought.[46] This holding is consistent with the narrow scope of the BFOQ, but it leaves intact the age restriction established by the FAA. Indeed, a subsequent decision of the D.C. Circuit upheld the FAA's restriction as not "arbitrary and capricious" under the Administrative Procedure Act because it was sufficiently related to maintaining airline safety.[47] It is difficult to

43. 472 U.S. at 414 (quoting Usery v. Tamiami Trail Tours, Inc., 531 F.2d at 235).

44. 469 U.S. 111 (1985).

45. *Id.* at 123 nn. 17 & 18.

46. *Id.* at 122–23.

47. Professional Pilots Fed'n v. FAA, 118 F.3d 758, 766–67 (D.C. Cir. 1997), *cert. denied*, 523 U.S. 1117 (1998). The court also held that the FAA regulations fell outside the scope of the ADEA be-

imagine a decision upholding a similar restriction on the basis of sex, or even a federal regulation imposing such a restriction in the first place.

B. Procedures and Remedies

The ADEA is enforced according to procedures drawn from both Title VII and the Fair Labor Standards Act (FLSA). This otherwise inexplicable combination of statutory provisions arises from the use of the procedures and remedies under the FLSA to enforce the Equal Pay Act. Following this model, the ADEA borrows most of the remedial provisions of the FLSA. Through a series of amendments, the ADEA gradually came to incorporate the procedures in Title VII on other issues, mainly those for exhausting administrative remedies and filing claims in a timely fashion. The end result is a system of procedures and remedies that is better explained by its development than its logic. If anything, the remedies available under the ADEA are slightly narrower than those available under Title VII, suggesting again that preventing age discrimination does not have quite the same priority as preventing discrimination on other grounds.

The ADEA allocates enforcement authority between public and private actions according to the provisions of the FLSA,[48] with one exception. The FLSA authorizes public actions by the Secretary of Labor, but by executive order, authority to enforce the ADEA (like the Equal Pay Act) has been transferred to the EEOC.[49] Actions by the EEOC need not be preceded by exhaustion of state administrative remedies or by filing a charge with the EEOC, but they must be preceded by attempted conciliation.[50] Public actions can preempt private actions if they are filed earlier, but private individuals have a right to intervene in public actions on their behalf.[51]

Following the model of Title VII, private actions under the ADEA must be preceded by filing a charge with the EEOC, followed by a waiting period to allow the EEOC to attempt conciliation.[52] In states that do not have an agency that enforces a state law against employment discrimination on the basis of age, the charge must be filed with the EEOC within 180 days of the alleged discrimination.[53] In states that do have an appropriate agency, the charge must be

---

cause they were not issued in its capacity as an employer. *Id.* at 763.

48. 29 U.S.C. § 626(b) (2000).

49. Reorganization Plan No. 1 of 1978, § 2, 5 U.S.C. app. at 1366 (2000).

50. 29 U.S.C. § 626(b) (2000).

51. *Id.* § 216(b), (c).

52. *Id.* § 626(d).

53. *Id.* § 626(d)(1).

filed with the EEOC within 300 days of the alleged discrimination or 30 days of notice of termination of state proceedings, whichever is earlier.[54] The ADEA explicitly grants the parties a right to a jury trial.[55]

The limitations for filing actions under the ADEA originally were the same as those under the Equal Pay Act and the FLSA, but when the EEOC experienced delays in processing charges, many individual plaintiffs lost their claims under these limitations. Congress responded, first by extending the limitations for such delayed claims,[56] and then by changing the limitations period so that it was the same under the ADEA as under Title VII. Individuals must now file an action in court within 90 days of receipt of a right-to-sue letter.[57] The effect of this amendment is to relieve the EEOC of any explicit limitations for filing its actions, apparently subject only to the same doctrine of laches that applies to EEOC actions under Title VII.[58]

Remedies under the ADEA again are the same as under the Equal Pay Act and the FLSA, with the qualification that liquidated damages, in an amount equal to actual damages, are payable only for "willful violations" and that the court is authorized to grant "such legal or equitable relief as may be appropriate to effectuate the purposes of this chapter."[59] Under the Eleventh Amendment, however, private individuals cannot recover back pay or damages from states or their instrumentalities.[60] The equitable remedies available under the ADEA have given rise to some disagreement over the allocation of issues between judge and jury. In particular, in some circuits, awards of front pay are determined wholly by the judge,[61] while in others, the judge makes an initial determination that front pay should be awarded and the jury decides the amount of the award.[62]

In *Trans World Airlines v. Thurston*,[63] the Supreme Court considered the meaning of "willful violations" sufficient for an award of liquidated damages. The Court agreed with the standard articulated by the court of appeals in this case, but disagreed over

54. *Id.* § 626(d)(2).

55. *Id.* § 626(c)(2).

56. Pub. L. No. 100–283, 102 Stat. 78 (1988).

57. 29 U.S.C. § 626(e) (2000).

58. Occidental Life Ins. Co. v. EEOC, 432 U.S. 355, 358–66, 372–73 (1977).

59. *Id.* § 626(b).

60. Kimel v. Florida Board of Regents, 528 U.S. 62 (2000).

61. Dominic v. Consolidated Edison Co., 822 F.2d 1249, 1258 (2d Cir. 1987).

62. Roush v. KFC Nat'l Mgmt. Co., 10 F.3d 392, 398 & n.10 (6th Cir. 1993); Maxfield v. Sinclair Int'l, 766 F.2d 788, 796 (3d Cir. 1985), *cert. denied*, 474 U.S. 1057 (1986).

63. 469 U.S. 111 (1985).

its application. The standard was whether " 'the employer ... knew or showed reckless disregard for the matter of whether its conduct was prohibited by the ADEA.' "[64] The Court interpreted this standard to be substantially the same as that for determining willfulness under the provision for criminal penalties in the FLSA.[65] On the record before it, the Court held that the employer had not acted willfully because it had sought the advice of counsel and had negotiated with the union to modify its collective bargaining agreement to conform to the act. In a subsequent case, the Third Circuit has interpreted *Thurston* to require "some additional evidence of outrageous conduct,"[66] but the Eleventh Circuit has disagreed.[67] The Supreme Court itself has made clear that *Thurston* requires more than unreasonable action by the defendant.[68]

Again like Title VII, the ADEA creates special procedures for claims by federal employees. The EEOC has succeeded the Civil Service Commission as the agency that adjudicates age discrimination complaints by federal employees.[69] Federal employees can pursue their claims either through administrative proceedings, in which case they must follow the same procedures as under Title VII,[70] or they can proceed directly to court. If the latter, they must file a notice of intent to sue with the EEOC within 180 days of the alleged discrimination and no less than 30 days before they file an action in court.[71] The action in court must be commenced within an appropriate limitation period borrowed either from state or federal law.[72] The act authorizes actions in federal court for "such legal or equitable relief as will effectuate the purposes of this chapter."[73]

C. Implications of the ADEA

This chapter has pointed out the limitations of the ADEA, particularly when it is compared to the prohibitions against discrimination in Title VII. The latter prohibitions have a stronger

---

64. *Id.* at 128–29 (quoting Air Line Pilots Ass'n v. Trans World Airlines, 713 F.2d 940, 956 (2d Cir. 1983)).

65. 29 U.S.C. § 216(a) (2000); 469 U.S. at 125–26.

66. Dreyer v. Arco Chemical Co., 801 F.2d 651, 658 (3d Cir. 1986), *cert. denied*, 480 U.S. 906 (1987).

67. Lindsey v. American Cast Iron Pipe Co., 810 F.2d 1094, 1099–1101 (11th Cir. 1987). The circuits have also divided on the question whether an award of liquidated damages precludes an award of prejudgment interest. *See id.* at 1102 & n.7; Starceski v. Westinghouse Elec. Corp., 54 F.3d 1089, 1101–03 (3d Cir. 1995).

68. McLaughlin v. Richland Shoe Co., 486 U.S. 128, 135 & n.13 (1988). The same standard also governs determination of willfulness for the three-year limitation that applies to claims under the Equal Pay Act. *Id.* at 131.

69. 29 U.S.C. § 633a(a) (2000); Reorganization Plan No. 1 of 1978, § 2, 5 U.S.C. app. at 1366 (2000).

70. *See* Chapter VIII.D *supra.*

71. 29 U.S.C. § 633a(d) (2000).

72. Stevens v. Department of the Treasury, 500 U.S. 1, 7 (1991).

73. 29 U.S.C. § 633a(c) (2000).

basis in the historical and remedial perspectives, resting ultimately on the need to compensate for the cumulative effects of past discrimination. The ADEA, by contrast, is not aimed at protecting an historically disfavored group, but at protecting all persons who are at least 40 years old. Many white males, and others who are not victims of systematic discrimination, fall within the protection of the act. The breadth of the act's coverage supports restrictions on the scope of its prohibitions, or so this chapter has argued.

Nevertheless, an opposite and equally valuable lesson can be drawn from the breadth of the ADEA. It is that laws against employment discrimination protect the majority as well as the minority and that everyone benefits from general prohibitions against discrimination in public life. Paradoxically, in identifying a genuine protected class of older workers, the ADEA has broadened, not narrowed, the coverage of the civil rights laws, extending the principle against discrimination to groups that do not usually benefit from its protection. In doing so, the ADEA has also broadened the base of popular support for these laws, both in the legislature and in the process of enforcement and compliance that determines their ultimate effectiveness. In going beyond traditional civil rights groups, the ADEA has reinforced the willingness of the majority to support civil rights laws, a condition of any effective legislation in a democratic society.

Chapter XII

DISABILITIES

Two federal statutes prohibit discrimination on the basis of disability: the Rehabilitation Act of 1973 and the Americans with Disabilities Act of 1990 (ADA). The principal difference between the two statutes is in coverage: the Rehabilitation Act applies to the federal government, federally funded programs, and federal contractors;[1] the ADA applies to all employers with at least fifteen employees, except the federal government.[2] Both acts also apply to activities other than employment, and again, the ADA is broader because it covers all public services and public accommodations, the latter including public accommodations operated by private entities.[3] Much of the case law has developed under the earlier of the two statutes, the Rehabilitation Act, but applies also to the ADA with only a few modifications.

Despite the differences in coverage of the two statutes, they have the same fundamental aim: to increase the opportunities in public life, and particularly in employment, for disabled individuals. Both offer a variety of means of achieving this aim and both take the remedial perspective in a new and surprising direction, compensating for natural disadvantages in addition to the consequences of past discrimination. This is accomplished through the duty of reasonable accommodation, which requires employers to adjust the requirements of employment to the needs of disabled individuals, so long as these adjustments can be made without undue hardship. This development, although significant as a matter of legal doctrine, has turned out to be difficult to implement in practice, leading the interpretation of the Rehabilitation Act and the ADA to depend on the alternative perspectives drawn from history and economics and on analogies to other statutes, such as Title VII.

In fact, the duty of reasonable accommodation has its doctrinal source in the duty to accommodate religious practices under Title VII. As discussed earlier,[4] however, constitutional questions under the religion clauses of the First Amendment have caused the duty of reasonable accommodation under Title VII to be narrowly interpreted. No such impediments prevent a broad interpretation of the

---

1. §§ 501–504a, codified as 29 U.S.C.A. §§ 791–94a (2000).

2. § 101(5), codified as 42 U.S.C. § 12111(5) (2000).

3. §§ 201 et seq., 301 et seq., codified as 42 U.S.C. §§ 12131 et seq., 12181 et seq. (2000).

4. See Chapter VII.B supra.

duty of reasonable accommodation under the disabilities statutes. For the same reason, claims of reverse discrimination by individuals are not available under either constitutional or statutory law. The Rehabilitation Act and the ADA identify a genuine "protected class" of disabled individuals who receive special protection. Any classification on this basis is subject only to the most lenient constitutional scrutiny for a rational basis in fact.[5]

In this respect also, the duty of reasonable accommodation goes beyond those provisions in Title VII that seek to compensate for natural conditions, such as pregnancy and childbirth, that create obstacles to the full employment of women.[6] Such natural conditions are found only temporarily among individual women, whereas individuals with disabilities, almost by definition, suffer from more permanent conditions. Purely as a matter of legal doctrine, the duty of reasonable accommodation offers substantial assistance to individuals with disabilities in overcoming traditional barriers to employment.

Yet the duty of reasonable accommodation has not fulfilled its initial promise, mainly because of decisions that narrowly interpret the Rehabilitation Act and the ADA to cover only individuals who suffer from impairments serious enough to qualify as "disabilities" within the meaning of these statutes, yet are not so disabled that they are incapable of performing the essential functions of the jobs that they seek. The effect of these narrowing decisions has been to return the interpretation of these statutes to the model of racial discrimination, emphasizing patterns of past discrimination and the efficiency to be gained by employers and employees alike in eliminating discrimination. On this view, relying on the historical and economic perspectives, individuals with disabilities have suffered only from practices that have stigmatized them as unworthy of employment and discrimination against them must be prohibited only in order to promote overall efficiency. Employers are therefore required, at most, to make minimal adjustments in the workplace to take advantage of the skills and abilities that disabled employees possess.

Perhaps for this reason, plaintiffs who bring disability discrimination claims have experienced a remarkably low level of success, less than ten percent in claims litigated to judgment.[7] Other studies

5. City of Cleburne v. Cleburne Living Center, 473 U.S. 432, 442–47 (1985); New York City Transit Auth. v. Beazer, 440 U.S. 568, 587–94 (1979).

6. *See* Chapter VI. D *supra.*

7. *See* Ruth Colker, The Americans with Disabilities Act: A Windfall for Defendants, 34 Harv. C.R.-C.L. L. Rev. 99 (1999).

find a general absence of any increase in employment of individuals with disabilities after passage of the ADA, although these studies stop short of proving that this shortfall in employment results from the ineffectiveness of the ADA, as opposed to other factors.[8] The overall effect of these studies have led some authors to call for a renewed emphasis on social welfare approach to protecting individuals with disabilities rather than relying mainly on a model of discrimination.[9]

Even retaining a model of discrimination, however, requires modification from the usual standards of colorblindness. Discrimination against an individual with a disability cannot be easily disentangled from consideration the consequences of the disability itself. An employer who refuses to hire blind employees does not usually do so because of any stigma attached to being blind, but because blind employees would not perform as well on the job. The consequences of being blind, for most forms of employment, are indistinguishable from the status of being blind. Any robust prohibition against discrimination on the basis of disability must therefore impose some affirmative obligation upon employers to compensate, to some extent, for the natural consequences of covered disabilities. Such an obligation, whatever doctrinal form it takes, must therefore rely on a remedial perspective, and one directed not only to the consequences of past discrimination, but also to the natural and social consequences of disabilities, however they are caused. The resulting tension in the law of disability discrimination can be found in a variety of different statutory provisions and legal doctrines.

This chapter begins chronologically, with the Rehabilitation Act and a discussion of its prohibitions against employment discrimination. The next section discusses the ADA and its additions to the coverage of the Rehabilitation Act. The following sections address two fundamental issues common to both statutes: the definition of protected individuals with a disability and the scope of the duty of reasonable accommodation.

A.   The Rehabilitation Act of 1973

The Rehabilitation Act has three different provisions that apply to employment: section 501, which prohibits discrimination

8. *See* Christine Jolls & J.J. Prescott, Disaggregating Employment Protection: The Case of Disability Discrimination., Nat'l Bureau of Econ. Res. Working Paper Series, vol. 10740 (2004) (available at   http://www.nber.org/papers/w10740)   (finding state-by-state variations in employment of individuals with disabilities after enactment of the ADA).

9. Samuel R. Bagenstos, The Future of Disability Law, 114 Yale L.J. 1 (2004).

and requires affirmative action on the basis of disability by federal agencies;[10] section 503, which requires federal contractors to "take affirmative action to employ and advance in employment qualified handicapped individuals";[11] and section 504, which prohibits discrimination against otherwise qualified handicapped individuals in federally assisted programs.[12] These provisions all depend upon federal participation as a condition of coverage, invoking a model of federal regulation that dates back at least to the Civil Rights Act of 1964. Title VI of that act prohibited racial discrimination by the recipients of federal funds.[13] The extent of federal regulation under the Rehabilitation Act depends upon the extent of federal involvement in the program. Just to take one example, sections 501 and 503 impose an obligation upon federal agencies and federal contractors to engage in affirmative action, but section 504 does not require recipients of federal funds to do so.

The obligation to engage in affirmative action, like others imposed by the Rehabilitation Act, is qualified in practice by the enforcement provisions of the statute. Federal employees have a cause of action for any complaint filed under section 501,[14] but employees of federal contractors do not.[15] Litigation over affirmative action has therefore arisen mainly in claims by federal employees, and mainly by the indirect means of augmenting the duty of federal agencies to accommodate individuals with disabilities.[16] Following regulations of the EEOC, the lower federal courts have required the federal government to be "a model employer" of individuals with disabilities.[17]

10. § 501, codified as 29 U.S.C. § 791 (2000).

11. § 503, codified as 29 U.S.C. § 493 (2000).

12. § 504, codified as 29 U.S.C. § 494 (2000). Section 504 prohibits employment discrimination by recipients of federal funds, whether or not the purpose of such assistance is to provide employment. Consolidated Rail Corp. v. Darrone, 465 U.S. 624 (1984). This provision also applies to programs by federal agencies and by the Postal Service. In addition, the Rehabilitation Act itself provides various special services for individuals with disabilities, such as vocational rehabilitation and federal training programs. §§ 100 *et seq.*, §§ 300 *et seq.*, codified as 29 U.S.C. §§ 720 *et seq.*, §§ 770 *et seq.* (2000).

13. 42 U.S.C. § 2000d *et seq.* (2000). This title, however, did not apply to employment discrimination, which was covered only by Title VII.

14. § 505(a)(1), codified as 29 U.S.C. § 794a(a)(1) (2000).

15. *E.g.*, D'Amato v. Wisconsin Gas Co., 760 F.2d 1474, 1478 (7th Cir. 1985); *see* Consolidated Rail Corp. v. Darrone, 465 U.S. 624, 630 n.9 (1984) (reserving this question); New York City Transit Authority v. Beazer, 440 U.S. 568, 580 & n.17 (1979) (same).

16. Gardner v. Morris, 752 F.2d 1271, 1280 (8th Cir. 1985); Hall v. United States Postal Service, 857 F.2d 1073, 1080 (6th Cir. 1988); Mantolete v. Bolger, 767 F.2d 1416, 1423 (9th Cir. 1985).

17. 29 C.F.R. § 1613.703 (2006).

Employees in programs receiving federal financial assistance, like federal employees, have a cause of action under the Rehabilitation Act.[18] They can assert claims for discrimination under section 504. This section does not require affirmative action, but it does prohibit practices with adverse effects upon individuals with disabilities under the theory of disparate impact.[19] This requirement again has, at most, an indirect effect on actual litigation, which focuses on the duty of reasonable accommodation as the principal means of requiring employers to compensate for the adverse effects of neutral practices upon individuals with disabilities.

The coverage provisions of the Rehabilitation Act extend only to an "individual with a disability," which is defined as "any person who (i) has a physical or mental impairment which substantially limits one or more of such person's major life activities, (ii) has a record of such an impairment, or (iii) is regarded as having such an impairment."[20] The ADA uses essentially the same language in defining a "disability," so that this issue of coverage is common to the two statutes, and for that reason, is taken up later in this chapter.[21]

Several other issues of coverage and remedies, however, are unique to the Rehabilitation Act. The act is subject to exceptions for various disabilities that Congress found to be morally questionable,[22] and sections 503 and 504 are subject to additional exceptions for alcoholism, and for infectious diseases that "constitute a direct threat to the health or safety of other individuals" or that prevent the infected individual from performing the duties of the job.[23] Under section 504, the scope of a federally assisted "program or activity" was initially interpreted narrowly by the Supreme Court to include only activities of a recipient that actually received federal funds.[24] Congress responded by adding provisions that broadly defined these terms to include all of the operations of an organization if any part of it received federal financial assistance.[25]

In separate legislation, Congress also tried to supersede a decision of the Supreme Court that prevented the recovery of

18. § 505(a)(2), codified as 29 U.S.C. § 794a(a)(2) (2000). Only employees of federal contractors are left without a private right of action under the Rehabilitation Act, but virtually all such employees now have claims under the ADA.

19. Alexander v. Choate, 469 U.S. 287 (1985).

20. § 7(8)(B), codified as 29 U.S.C.§ 706(8)(B) (2000).

21. *See* Section C *infra.*

22. § 7(8)(C), (E), (F), (22) codified as 29 U.S.C. § 706(8)(C), (E), (F), (22) (2000).

23. § 7(8)(C)(v), (D) codified as 29 U.S.C. § 706(8)(C)(v), (D) (2000).

24. Grove City College v. Bell, 465 U.S. 555 (1984).

25. § 504(b), codified as 29 U.S.C. § 794(b) (2000).

damages against states and their instrumentalities.[26] These amendments, however, might exceed the power of Congress to abrogate state immunity under the Eleventh Amendment,[27] depending on how broadly the Supreme Court interprets a decision under the ADA raising a similar issue.[28] Nevertheless, monetary remedies remain available other recipients of federal funds, including private defendants and localities, on the same terms as under Title VI of the Civil Rights Act of 1964.[29] These remedies include the award of back pay[30] and attorney's fees.[31] In provisions added by the Civil Rights Act of 1991, damages and the right to jury trial are available for intentional violations of sections 501 and 504.[32] An employer, however, has a defense of good faith effort to provide a reasonable accommodation to a claim for damages for failure to make such an accommodation.[33]

B. The Americans with Disabilities Act

Just as the Rehabilitation Act is modeled on Title VI of the Civil Rights Act of 1964, the ADA is modeled on Title VII. The fundamental prohibition in the ADA against discrimination in employment follows the corresponding prohibition in Title VII.[34] It is augmented by a prohibition against retaliation, again modeled on the corresponding prohibition in Title VII.[35] The ADA departs from Title VII in offering a definition of "discriminate," although it does so by listing a series of activities that are derived, in one way or another, from Title VII.

The first of these is a prohibition against segregation.[36] Several examples are concerned with evasion of the ADA by contracting for

26. 42 U.S.C. § 2000d–7(a) (2000). The overruled decision is Atascadero State Hospital v. Scanlon, 473 U.S. 234 (1985).

27. Seminole Tribes of Florida v. Florida, 517 U.S. 44, 72–73 (1996) (Congress cannot abrogate the immunity of the states under the Eleventh Amendment by exercising its powers under the Commerce Clause); City of Boerne v. Flores, 521 U.S. 507, 516–20 (1997) (limiting the powers of Congress under the Fourteenth Amendment, under which it could abrogate the immunity of the states under the Eleventh Amendment).

28. Board of Trustees v. Garrett, 531 U.S. 356 (2001). This case, however, did not concern the power of Congress to attach conditions to federal spending, which would be involved in abrogating state immunity or obtaining state consent for claims under section 504.

29. § 505(a)(2), codified as 29 U.S.C. § 794a(a)(2) (2000).

30. Consolidated Rail Corp. v. Darrone, 465 U.S. 624 (1984).

31. § 505(a)(2), codified as 29 U.S.C. § 794a(a)(2) (2000).

32. 42 U.S.C. § 1981a(a)(2) (2000).

33. *Id.* § 1981a(a)(3).

34. § 102(a), codified as 42 U.S.C. § 12112(a) (2000).

35. § 503, codified as 42 U.S.C. § 12203 (2000).

36. § 102(b)(1), codified as 42 U.S.C. § 12112(b)(1) (2000).

discrimination by others or by perpetuating the effects of such discrimination.[37] These examples follow the law that has developed in decisions under Title VII on the issue of agency,[38] or under the theory of disparate impact.[39] The theory of disparate impact itself is codified in terms that were then later incorporated back into Title VII.[40] A unique prohibition imposes detailed restrictions on medical examinations and inquiries, prohibiting most such examinations and inquiries before an offer of employment is made, but not before an applicant actually begins employment.[41] Another subdivision codifies the duty of reasonable accommodation,[42] which was taken from regulations under the Rehabilitation Act and which is discussed later in this chapter.[43]

The ADA also contains a number of special exceptions and defenses. Several of the exceptions are modeled on, or even taken from, the exceptions to the Rehabilitation Act for conditions that Congress found unworthy of coverage. These exceptions concern the illegal use of drugs and alcohol,[44] transvestitism, homosexuality, and similar sexually related conditions,[45] compulsive gambling, kleptomania, and pyromania.[46] Other provisions are unique to the ADA: a general defense, apparently to claims for disparate treatment as well as disparate impact, that a job requirement is "job-related and consistent with business necessity" and not capable of reasonable accommodation;[47] an exception for infectious and communicable diseases, but again subject to the duty of reasonable accommodation;[48] an exception for insurance plans, provided that they are not used as a subterfuge to avoid the purposes of the law;[49] and a specific defense for exclusion of an individual who poses "a direct threat to the health or safety of other individuals in the

---

37. § 102(b)(2), (3), codified as 42 U.S.C. 12112(b)(2), (3) (2000). The ADA also prohibits discrimination based on the disability of a related or associated individual. § 702(b)(4), codified as 42 U.S.C. § 12112(b)(4) (2000).

38. Arizona Governing Committee v. Norris, 463 U.S. 1073, 1086 & n.16 (1983); Meritor Savings Bank v. Vinson, 477 U.S. 57, 63 (1986).

39. Griggs v. Duke Power Co., 401 U.S. 424 (1971); Albemarle Paper Co. v. Moody, 422 U.S. 405, 424 (1975).

40. Raytheon v. Hernandez, 540 U.S. 44 (2003).

41. § 102(d), codified as 42 U.S.C. § 12112(d) (2000).

42. § 101(9), codified as 42 U.S.C. § 12111(9) (2000).

43. *See* Section D *infra.*

44. §§ 104, 510, 511(b)(3) codified as 42 U.S.C. §§ 12114, 12210, 12211(b)(3) (2000).

45. §§ 508, 511(a), (b)(1), codified as 42 U.S.C. §§ 12208, 12211(a), (b)(1) (2000).

46. § 511(b)(2), codified as 42 U.S.C. § 12211(b)(2) (2000).

47. § 103(a), codified as 42 U.S.C. § 12113(a) (2000).

48. § 103(d), codified as 42 U.S.C. § 12113(d) (2000).

49. § 501(c), codified as 42 U.S.C. § 12201(c) (2000).

workplace."[50] This last defense was extended by regulations of the EEOC, later approved by the Supreme Court, to individuals who pose a threat to themselves in the workplace.[51]

The provisions of the ADA on coverage and remedies also follow Title VII, representing a significant expansion upon the prohibitions in the Rehabilitation Act. The ADA covers all employers with fifteen or more employees,[52] including employees of state and local government, but not the federal government.[53] Procedures and remedies under the ADA simply follow those under Title VII.[54] Damages and the right to jury trial are available for intentional violations of the ADA on the same terms as violations of Title VII.[55] As under the Rehabilitation Act, however, no damages are available for failure to make a reasonable accommodation if the employer has made a good faith effort to provide a reasonable accommodation in consultation with the individual with disabilities.[56]

C. Coverage of Disabilities

Both the Rehabilitation Act and the ADA define covered individuals in two basic ways: first, they must suffer from an impairment that is severe enough that it "substantially limits one or more of the major life activities";[57] but second, they must still be able "with or without reasonable accommodation" to "perform the essential functions of the employment position" that they seek.[58] The first of these requirements is taken up in this section. The second, because it concerns the duty of reasonable accommodation, is taken up in the next section.

50. § 103(b), codified as 42 U.S.C. § 12113(b) (2000).

51. Chevron U.S.A., Inc. v. Echazabal, 536 U.S. 73 (2002).

52. § 101(5)(A), codified as 42 U.S.C. § 12111(5)(A) (2000).

53. An "employer" is defined as a "person," which in turn is defined in the same way as under Title VII, to include state and local government. § 101(5)(A), (7), codified as 42 U.S.C. § 12111(5)(A), (7) (2000). The federal government is largely excluded from the definition of "employer," leaving federal employees with their remedies under the Rehabilitation Act. § 101(5)(B), codified as 42 U.S.C. § 12111(7) (2000). As under Title VII, however, special procedures apply to employees of Congress. § 509, codified as 42 U.S.C. §.12209

(2000). The ADA also contains the same provisions for coverage in foreign countries as Title VII, creating exceptions for compliance with the laws of other countries and for foreign corporations not controlled by a covered employer. § 102(c), codified as 42 U.S.C. § 12112(c) (2000).

54. § 107(a), codified as 42 U.S.C. § 12117(a) (2000).

55. 42 U.S.C. § 1981a(a)(2) (2000).

56. *Id.* § 1981a(a)(3).

57. Rehabilitation Act § 7(8)(B), codified as 29 U.S.C. § 706(8)(B) (2000); ADA § 3(2), codified as 42 U.S.C. § 12102(2) (2000).

58. § 101(8), codified as 42 U.S.C. § 12111(8) (2000).

According to the terms of the statutes, the individual need not actually suffer from the impairment that is sufficient for coverage. It is enough if the individual has "a record of such an impairment" or is "regarded as having such an impairment."[59] But it is the nature of the impairment itself that has most frequently given rise to litigation. The decisions of the Supreme Court on this issue have been both expansive in some respects and restrictive in others.

In *School Board v. Arline*,[60] the Supreme Court held that an individual could be disabled by a contagious disease, in that case, tuberculosis. The Court relied both upon the breadth of the statutory definition under the Rehabilitation Act and on regulations that broadly define the terms "physical or mental impairment" and "major life activities" used in the definition.[61] Because the plaintiff had been hospitalized for tuberculosis, although several decades before she was discharged from her position as a public school teacher, she had a record of an impairment sufficient for coverage under the statute. Moreover, she was not excluded from coverage because tuberculosis is contagious, since the contagiousness of the disease went only to the question, reserved by the Court, whether the plaintiff was "otherwise qualified" for her position as a school teacher.[62] The initial question of coverage was different from the question whether she would ultimately prevail on her claim of discriminatory discharge.

Another infectious disease, but one that is more controversial, was also held to be covered by the Supreme Court. In *Bragdon v. Abbott*,[63] the plaintiff was infected with HIV, the virus that causes AIDS. She had been refused treatment by a dentist and brought suit under Title III of the ADA, which prohibits discrimination in public accommodations against covered individuals, defined in the same terms as for Title I, which prohibits discrimination in employment. The Court held that being infected with the virus, even without having full-blown AIDS, interfered with the major life activity of reproduction, since it created a substantial risk of infection of any child born to a woman with the virus. Presumably, the same reasoning would apply to men infected with the virus, since they would infect their partners who would, in turn, infect any children born to them. Again, however, the contagiousness of the disease was not a reason to deny coverage, although it raised an issue of safety to be determined later in the litigation.

---

59. Rehabilitation Act § 7(8)(B), codified as 29 U.S.C. § 706(8)(B) (2000); ADA § 3(2), codified as 42 U.S.C. § 12102(2) (2000).

60. 480 U.S. 273 (1987).

61. *Id.* at 278.

62. *Id.* at 287.

63. 524 U.S. 624 (1998).

A more restrictive decision on covered disabilities is *Sutton v. United Air Lines, Inc.*,[64] which required mitigating measures to be taken into account in assessing the degree of impairment caused by an individual's disability. The plaintiffs in *Sutton* were twin sisters who sought positions as commercial airline pilots, but who were denied employment because they had particularly poor eyesight. The Supreme Court held that this decision did not violate the ADA, although on grounds that are more than a little paradoxical. The Court held that the plaintiffs were not disabled by their poor eyesight, even though the defendant found them to be disqualified for that reason. The Court reached this conclusion, moreover, because the plaintiffs could have corrected their vision with eyeglasses, seemingly removing the substance of the defendant's objection to their employment.

By analogy perhaps to the defense of contributory negligence in tort cases, the Court could have required plaintiffs to take reasonable steps to mitigate the consequences of their disability. The Sutton sisters should not have been allowed to prevail by refusing to wear eyeglasses. But in tort law, precautions taken by the plaintiff defeat the defense of contributory negligence, thus allowing the plaintiff to recover for the defendant's negligence. Under *Sutton*, a plaintiff who has taken reasonable mitigating measures cannot recover at all because her condition falls outside the coverage of the ADA. In terms of the immediate incentives that it provides to plaintiffs, the decision in *Sutton* does not seem to make much sense.

The decision does, however, make sense as a necessary limit on any scheme of remedial justice. The Suttons' disability was not covered by the ADA because it fell below the lower limit on impairments necessary to trigger the protection of the act. Just as a program of disability insurance cannot cover all impairments, no matter how minor or temporary, the ADA cannot cover all disabling conditions regardless of how little they detract from normal abilities. Otherwise, everyone could claim special advantages, and in the end, no one would receive them. At some point, disabilities become so minor that those who suffer from them no longer need the law's assistance. These individuals can be required to take care of themselves because they are in a better position to do so than anyone else. The coverage of the ADA is properly restricted to those who are in greater need, or in the terms used by the act, to those with a condition that "substantially limits one or more of the major life activities."

64. 527 U.S. 471 (1999).

Perhaps *Sutton* interpreted this phrase too narrowly, but it is apparent that at some point, the statutory language must be given a limiting interpretation. In any event, in two companion cases, the Court made clear that the effects of a disability must be evaluated in its treated form. In one of the cases, the plaintiff suffered from a visual impairment—blindness in one eye—that could be treated with corrective glasses, like the impairment in *Sutton*.[65] In the other, the plaintiff suffered from high blood pressure, which could be treated so that he could obtain employment in a wide range of other occupations.[66]

Both of these cases also resemble *Sutton* in implicating issues of safety in transportation. The plaintiffs in both cases sought jobs as truck drivers, and in one of the cases, government regulations provided an additional ground for the employer's refusal to hire the plaintiff.[67] Adding to the paradoxical nature of *Sutton* and its companion cases, concerns for safety seem to have a greater role in finding disabilities to be too minor to be covered by the ADA. If the disabilities are sufficiently severe, the plaintiff has met the initial hurdle for obtaining coverage, leaving the issues of safety to be determined at a later stage in the litigation, as in *Arline* and *Bragdon*. Otherwise, if it is too minor, and seemingly poses a smaller risk to others, it is not covered by the statute at all.

The Supreme Court addressed the last of these issues in *Toyota Manufacturing v. Williams*,[68] a case in which the plaintiff claimed that she was disabled because she suffered from carpal tunnel syndrome. The plaintiff's evidence of a physical impairment was sufficient, but she failed to show that it was one that "substantially limits one or more major life activities." According to the Court, "to be substantially limited in performing manual tasks, an individual must have an impairment that prevents or severely restricts the individual from doing activities that are of central importance to most people's daily lives."[69] These activities include "such basic abilities as walking, seeing, and hearing" and such mundane tasks as "household chores, bathing, and brushing one's teeth."[70] The Court also made clear that the impairment must be "permanent or long term."[71]

As in *Sutton*, the Court again avoided the question whether working itself constitutes a major life activity, but narrowed the

65. Albertson's, Inc. v. Kirkingburg, 527 U.S. 555, 565–66 (1999).

66. Murphy v. UPS, Inc., 527 U.S. 516, 521 (1999).

67. *Albertson's*, 527 U.S. at 570.

68. 534 U.S. 184 (2002).

69. *Id.* at 198.

70. *Id.* at 197, 202.

71. *Id.* at 198.

range of affected activities which triggered a finding of disability under the statute.[72] The Court's continuing concern appeared to be in preventing the coverage of the statute from reaching commonly occurring disabilities, particularly those, like carpal tunnel syndrome, that might appear in less severe form in broad segments of the population. Going so far to restrict coverage of the statute, however, creates the corresponding risk of preventing deserving plaintiffs from obtaining coverage at all. It may also contribute to the very low success rate for plaintiffs who bring disability claims.

D. The Duty of Reasonable Accommodation

The duty of reasonable accommodation enters into the definition both of coverage and of affirmative obligations under the Rehabilitation Act and the ADA. As a question of coverage, it represents the opposite side of the coin from disabilities that are too minor to deserve protection. Disabilities that are too severe to be remedied through reasonable accommodation render an individual unqualified and therefore outside the statutes' protection. As a question of affirmative obligations, reasonable accommodation represents the central doctrinal innovation of the Rehabilitation Act and the ADA.

The intersection of questions of coverage and reasonable accommodation are apparent under both statutes. Section 504 of the Rehabilitation Act protects only "a qualified handicapped individual" from discrimination. Regulations give such an individual a right to reasonable accommodation, implicitly making the question whether they are qualified depend upon whether a reasonable accommodation is available for them.[73] So, too, under the ADA, the general duty not to discriminate applies only to "a qualified individual with a disability." This phrase, in turn, is defined as "an individual with a disability who, with or without reasonable accommodation, can perform the essential functions of the employment position that such individual holds or desires."[74] This subsection of the statute goes on to make the employer's judgment relevant, but not dispositive, of what constitutes the essential functions of the job. The employer can also invoke "undue hardship" as a defense to a claim of reasonable accommodation.[75] The individual's disability, the essential functions of the job, the accommodations available,

---

72. *Id.* at 200–01.

73. 29 C.F.R. § 32.13(a), (c) (2006). For federal agencies, the regulation is 29 C.F.R. § 1613, 704(a) (2006).

74. § 101(8), 42 U.S.C. § 12111(8) (2000).

75. §§ 101(10), 102(5)(A), codified as 42 U.S.C. §§ 12111(10), 12112(5)(A) (2000).

and the hardship to the employer all are closely related. Under both statutes, all of these elements define both the coverage of protected individuals and the obligations of employers.

None of these interrelated elements appears to be so fundamental that the others can be derived from it. Yet some of these elements can be taken as fixed, at least over the short run in which most cases are decided. If the plaintiff has already been found to suffer from a covered disability (the issue discussed in the previous section), the nature of the disability and the position that the plaintiff seeks will determine the range of possible accommodations. A plaintiff with a bad back can only be accommodated by measures that reduce the amount of lifting necessary in his job or that provide assistance in doing the lifting that is necessary. The parties are not likely to contest these issues.

They are more likely to argue over which of the possible accommodations compromise the essential functions of the job and which would impose an undue hardship upon the employer. These issues are deeply interrelated as well. The essential functions of the job can be changed by job restructuring, which is one of the reasonable accommodations listed in the statute.[76] Since any job could be changed to compensate for any disability—just by tailoring its requirements to what the individual with disabilities could do— the crucial question in many cases is whether a proposed job restructuring would cause undue hardship to the employer. This is just another way of framing the more general question of the scope of the employer's duty to accommodate.

These issues also raise the problem of determining where the plaintiff's burden of proof leaves off and the defendant's burden of proof begins. The plaintiff has the initial burden of proving that he or she is a "qualified individual with a disability."[77] The regulations under the Rehabilitation Act, and the explicit terms of the ADA, both assign to the employer the burden of proving that a proposed accommodation would result in "an undue hardship on the operation of its program."[78] These sources of law, however, leave to judicial decisions the task of disentangling these interrelated issues so that both the plaintiff and the defendant bear clearly defined burdens of proof.

The Supreme Court first addressed this problem in a decision under the Rehabilitation Act, *Southeastern Community College v.*

---

76. § 101(9)(B), codified as 42 U.S.C. § 12111(9)(B) (2000).

77. Cleveland v. Policy Management Sys. Corp., 526 U.S. 795, 806 (1999).

78. 29 C.F.R. §§ 32.13(a), 1613.704(a) (2006); § 102(5)(A), codified as 42 U.S.C. § 12112(5)(A) (2000).

Davis.[79] That case involved admission to a clinical training program for registered nurses, operated by a community college that received federal funds. Although the case did not concern employment, it raised closely analogous issues. The plaintiff had a severe hearing impairment and was denied admission to the program for that reason. The Court held that the community college was not required to make "substantial" or "fundamental" changes in its educational program to accommodate the plaintiff.[80]

The Court interpreted the phrase "otherwise qualified handicapped individual" to refer only to those who meet all of the nondiscriminatory qualifications for a job despite their disabilities. The limitations imposed by their disabilities could be taken into account in determining eligibility.[81] More generally, the Court held that the duty of reasonable accommodation, imposed upon recipients of federal funds under section 504, did not amount to a broad duty of affirmative action like that imposed upon federal agencies under section 501 or upon federal contractors under section 503.[82]

Consistently with this reasoning, the lower federal courts have imposed a heavier duty of accommodation upon federal agencies than upon private employers, following the regulation, quoted earlier, that "the Federal Government shall become a model employer of handicapped individuals."[83] With this qualification, most of the decisions on the duty to accommodate under the Rehabilitation Act support at least as strong a duty under the ADA, which specifically provides that the duties it imposes can only be broader, not narrower, than those under the Rehabilitation Act.[84]

The regulations under the Rehabilitation Act offer a list of accommodations that might be tried and factors that might be taken into account.[85] The statutory language of the ADA follows the same pattern in defining the duty of reasonable accommodation under the ADA by a series of examples, which nevertheless are not meant to be exhaustive: making facilities accessible to individuals with disabilities, restructuring jobs, modifying equipment and tests, providing readers and interpreters, and providing "other similar accommodations for individuals with disabilities."[86]

The definition of "undue hardship" in the ADA, like the definition of "reasonable accommodation," follows regulations is-

---

79. 442 U.S. 397 (1979).

80. *Id.* at 410–11.

81. *Id.* at 405–06.

82. *Id.* at 407–12.

83. 29 C.F.R. § 1613.703 (2006). *See* Section A *supra.*

84. § 501(a), codified as 42 U.S.C. § 12201(a) (2000).

85. 29 C.F.R. §§ 32.13(b), (c), 1613.704(b), (c) (2006).

86. § 101(9)(B), codified as 42 U.S.C. § 12111(9)(B) (2000).

sued under the Rehabilitation Act.[87] "Undue hardship" under the ADA "means an action requiring significant difficulty or expense, when considered in light of" four enumerated factors.[88] These factors themselves are framed very broadly, in terms of the nature and cost of the accommodation, the nature and financial resources of the facility and of the employer (the latter are two separate factors), and the type of operations.[89] If any confirmation were needed, the legislative history makes clear that Congress intended to impose no definite rules about what constitutes undue hardship, such as a certain percentage of the pay for the position in question.[90]

The Supreme Court attempted to give these provisions more definite content in *US Airways Inc. v. Barnett*,[91] a case involving an employee's request for accommodation of his bad back by transfer to a less strenuous position, one that was not otherwise open to him under the terms of the employer's seniority system. When the employer failed to make an exception to the seniority system for his benefit, he sued. As the case came to the Supreme Court, it raised the question of who had to prove that an exception to the seniority system was necessary: whether this issue was part of the plaintiff's burden of proof on reasonable accommodation or whether it was part of the defendant's burden of proof on undue hardship.[92] Because the ADA defines "reasonable accommodation" and "undue hardship" with lists of examples and factors to be taken into account, it does not precisely identify what makes an accommodation "reasonable" or what makes a hardship "undue." The statute leaves open the question of how a reasonable accommodation could still cause undue hardship and what, precisely, each party must prove in this situation.

The ADA assigns the burden of proof on the general issues of reasonable accommodation and undue hardship apparently according to the parties' access to evidence. The plaintiff has better knowledge of what accommodations are reasonable—what steps could be taken to compensate for his disability—and the defendant has better knowledge of undue hardship—what steps would be too costly for it to take. These generalizations may not be invariably

---

87. 34 C.F.R. § 104.12(c); 45 C.F.R. § 84.12(c) (2006).

88. § 101(10)(A), codified as 42 U.S.C. § 12111(10)(A) (2000).

89. § 101(10)(B), codified as 42 U.S.C. 12111(10)(B) (2000).

90. 136 Cong. Rec. H2470, H2475 (daily ed. May 17, 1990) (rejecting an amendment that would have established a presumption of undue hardship at 10% of annual salary); H.R. Rep. No. 101–485, 101st Cong. 2d Sess. pt. 3 at 41 (1990) (rejecting per se rule of undue hardship).

91. 535 U.S. 391 (2002).

92. *See* § 102(5)(A), codified as 42 U.S.C. § 12112(5)(A) (2000).

true, but they are augmented by the "interactive process" that the ADA encourages employers to engage in, by relieving them of liability for damages if they do so.[93] The employee initiates the process by suggesting a proposed accommodation and the employer responds, accepting or rejecting it or offering its own proposed accommodation.

In *US Airways*, the Supreme Court took the same practical approach to defining the burden of proof, requiring the plaintiff to prove that an accommodation is reasonable "ordinarily or in the run of cases,"[94] in terms of effectiveness and the burdens that it places on the employer and other employees. The defendant then has the burden of proving undue hardship "in the particular circumstances" of each case.[95] With respect to the particular accommodation in *US Airways*, involving a seniority system, the plaintiff has the added initial burden of showing "special circumstances" that justify a departure from the system's ordinary operation.[96] This specification of the burden of proof facilitates motions for summary judgment by forcing the plaintiff to submit evidence that the proposed accommodation is reasonable "ordinarily or in the run of cases," and for seniority systems, that an exception is warranted by "special circumstances." Failure to do so results in summary judgment for the defendant.

Before *US Airways*, the federal circuits had taken variety of different approaches to the burden of proof. Most of these variations involved slight differences in formulating what each party had to prove. Some, however, were more consequential. Two leading cases, one cited favorably in *US Airways*, and the other passed over without citation, exemplify the different approaches. The first, *Borkowski v. Valley Central School District*,[97] was decided under the Rehabilitation Act, and the other, *Vande Zande v. Wisconsin Department of Administration*,[98] was decided under the ADA. Yet both addressed the same issue: how to divide the burden of proof between the plaintiff and the defendant on the duty of reasonable accommodation and the defense of undue hardship. Both decisions place upon the plaintiff the burden of proposing some form of reasonable accommodation and both also impose upon the defendant the burden of proving that a particular accommodation is too costly to be implemented. The difference between the two decisions lies in how much the plaintiff must prove in order to establish that a proposed accommodation is "reasonable."

---

93. 42 U.S.C. § 1981a(a)(3) (2000).

94. *US Airways*, 535 U.S. at 401.

95. *Id.* at 402.

96. *Id.* at 405.

97. 63 F.3d 131 (2d Cir. 1995).

98. 44 F.3d 538 (7th Cir. 1995).

In *Borkowski*, Judge Calabresi resolved the overlap between the open-ended definitions of "reasonable accommodation" and "undue hardship" in favor of the plaintiff, requiring her to make only a minimal showing that her proposed accommodation was cost-effective. On his view, the plaintiff has only the burden of producing evidence (not the burden of persuasion) that the costs of a proposed accommodation "are not clearly disproportionate to the benefits that it will produce."[99] The remainder of the burden of production, and all of the burden of persuasion, falls on the defendant in establishing cost as an "undue hardship." Accordingly, Judge Calabresi concluded that the plaintiff had presented sufficient evidence to survive a motion for summary judgment.

By contrast, in *Vande Zande*, Judge Posner imposed a heavier burden on the plaintiff to show that a proposed accommodation is "reasonable in the sense both of efficacious and of proportional to costs."[100] On the record presented in *Vande Zande*, the plaintiff had not made this showing and summary judgment was therefore properly entered against her. The accommodations that she proposed were too costly in comparison to the benefits that they conferred on both her and her employer in making her better able to perform her job.

Although the difference between these two decisions, and the standards that they articulate, may be subtle, it is nevertheless significant, particularly in close cases resolved on summary judgment. *Borkowski* gives the plaintiff a greater chance of going to trial, or what amounts to the same thing, a greater chance of obtaining a favorable settlement and more extensive accommodations. *Vande Zande* makes it more difficult for the plaintiff to get past summary judgment and so obtain the relief that she seeks, either by judicial decision or by settlement. On the issue of reasonable accommodation, as elsewhere in employment discrimination law, allocation of the burden of proof often is crucial.

The Supreme Court has also addressed burdens of proof and the standards for summary judgment under the ADA, although in a case concerned with the narrow issue of the plaintiff's prior representation that she was "totally disabled" in seeking disability benefits. In *Cleveland v. Policy Management Systems Corp.*,[101] the Supreme Court held that an application for benefits under the Social Security Disability Insurance (SSDI) program did not necessarily preclude an individual from establishing coverage under the ADA. Under the SSDI program, covered disabilities are determined

---

99. 63 F.3d at 138.   **101.** 526 U.S. 795 (1999).
100. 44 F.3d at 543.

by applying a set of presumptions that have no counterpart under the ADA. Moreover, the ultimate award of benefits depends upon the existence of a disability alone, without considering the possibility of reasonable accommodation. Because of the difference between the issues under the ADA and under the SSDI, the plaintiff could survive a motion for summary judgment by the employer based solely on her representation of total disability in her application for SSDI benefits. Nevertheless, the burden of proof remained upon the plaintiff to establish that she was "otherwise qualified" for the position that she sought from the employer.

The preceding discussion has emphasized litigation over the duty of reasonable accommodation, but many requests for accommodation are resolved short of litigation. As noted earlier, the ADA encourages this approach by relieving an employer of liability for damages if he has made a good faith effort to provide a reasonable accommodation in consultation with the individual with disabilities.[102] The judicial decisions, even before enactment of this provision in the ADA, also recognized that employers are well advised to consult in good faith with potential plaintiffs over proposed accommodation. Few decisions, in fact, have imposed any form of liability upon employers when they have undertaken these efforts and granted a partial accommodation to the plaintiff.[103] Conversely, many of those in which employers have been held liable have involved an outright refusal to consider any accommodation at all.[104] Such decisions impose a duty, at least as a practical matter, to confer with one another over proposed accommodations, again bringing out the importance of voluntary action in remedying systematic disadvantages in employment opportunities. As with affirmative action under Title VII, the broader the remedial goal, the more it depends upon the initiative of employers to reach voluntary agreements with their employees.

---

102. 42 U.S.C. § 1981a(a)(3) (2000).

103. *E.g.,* Guice–Mills v. Derwinski, 967 F.2d 794, 798 (2d Cir. 1992); Shea v. Tisch, 870 F.2d 786, 789–90 (1st Cir. 1989).

104. *E.g.,* Stutts v. Freeman, 694 F.2d 666, 669 (11th Cir. 1983); Cain v. Hyatt, 734 F.Supp. 671, 682–83 (E.D. Pa. 1990).

Chapter XIII

STATE LAWS

Just as the modern law of employment discrimination began with state law, it is fitting to conclude this survey with an account of where state law stands today. When Title VII was enacted, 21 states had laws against employment discrimination, limited mainly to discrimination on the basis of race, national origin, and religion.[1] Discrimination on the basis of sex was generally prohibited only in a handful of states, although almost half had requirements of equal pay for equal work. This situation changed rapidly after the passage of Title VII, whose enforcement provisions established a system of "cooperative federalism" requiring resort to state and local administrative remedies before filing a charge under Title VII. Today, all the states except Alabama have laws prohibiting discrimination on the same grounds as Title VII, and even Alabama has joined the remainder of the states in prohibiting discrimination on the basis of age and disability.[2] A number of localities have also passed ordinances against discrimination and have enforced them through agencies that receive deference from the EEOC.[3]

State law initially contributed to the law of employment discrimination by providing a model for the federal laws such as Title VII. It does so now by extending coverage, in a modest way to smaller employers, but in a more innovative fashion to additional grounds of prohibited discrimination, such as marital status and sexual orientation. Procedurally, state laws have also offered a wider and more effective array of administrative remedies than federal law. In all of these respects, state laws continue to provide models for possible changes in federal law.

A. Substantive Provisions

State laws against employment discrimination generally follow federal law, both in their explicit provisions and in how those provisions are interpreted. Only occasionally does state law depart from federal law in the areas in which both overlap. The most

---

1. *See* William M. Landes, The Economics of Fair Employment Laws, 76 J. Pol. Econ. 507, 507 n. 1 (1968).

2. *See* Bureau of National Affairs, 8A Labor Relations Reporter: Fair Employ-

ment Practices Manual 451:52–53 (2005). These figures include the District of Columbia and Puerto Rico.

3. *See* 29 C.F.R. § 1601.80 (2006).

significant differences arise in the area in which state law does not overlap with federal law, but in which it extends its coverage further.

The coverage of state law can extend further because, both figuratively and practically, it is closer to the individuals and firms that fall within its scope. This proximity increases the political support for laws against employment discrimination, just as much as the fact that these laws have now been enacted by nearly all the states. The coverage of state law can therefore be more extensive, reaching employers that are not covered by Title VII. Some, but not all, of the state laws against employment discrimination reach employers with fewer than the threshold of fifteen employees that triggers coverage under Title VII.[4] State laws can also have special provisions which, although they overlap to a large extent with Title VII, provide additional remedies with respect to state employment and state contracts.[5]

State laws also differ from federal law in covering additional grounds of discrimination. These range from discrimination on the basis of sexual orientation, now prohibited by seventeen states and the District of Columbia to discrimination on the basis of use (or nonuse) of tobacco.[6] Discrimination on the basis of marital status is another common form of discrimination prohibited under state law.[7] The significance of these added grounds of discrimination lies in their use as a model for other states and the federal government. Thus, bills have repeatedly been introduced in Congress to amend Title VII to prohibit discrimination on the basis of sexual orientation. Discrimination on this basis, of course, has been controversial and has resulted in constitutional decisions that protect the right of private associations to restrict their membership under the First Amendment.[8]

Such decisions do not apply with full force to employers who hold themselves out to deal with the general public, but they indicate the kind of objections raised to any prohibition against newly recognized forms of discrimination. A legal prohibition would not be necessary unless the underlying discrimination were widespread, at least in some parts of the country or some segments of

---

4. *E.g.*, Cal. Gov't Code Ann. § 12926(d) (2005) (coverage of employers with five or more employees); N.Y. Exec. Law Ann. § 292.5 (2007) (coverage of employers with four or more employees).

5. *E.g.*, Tex. Civ. Prac. & Rem. Code Ann. §§ 106.001 (2005); Va. Code Ann. §§ 2.2–4200 (2005).

6. *See* Bureau of National Affairs, 8A Labor Relations Reporter: Fair Employment Practices Manual 451:52–53 (2005).

7. *Id.*

8. Boy Scouts of America v. Dale, 530 U.S. 640 (2000).

society. Yet if it is widespread, employers and others subject to the prohibition face the cost of conforming their behavior and expectations, as well as those of their managers, employees, and customers, to the newly imposed requirements of the law. State laws provide a welcome means of testing the implementation and enforcement of such expanded prohibitions against discrimination. As Justice Brandeis's laboratories for social experiments, the states enable newly proposed laws to be tested by experience before they are enacted more widely.

B. Procedures and Remedies

State laws typically confer more enforcement authority on administrative agencies than federal law confers on the EEOC. In addition to the functions of investigation and conciliation performed by the EEOC, state agencies usually have the power to adjudicate charges of discrimination and to issue a broad array of remedies, including cease-and-desist orders, back pay, and attorney's fees.[9] Although such orders are not the equivalent of judgments entered by a court, they achieve this status after they have received judicial review and become enforceable like any other judgment.

The added administrative remedies under state law give victims of discrimination a less expensive alternative to filing a lawsuit in court. They can often proceed without the assistance of an attorney, and even if they need one to present their claim, the expenses of administrative proceedings are generally less than those of litigation. Of course, they cannot be guaranteed an expeditious and inexpensive determination of their claims, but they do have a wider choice than they have under federal law, where all of the significant remedies for private employees are available only in court.

Resorting to state administrative remedies does not foreclose relief under Title VII and the other federal laws against employment discrimination. Only if a state court renders a judgment in review of state administrative proceedings do its findings and conclusions have any preclusive effect on a subsequent judgment on a federal claim.[10] Otherwise, resort to state agency is only a prerequisite to filing with the EEOC and eventually to filing a claim in court. Title VII encouraged the adoption of state laws against discrimination precisely by requiring the exhaustion of state admin-

---

9. *E.g.*, Fla. Stat. Ann. § 760.11 (2005); Ill. Comp. Stat. Ann. ch. 775 §§ 5/8A–103,–104 (2006).

10. Kremer v. Chemical Constr. Corp., 456 U.S. 461, 476–77 (1982).

istrative remedies and by authorizing the EEOC to enter into cooperative agreements with state agencies.[11]

Just like the expanded coverage of state law, the expanded role of state agencies can also serve as a model for revising the procedures for enforcing federal laws. As employment discrimination claims have increased in number and familiarity, the need for full-fledged adjudication has diminished. Routine claims no longer need the interpretive skills of federal judges which were required in the early decades of enforcement of Title VII. And more recently enacted statutes, such as the ADA, eventually will be filled in by judicial interpretation, leaving the remaining questions of interpretation to be settled through judicial review of administrative decisions. An enhanced role for administrative agencies, although it was initially rejected by Congress in the enactment of Title VII, can become the standard means of enforcing the statute. At this time, as at the beginning of the Civil Rights Era, state law can serve as the model for federal legislation.

11. §§ 706(c), (d), 709(b), codified as 42 U.S.C. §§ 2000e–5(c),–8(b) (2000).

TABLE OF CASES

References are to Pages.

241

*

INDEX

WAGE AND SALARY DISCRIMINATION
  See also Equal Pay Act, this index
Statistical evidence, 66–67
Title VII claims for sex discrimination,
    119–22

WRONGFUL DISCHARGE LAW
Employment discrimination law com-
    pared, 52–53, 206

†